Punishing Criminals

PUNISHING CRIMINALS

Concerning a Very Old and

Painful Question

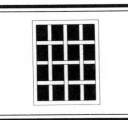

Ernest van den Haag

Basic Books, Inc., Publishers   New York

After such knowledge, what forgiveness?

T. S. ELIOT, *Gerontion*

Contents

41234

PART THREE

KINDS OF PUNISHMENT

Acknowledgments

Many good friends have helped me by reading the manuscript of this book. They succeeded in preventing at least some errors. I could not name all, nor assess their contributions without losing some, so I will cop out and name none. But I gladly make some exceptions. James Q. Wilson suggested major improvements in style and substance. I am grateful for his gift of time and wisdom. I am grateful also to Robert Martinson for originally drawing my attention to the unresponsiveness of the crime rate to incapacitation, a matter usually neglected. Judge Fred Berman was kind enough to give me a bench-eye view of our court system by inviting me to sit with him as *amicus curiae.* Crime Deterrence and Offender Career (O.E.O. grant 20071 G) has given me time to think, to do research, and to write this book. Prior to that, a Senior Fellowship from the National Endowment for the Humanities greatly helped to get me started. I am grateful to the U.S. taxpayer. Midge Decter was the editor one dreams about: tactful, helpful, and congenial. My friend Susan Skorski, who did the index, also helped to make this the best of all possible books I could write. I wish I could conclude with Voltaire's Candide that the best is necessarily good. But I shall be content, in Francis Bacon's words, "to excite the judgment briefly rather than to inform it tediously."

E.v.d.H.

PART ONE

THE INSTITUTION

OF PUNISHMENT

I

To Secure These Rights

Although they do many other things, the paramount duty, the *raison d'être*, of governments is to provide a legal order in which citizens can be secure in their lives, their liberties, and their pursuit of happiness. Whether originally granted by God, nature, society, or by the government itself (through a charter or constitution), these rights can be secured only by the government. For the rights of each citizen necessarily are the duties of all other citizens. Unless they give him what his rights entitle him to, and refrain from interfering with his rightful actions, no citizen can exercise his rights. Since not everybody can be counted on to volunteer his duties, our "unalienable" rights could easily be alienated; hence, according to our Declaration of Independence, "To secure these rights governments are instituted among men."

Governments secure rights and duties by specifying them through laws and by enforcing the laws. Laws regulate many activities; criminal (penal) laws, which concern us here, prohibit some activities (crimes) on pain of punishment (penalties). Punishment is administered by many agencies, which, by aggregation more than by systematic organization, form the "criminal justice system." By distributing punishments to those found guilty of violating penal laws, the criminal justice system directly and visibly dispenses "justice." Now, the total of what we call "social justice" depends on many other institutions that more or less equitably distribute income, or opportunities for advancement, or the good things of life generally. These distributions, not decided on directly by the criminal justice system, are referred to as "distributive justice"; only the distribution of punishments is referred to as "penal," or "criminal" justice. But in both cases the word "justice" connotes an ideal, not an evaluation of reality.

Basically, the criminal justice system deals with three questions.

1. What conduct is prohibited?
2. How is it decided that a person is guilty of prohibited conduct?
3. What is to be done with those found guilty?

I shall focus mostly on the third question, although the other two will be engaged when they are likely to shed light on punishment. Where relevant, I shall also try to indicate the relation of criminal to distributive justice.

Punishment has been the main device for enforcing laws ever since the mists of prehistory lifted. And questions about punishment have been with us since then. What exactly is punishment? What motivates us to punish? What do we intend to accomplish? Is punishment effective? Can punishment deter? What role does it play in determining crime rates? Why do people violate laws? Are they responsible? What kind and what degree of punishment, if any, is just and effective for what kind of crime and for what kind of criminal? Are there means other than punishment to enforce laws? Are these more promising than the present kinds of punishment? How is punishment related to the social order, to justice, and to charity? Could punishment—as is frequently argued—be replaced by other measures such as education, treatment, or redistribution of income and property? Finally, what can be said for and against the three major kinds of punishment now used: death, imprisonment, and fines (including conditional suspensions such as probation and parole), and for and against the alternatives that might be available?

These are perennial questions. In the U.S. they have become pressing because our rate of crime * has been rising. From 1966 to 1971 the number of crimes per 100,000 persons (the crime rate) rose by 74 percent. Robbery alone rose by 133 percent. Meanwhile, the rate of punishment has fallen. At present, ". . . the proportion of actual offenses that result in prison sentences is . . . estimated at being one percent of the total number of actual crimes committed, although it varies from crime to crime." [1] It may be that fines, or probation, have in some cases taken the place of prison. But whichever way one turns the matter, the proportion of crimes punished is low and the crime rate high. Ramsey Clark doubts that we "achieve one conviction for every fifty serious crimes." [2] As a result, the sense of public safety has diminished. Particularly in the bigger cities, many people are fearful of venturing on the streets by night, while parks are usable only in daylight and shopkeepers have armed themselves.

In part the rate of punishment is low because of the genuine difficulties of catching criminals and convicting them. But there are also hesitations about actually punishing criminals: the moral justification for punishment is questioned more and more intensely, and so is its usefulness. "The salient 20th century fact about criminal law is widespread skepticism of punishment," writes Jerome Hall.[3]

Attitudes toward crime and punishment have indeed changed greatly in the last century (reading Dostoyevsky will persuade anyone). Many people now believe that crime is as

---

* The crime rate in the U.S. is remarkably high by comparison with other countries. In 1972 New York experienced 8 times as many murders as Tokyo, 182 times as many robberies, and 7 times as many rapes—although it has only two-thirds of Tokyo's more than 11 million inhabitants. Comparison with crime rates in London and elsewhere also shows that New York crime rates are several hundred percent higher. (In the U.S. the New York crime rate is exceeded by several cities, such as Detroit.)

much the responsibility of the society victimized by it as of the criminal who commits it. Writers write of *The Crime of Punishment*.[4] They believe punishment morally unjustifiable and ineffective in enforcing laws, little more than a barbarous relic that merely satisfies an ignoble thirst for revenge. On the other hand, if the laws are not enforced, the citizens, in Lincoln's words "seeing their property destroyed, their families insulted and their lives endangered . . . become tired and disgusted with a government that offers them no protection."[5] Hence, there is insistence as well on the paramount duty of the government to enforce the laws. The issue hinges on the moral legitimacy and effectiveness of punishment as against alternative means of enforcing the laws—and, not least, on the justice of the laws themselves and of their enforcement.

Although the institution of punishment is as old as society, actual punishments, as well as the methods of dispensing them, have changed a great deal. Our present emphasis on incarceration as the main punitive or corrective device is less than two hundred years old and largely an American invention. In the past offenders were imprisoned mainly to hold them for trial. They were then sentenced to be fined, pilloried, flogged, mutilated, or put to death. The death penalty was used for many crimes, while now it is used for but a few, if at all. Corporal punishments, which together with the death penalty enabled past societies to do almost without prisons, have been abolished. On the other hand, probation (conditional liberty in place of incarceration) and parole (conditional release before the term of incarceration ends), quite recently introduced, have greatly reduced prison terms. These changes can be explained historically and sociologically. But my main concern will be with a critical analysis of the institution of punishment as currently practiced, or proposed.

Philosophers have lately taken to calling "rational reconstruction" the kind of analysis to which I mean to subject the whole problem of punishing lawbreakers. Indeed, my analysis will be as rational as I can make it. But I shall bear in mind (and I hope the reader will) that neither society itself nor its institutions (such as punishment) are cemented merely by reason, or rationally designed, or motivated. The social order can be rationally analyzed, but it is historically accumulated and actually held together, made to cohere, by affective bonds, by traditional institutions, and by functional needs. To analyze the regularities displayed by bees, whether in a hive or swarming, scientists may construct a rational theory to explain, to predict, and even to influence their behavior. Scientists can do so without attributing the rationality of their analysis to its subject and without imitating (or being infected by) its nonrationality. So with the analysis of the social institution of punishment.

II

Retribution, Vengeance, and the Future

━━━━━━━

Punishment Defined

"Punishment" is a deprivation, or suffering, imposed by law. Illness, loss, or wrongful imprisonment, although just as painful, are not punishment any more than pain, injury, or death, even when suffered by a fleeing suspect: suffering may be said to be punitive only when it is court-imposed retribution for violating laws. This definition of punishment, although stipulative, follows common usage rather closely. To be sure, any suffering can be described colloquially as "punishment." Yet, even in this loose usage "punishment" suggests some sort of retribution for past offenses—e.g., when parents "punish" children. Even when guilt was not established or retribution inflicted by a visible tribunal, it is quite often felt that, to deserve his misfortune, the person "punished" by pain or loss must have violated some law-like norm ordinarily thought to be sanctioned by a legitimate higher authority ("God punished him").*

* Arrests, indictments, or even police interrogations also tend to have some of the effects of punishment, because they make the threat of actual punishment more vivid and may inflict similar inconvenience.

Guilt: Two Kinds of Wrong

Conduct prohibited by law is wrong; to engage in it is to commit an offense. Legal guilt is incurred by doing what one knew (or could have known) to be wrong when one could have done otherwise. Laws may forbid two kinds of actions. An act generally accepted to be intrinsically evil—*malum in se* (e.g., murder)—is *prohibitum quia malum* (prohibited because bad); conversely, an act the government has found it necessary to prohibit—*malum prohibitum* (e.g., drunken driving or practicing medicine without a licence)—becomes *malum quia prohibitum* (bad because prohibited). Thus, acts are forbidden either because regarded as inherently wicked (murder) or because, although not intrinsically wicked (e.g., driving on the wrong side of the street), they interfere with securing some good. Once forbidden, acts become offenses because unlawful, whatever their moral quality.*

An intrinsic evil (*malum in se*) is often thought to be wrong "by nature"; usually, it is something no society can tolerate if it is to function and continue. And certainly it is a crime regarded as odious so that punishment for it expresses blame and denounces the offender. Non-intrinsic evils (*mala prohibita*) are unlawful where they occur, but might be lawful elsewhere or at other times (e.g., polygamy or carrying a gun). The distinction between the two kinds of evil is philosophically significant and has some legislative importance, but little relevance to the enforcement of laws. Courts need not ask what kind of evil they punish: offenses are offenses and punishable because they are prohibited, regardless of what led to the prohibition. Further, according to the maxim *nullum crimen (nulla poena) sine lege*—no crime (no punishment) without

* Those who value the moral quality of the prohibited act more highly than that of the prohibition may feel morally entitled to disobey, thereby committing the legal offense that is usually referred to as civil disobedience. See my *Political Violence and Civil Disobedience* (New York: Harper Torchbooks, 1972).

[preexisting] law—nothing is a crime unless the penal law prohibits it; and only crimes can be punished. Else, one could not know before one acts whether one is acting lawfully; courts could punish anything they dislike. In short, in meting out punishments courts apply the law and not an independent notion of justice (whether or not based on nature), except by interpreting the law.*

Retribution and Vengeance

Since punishment is imposed for a past offense, it can be more, but never less, than retribution. And, since retribution refers to past events, as does revenge, the two are easily confused. Thus, a Pennsylvania judge declared that retribution is ". . . the doctrine of legal revenge, or punishment merely for the sake of punishment" wherefore ". . . the refinement and humanizing of society has been in the direction of dispelling from penology any such theory." [6] This view is becoming ever more popular, as Jerome Hall points out: "Retribution is sharply disparaged as, at best, a disguised form of vengeance." [7] However, the differences between vengeance and retribution seem as important as the characteristics they share.

Vengeance is self-serving since it is arbitrarily (by his own authority) taken by anyone who feels injured and wishes to retaliate. Vengeance is not defined by preexisting rules nor proportioned to the injury avenged. And what is avenged need not even be a crime: jealous competitors, or lovers, may take revenge for grievances produced by quite lawful actions. Since it is not imposed, or regulated, by any legal authority, revenge can easily harm law-abiding citizens. Vendettas can become family affairs and be directed against relatives or asso-

* This ideal of legality was explicitly rejected by the Soviet Union and the Nazis. (Theoretically, it has been reestablished in the Soviet Union.) Like all ideals, it can only be approximated, even when accepted.

ciates of the alleged wrongdoer. Revenge is harmful to the legal order, too, as Francis Bacon stressed in 1597: "Revenge is a kind of wild justice, which, the more man's nature runs to, the more ought law to weed it out; for as for the first wrong, it doth but offend the law, but the revenge of that wrong putteth the law out of office." Only when it becomes regulated by custom does vengeance acquire some aspects of nascent law.*

Unlike vengeance, retribution is imposed by courts after a guilty plea, or a trial, in which the accused has been found guilty of committing a crime. Prescribed by the law broken, and proportioned to the gravity of the offense committed, retribution is not inflicted to gratify or compensate anyone who suffered a loss or was harmed by the crime—even if it does so—but to enforce the law and to vindicate the legal order.

The scales usually sported by the statue of justice symbolically suggest that society is the first victim of any crime and the individual harmed, if any, the second. Justice, blindfolded, so as not to be distracted by the person of the offender, or of his victim, weighs the gravity of the crime on her scales to reestablish the equilibrium disturbed by the offense through an equally weighty punishment.† (The difficulties raised by the phrase "equally weighty" will be discussed in Chap. XVI.) Retribution is to restore an objective order rather than to satisfy a subjective craving for revenge. This objective order was often thought to have a divine or "natural" source. But whatever its origin, a transpersonal social order objec-

---

* The Bible rejects vengeance. The Lord, speaking through Moses, commands (Leviticus 19: 18): "Thou shalt not avenge," and again (Romans 12: 19): "Vengeance is mine; I will repay," and (Hebrews 10: 30): "Vengeance belongeth unto me; I will recompense." Revenge is absorbed in the enforcement of laws by authority through retribution here and thereafter, which the Bible supports (Genesis 9: 6): "Whoso sheddeth man's blood, by man shall his blood be shed."

† As Prof. David Daube points out ("The Scales of Justice" *Juridical Review* 63, 1951), the scales in the original Egyptian image did not measure more or less of any quantity, but indicated total salvation, or perdition, the absence or presence of a quality decisive in the ultimate judgment of souls. Later, Roman and particularly Christian interpretations are nearer to the one used in the text.

tively does exist. If it is to continue, it must be vindicated through the punishment of offenders. The visual metaphor—and it is certainly no more—suggests that retribution would be needed to vindicate the legal order even if neither individuals nor groups wanted revenge. The social objective of retribution, the enforcement of laws, matters more than the individual wish and is quite independent of it. For it must be said, although as yet it has to be shown, that retributive punishment is indispensable to the maintenance of any social order, just or unjust.

Motives, Intentions, Effects

James Fitzjames Stephen was right about human motivation when he suggested that revenge plays a major role in retribution: "The criminal law stands to the passion of revenge in much the same relation as marriage to the sexual appetite." [8] But the individual motive—be it revenge or any other—does not exhaust the social objective of retribution. Motives—*why* one tries to achieve what one does—can neither justify nor discredit *what* one tries to achieve, one's intentions. Objectives can be justified, or rejected, independently of the motives that cause us to try to achieve them. At any rate, motives must remain somewhat conjectural when many persons are involved. Each may have a different motive. Even the same motive may produce different actions and intentions, while the same objective may spring from different motives. Finally, the effects actually achieved need not be those intended.

If retaliatory motives are as important as Stephen suggests, the abolition of legal retribution would not have the benign effects so often hoped for. Abolition would be no more likely to reduce "the passion of revenge," which finds sanctioned satisfaction in retribution, than the abolition of marriage would be to reduce the "sexual appetite," which finds sanctioned satisfaction in marriage. Marriage and retribution both serve to control impulses that might otherwise be gratified in socially more destructive ways.* When legal retribution is not imposed for what is felt to be wrong, or when retribution is felt to be less than deserved—when it is felt to be insufficient, not inclusive, certain, or severe enough—public control falters, and "the passion of revenge" tends to be gratified privately.

When the settlers in the American West deemed their legal authorities too weak to protect their property, they resorted to "lynch justice" to punish, without the formalities of a trial, individuals thought to be guilty of cattle rustling or of other acts the settlers wanted to curb and for which they wanted retribution. While it can be temporarily effective in curbing offenses, such informal penalization easily degenerates. The processes by which the identity of the suspect and his guilt are ascertained are haphazard and the penalties arbitrary. Very soon, instead of vindicating public order, lynching is used for personal revenge, or to impose the moral dictates of petty tyrants and to terrorize the community rather than criminals. The most effective remedy is the institution of a judicial system that deserves and gains the trust of the community by effectively protecting its order and satisfying its sense of justice. Ineluctably, some sort of lynch justice will appear, or reappear, wherever the legal system of the community is not effectively enforced.† In the United States lynch justice is as yet a fantasy.‡ It is public knowledge that in Brazil vigilantes (mainly police and military men) select individuals reputed to be troublemakers or gangsters, shoot them, and leave their bodies on roadsides with admonitory messages. Apparently, most of the victims are quite unsavory characters who slip

---

* Just as marriage does more than control the "sexual appetite," retribution does more than control "the passion of revenge."

† Vigilantes and informal rule-enforcing groups also may appear when the legal system enforces rules alien to the communal sense of justice. Thus, the original Sicilian Mafia and the legendary Robin Hood.

‡ In the movie *Death Wish* (released in 1974), the hero, finding the law ineffective, becomes a one-man avenger of crime.

through the wide net of Brazilian justice and make life insecure for law-abiding citizens. Some, though, are merely petty criminals. And some may be altogether innocent of any crime other than displeasing the vigilantes. Unless stopped in time and replaced by an effective judicial system, the Brazilian practice will degenerate and end up not by strengthening but by undermining public order.

The Influence of the Past

The laws that prescribe the punishment of the guilty also determine what makes one guilty—which acts are regarded as harmful enough to be prohibited. By threatening retributive punishment for these acts, the law intends to restrain people from doing in the future what the law forbids. When the threat is carried out against those who have disregarded it, the retribution actually imposed for a past offense influences the future, because people learn from the past.

Retribution affects the future in much the same way as the payment of debts does. Debts must be paid in the first place because they are owed, because one has promised to pay them. Retribution must be paid because it is owed, because it has been threatened, and a threat is a (negative) promise. The payment of debts (or of retribution) fulfills an obligation undertaken in the past. Once undertaken, obligations are independent of the current or future usefulness of meeting them. Nonetheless, keeping promises also affects the future, because the credibility of as yet unfulfilled promises depends on keeping past promises: if past threats were not carried out, present threats would become incredible and therefore ineffective in deterring anyone from crime. *Pacta sunt servanda:* promises must be kept, threats must be carried out. Else they won't be believed, there would be no point in making them, and those inclined to break the law would realize that the law has been bluffing. The present low rate of punishment may bring this about. So far it has not, because the law still has a great deal of credibility handed down from past generations. We may be consuming this stock of credibility, as we do other resources, at a perilous rate. Meanwhile, when one considers that no more than 1 percent of all offenders go to jail, it seems remarkable that our rising crime rate has not risen even more.

A Debt Owed by, or to, Society?

The notion of retribution as a payment of debts can be overextended or misapplied. Thus, it is often said that the criminal who has received his punishment has "paid his debt to society." This is a puzzling phrase.

Laws threaten, or promise, punishment for crimes. Society has obligated itself by threatening. It owes the carrying out of its threats. Society pays its debt by punishing the offender, however unwilling he is to accept payment. There is some verbal confusion only because when a debt is paid in the form of suffering, the recipient usually feels that he has paid, rather than received, something. Still, when I make good my promise, or threat, to make you suffer if . . . , I, not you, meet my obligation by making you "pay" for your misdeed. My promise, or threat, was to exact a payment (suffering), however unwilling you are to pay. I, not you, then owed the exaction by virtue of my promise. The confusion is immaterial as long as one does not conclude that suffering the punishment exonerates the sufferer *a posteriori* (he has "paid his debt"); or, worse, that his punishment entitled him to do what he is punished for, because, after all, "he paid for it." The price exacted for having violated the law is not meant to be a retroactive license.

Apart from verbal confusions, the idea that the criminal "pays his debt" when punished assumes that all members of society *qua* members have made a tacit promise to obey its laws, a promise that the criminal has broken. He then "pays his debt" when he compensates society for his broken promise. This assumption—which goes back to Plato—presumes that a membership that is not voluntary, and cannot be avoided, implies a promise of the member, made without his assent. This seems questionable. And if he did not promise to do anything, or to pay for not doing it, the lawbreaker had no promise to keep and no debt to pay for not keeping it, unless in "accepting" his punishment and repenting his offense he assumes a debt and makes the promise he broke—a rather strained conception. Anyway, few offenders "accept" punishment and fewer still repent their offenses.

True, since we all benefit from even the worst social order—human beings cannot exist but in society, and society is inconceivable without some order—we all owe society some allegiance in exchange. Hence the idea of an implied promise. Shared by many philosophers, such as J. J. Rousseau and John Locke, the idea loses what explanatory advantages it has as a metaphor when taken too literally and treated as though an actual contract were involved, rather than an implied general moral obligation that many people reject. A less literal and more reasonable interpretation would have the offender owe a debt to society because by his offense he deprived it of an intangible yet important good: public security and trust. Something may be owed even if the debtor never consented to owe it (there are parallels in many tort matters) simply because he deprived others of it.

Still, retributive punishment is the payment of a debt to, at least as much as by, the offender. By fulfilling his current duty to submit to court-imposed retribution for a past offense, the offender merely receives the payment (retribution) and avoids a different violation and an additional punishment. Retribution pays a debt to law-abiding citizens as well. They were threatened with punishment and refrained from unlawful acts.

Unless the threat is carried out against those who did not refrain, the law-abiding citizens were fooled.*

Monetary restitution, finally, is a debt the offender owes the victim of his offense. It is quite unnecessarily neglected in our present legal practices. After all, the fact that someone *stole* my TV set—that he took it without my permission, in violation of the law—need not cancel his civil liability to compensate me for the loss.† However, restitution is independent of punishment and cannot replace it. Punishment is not primarily concerned with the actual loss or damage caused by the prohibited act but with the vindication of the prohibition, and of all legal prohibitions, with the integrity of the legal order. Murder is punished because wrong. The punishment threatened by society proclaims the wrongness of the act punished and means to deter potential offenders from it, rather than to compensate individual victims.

Retribution as Price

If we keep in mind that society owes the exaction, it is helpful to conceive of retribution as the price exacted from the offender for his offense, the cost to him. Cost is a major element

---

* Conceiving of the threat of punishment as a promise made to the offender, some German philosophers (e.g., Kant and Hegel) were led to insist that the human dignity of the criminal requires that the threat be carried out, that society owes him his punishment. But a promise need not be kept if both parties consent. And a threat, unlike a promise, can be withdrawn unilaterally by the party that made it. The consent of those for whom the threat functions as a promise—here, nonoffenders—is needed; that of the offender who was threatened is not.

† Legally, it does not at present—victims may recover by separate tort action. In practice such actions are made futile by the law, which puts the burden of undertaking them on the victim and makes civil judgments against offenders very hard to enforce. It would be quite feasible to impose restitution on the offender during the penal proceedings, as is done in some European countries (see Articles 2–10 in the French Code of Criminal Procedure).

in controlling the supply of crime (or of anything else), for, given the expected (gross) gain, cost determines the profitability of an action, the *net* advantage to be gained. But no cost most people are actually willing to suffer can be sufficient: the price exacted for crime is meant to be prohibitive, although it can never be altogether so because some offenders cannot be deterred by any cost, no matter how high. Crime, therefore, will always be with us. To be sure, if the costs were higher, more offenders might be deterred. Yet often a higher cost cannot, or should not, be exacted—another reason crime will stay with us. The mutilation of offenders, for example, might be an effectively prohibitive cost; at least it might prove a greater deterrent than temporary incarceration. But we would rather deter fewer offenders if the cost of deterring more is the punitive mutilation of those convicted. Values such as compassion for the guilty and protection of the possibly innocent set limits to the severity and certainty of punishment and, therefore, make even some deterrable crime unavoidable. Still, by deterring some would-be offenders, the imposition of any cost reduces the crime rate relative to what it would be otherwise. This is one of the main purposes of punishment.

Are Legal Threats Needed?

Granted that, unless carried out, legal threats are not credible and therefore not effective, are they necessary to begin with? Would people obey the law without credible threats?

Physical laws are unavoidably obeyed. They are self-enforcing. To defy the law of gravity is to defeat one's purpose and to suffer injury. Experience soon teaches us to attain what we wish by conforming to physical laws. Few people know how to calculate the exact effects of gravity, or of the consequences of ignoring it, and very few make such calculations in everyday life. Yet we avoid actions which the law of gravity would defeat, make dangerous, painful, or injurious. Habituation rather than rational calculation produces this avoidance. Rationality is not required. Animals, too, learn to conform to physical laws. Our experience with nature, often vicarious and seldom formulated, is gradually internalized to guide conduct from within. Internalized experience effectively deters us from trying to do what nature makes impossible, unprofitable, dangerous, or painful.* Unless bent on suicide, we do not cut our throats or jump from the fiftieth floor. Few of us even conceive of defying gravity.

The laws legislated by society are not self-enforcing. They become effective only when society does for them what nature does for its law—when society defeats the purpose of those who ignore its laws, or inflicts punishment, which makes defying them dangerous, disadvantageous, painful, and, above all, odious. Disregard of physical laws is naturally dangerous and unprofitable; disregard of legal laws must be made so socially, if people are to be deterred from disregarding them: lawbreaking cannot be allowed to produce the results sought by lawbreakers.

The law of gravity operates unfailingly. We cannot expect as much from legal laws. But if lawbreaking cannot be made impossible, society can try to make the cost of crime high and certain enough to deter most prospective offenders. Punishment, in the words of Jeremy Bentham, "is an artificial consequence annexed by political authority to an offensive act" to make it unrewarding. Crime always will remain with us, just as fires will be with us, or weeds, for an infinite variety of reasons. No society can altogether prevent or eradicate offenses. As Émile Durkheim stressed, crime is "normal": offensive conduct must be legally prohibited only because at least some people are inclined to it; not all can be restrained by the prohibition and by the threat of punishment, however severe. But most can be. The issue is how best to control and

---

* Some innate impulses may play a role as well, but the distinction is immaterial here.

minimize crime—by what precautions and by what punishments.

Why do people not volunteer to abide by the law without the threat of punishment? Ideally they would. But this ideal did not work out well in the Garden of Eden—which is why we are here. There is no reason to believe that it will work as long as we are. What the laws prohibit because disadvantageous to society can be advantageous to some individuals; or they may think it is. Society must try to make prohibited acts clearly disadvantageous to all if its laws are to be heeded. On occasion you may think it to your advantage to steal or cheat. But it is not to the advantage of society to allow theft or fraud (wherefore the very names of these acts bear a pejorative connotation). Social threats must offset the temptation to gratify individual wishes by unlawful means. Laws would be redundant if nobody wanted to do what they forbid. Even in the Garden of Eden, where the lawgiver was wiser and more just and the law less burdensome than it has been since, our legendary parents yielded to the temptation to violate it. The social order was perfect but they were not, and the law was violated. We have learned from this experience that "it is essential to the idea of a law that it be attended with a sanction . . . a punishment for disobedience" (Alexander Hamilton), which must be sufficient "to outweigh the profit of the offense" (Jeremy Bentham). And we have also learned that punishments cannot "outweigh the profit of the offense" for everybody, always. They can, however, much of the time.

Our inborn impulses permit and sometimes impel us to do what society cannot tolerate, what laws must forbid. In the process of socialization, we internalize, to some degree, the restraints on our impulses which society must require.* But internalized restraints occasionally prove insufficient for nearly

---

* Failure to internalize any restraints would make us less than human. Internalizing too many restraints, or the wrong ones, may incapacitate us for ordinary living and happiness.

all of us, and with some of us they take hold only precariously or not at all. All of us, then, in some situations are tempted to do what the law forbids. Many more than are ever brought to the attention of the criminal justice system yield to the temptation when discovery seems unlikely, if sociologists such as Cressey and Sutherland[9] are to be believed. If we take seriously the answers of anonymous respondents to questionnaires, few of us go through life without breaking laws, though most of us escape punishment. Most people, however, are law-abiding at least most of the time. The threat of punishment keeps it so.

Retribution as Fairness to the Law-abiding

Some are caught when they yield to temptation. Were they not punished, those who did restrain themselves would feel cheated. They would be. To get what they wanted they, too, could have broken the law. But to some extent, if not exclusively, they were restrained by the prohibition and by the threat of punishment, which they took seriously. If this threat were to prove altogether empty, those who did not break the law would have been deceived. They would resent it. If they are to continue to be restrained, every effort must be made to punish those who have not been. If tax evaders were permitted to benefit from evasion, honest taxpayers would feel they had been cheated. Unless convinced that tax evasion is unprofitable, they would, in time, want to benefit from it, too. So with other crimes. Internalized restraints are all too easily eroded. For if crimes are profitable, refraining from them is not.

Thus, legal threats must be carried out for three overlapping reasons: (1) because threats were made and become obligations of the society that made them; (2) because otherwise the threats would not remain credible and effective in restraining those tempted to break the law; and (3) to avoid cheating those who remained law-abiding.

Threats as Reinforcement

Optimists, who reject the Christian doctrine of the Fall and the psychoanalytic doctrine of an asocial "Id," tell us that we are born good and honest. If so, we find it easy to overcome this difficulty when we are not threatened by disapproval and, ultimately, by material punishment. "The sense of justice," David Hume pointed out, ". . . arises artificially from education and human conventions." [10] Psychoanalysts have specified that "all morality is restriction and modification of internal strivings. If man were good by nature, no morality would be needed; he would always want to do what he should." * As it is, morality—the willingness to do what is right even when it is not advantageous or pleasant—is needed; so is reinforcement by the threats of the law.

A society in the "state of nature" imagined by Thomas Hobbes where *homo homini lupus,* where men act like wild beasts,† would be self-destructive and too unstable to function. The Hobbesian *bellum omnium contra omnes*—"the warfare of all against all"—precludes society by precluding social order. Threats are not enough to maintain it. No society could continue unless most of its members wanted to be law-abiding, at least in major matters. They do because they have been brought up to be law-abiding, to internalize the re-

---

* Hume and Robert Waelder ("The Concept of Justice and the Quest for a Perfectly Just Society," 115 *U. Pa. L. Rev.* 1, 1966), pose but do not answer the question: In what direction and how far should "the sense of justice" go? But that question can arise only because the sense of justice is not inborn to the extent of answering it. Only the possibility to develop it is inborn, as it is for anything we do.

† Since Hobbes wrote, ethologists have found that wild beasts, within most species, do not actually act toward each other as Hobbes had imagined.

straints which the law imposes. However, credible legal threats are indispensable not only to the original internalization but also to the continuous reinforcement of restraints. The relationship between internal and external restraints is not alternative but cumulative.

Few of us will reinsert the coin into a public phone when it is accidentally returned after a call is completed.* Or, to paraphrase Jerome Hall, most passengers buy tickets for a train ride; only a few try to cheat. However, if it became known that there are no conductors on trains anymore, the habit of paying would soon disappear. Driven only by their internalized moral sense, unsupported by conductors or policemen, fewer and fewer passengers would buy tickets. Cheating might even be accepted enough to lose its disrepute. Ultimately, those who pay might be as few as those are who now cheat. (If the cost were negligible, people might continue to pay so as not to be regarded as cheap and dishonest. But not if the cost were significant.)

Unlike law violators, law-abiding persons habitually assume that lawbreaking will be discovered and punished. It is this assumption, albeit unconscious, that keeps them honest. Without it, sainthood rather than mere honesty would be required for people to act honestly. Saints are as rare as they are admirable. Hence, if the assumption now made by law-abiding citizens—that the laws are enforced—were to become wholly unrealistic, the law would become ineffective in regulating conduct.

---

* An illustration the economist Frank H. Knight was fond of.

III

Justice and Utility

▬▬▬

Justice Separated from Utility

Do we punish for the sake of utility—to modify the future behavior of the convict (and of others)—or do we punish for the sake of justice? If the answer is utility, why does a person's past guilt matter more than the probability of his committing offenses in the future? Why does past guilt matter at all? If the answer is justice, wherein is it proper to punish for the sake of justice? What obligation is to be honored, what benefit is to be expected? What exactly is meant by *justice?*

The relationship between the utility and the justice of punishment, between possible future social benefits and guilt-based retribution, has long puzzled philosophers and practitioners alike. It has troubled and divided "Retributionists," who stress justice, and guilt incurred in the past, and "Utilitarians," who look for future benefits from punishment. Many have insisted on one doctrine of punishment at the expense, or even to the exclusion, of the other. No such choice need be made, for, although utility and justice often do compete in the criminal justice system, they do not exclude each other. Both are always present in the system; each must prevail in a different phase of the process. Once the different phases of the criminal justice process are distinguished, the relationship of punishment to justice and to utility becomes clear.

It is in the legislative phase of the criminal justice system that utility must prevail. Utility is the main purpose of *making* laws and of *prescribing* punishments for violators. But justice must prevail in the judicial phase, when penalties are *distributed* to individual offenders. Retribution must be suffered by individual offenders because it is just, deserved by their offenses, not because it is useful to society. Hence, utility (mainly) in prescribing, justice in distributing punishment.

Acts are prohibited on pain of punishment because the prohibition, reinforced by the threat of punishment, is meant to keep people from doing what is prohibited. Social benefits are expected from the non-performance of the prohibited acts. It is for the sake of these benefits that punishment is threatened. From the punishment actually dispensed no benefit need be expected beyond the benefit inherent in doing what had been threatened. Utility was expected from the *threat* of punishment, which was to produce the non-performance of the forbidden act. The punishment actually imposed is useful simply by carrying out the threat, which, if not carried out, would not be an effective threat, and therefore not useful. Thus, if the threat is useful, punishment is, because it makes the threat effective. Punishment can, but need not have other use beyond this one.

Justice is done by distributing punishments to offenders according to what is deserved by their offenses as specified by law. Legal justice involves neither less nor more than honoring the obligation to enforce the laws, which the government undertook in the very act of making them. Benefits, such as the rehabilitation of offenders, the protection of society from them while they are incapacitated, or, even more, the deterrence of others, are welcome, of course. But they are not necessary—and never sufficient—for punishment, and they are altogether irrelevant to making punishment just.

The advantage to be secured by legislation that prohibits

some acts under pain of punishment may be moral; it may be justice itself, as when the law protects an unpopular minority or a suspect from lynching; or the advantage may be something thought useful apart from justice, as when the law institutes one-way streets. The original prohibition, the threat, and what is threatened—the punishment yet to be distributed to offenders—are instituted for the sake of the future benefits, material or moral, to be produced by keeping people from doing what the law prohibits. The carrying out of the threat in general is useful by making it credible. But the distribution of the threatened punishments to specific offenders is an act of retributive justice. Offenders deserve punishment because they are guilty of violating preexisting laws, because they did wrong. In the words of Immanuel Kant: "Punishment can never be administered merely as a means for promoting another good either with regard to the criminal himself [rehabilitation] or to civil society [deterrence, or incapacitation], but must in all cases be imposed only because the individual on whom it is inflicted has committed a crime."

No amount of utility, then, could make the incarceration of an innocent person just, nor is utility required for the punishment of a guilty person. Still, Kant's "merely" suggests that punishment can have additional purposes. Actually, we do want just punishments to be useful as well, and useful laws to be just as well. However, useful laws cannot always be just, and just punishments cannot always be useful. One can define away the possible conflict and identify justice with usefulness only if one ignores the frequent competition between laws, or sentences, which might be useful by bringing future benefits and what is felt to be just, i.e., deserved by past guilt. This competition occurs because in practice legislators, who prescribe punishments, do not focus exclusively on usefulness, and courts, which distribute penalties, do not confine themselves exclusively to justice. When the phases of the criminal justice system are not wholly separate—and they can never be altogether discontinuous—the demands of justice may compete with the requirements of utility.

The Desire for Justice

Even though the basic purpose of legislation is future usefulness, laws often reflect the desire for justice, for retribution according to what is deserved, more than the desire for effective and beneficial restrictions on future behavior (utility). Hence, laws may prescribe punishment other than would be apposite if usefulness in influencing future conduct were always decisive. The punishment prescribed may reflect what people feel is deserved by the offense rather than what would minimize it in the future.

If laws aimed only at utility, they would threaten the most severe punishment for whatever causes the most serious and frequent injuries, wherever the threat might restrain people. We should then punish vehicular homicide (negligent manslaughter) by drunken drivers more severely than deliberate murder. The former victimizes more people by far than murder, is no less serious for the victims, and is not caused by passion or malevolence, which produce crimes hard to restrain. Homicidal drunken driving probably could be deterred more frequently than murder by the effective threat of severe punishment. Yet we punish murder more severely. Murderers have intentionally committed a wrong, whereas the drunken driver did not intend to kill. We feel that he deserves less retribution because guilt depends on intent as well as on the effect produced.*

---

* Generally, *mens rea* (evil intent) is necessary in some degree for an act to be a crime and also aggravates its criminality; whereas absence of *mens rea* at the least mitigates it. So, however, does ineffectiveness: an attempted but unsuccessful crime, however malevolent the intent, is punished less severely than a successful one. Thus, both effect and intent count—although the effect quite often is a matter of luck, as in the lethal or nonlethal outcome of an assault.

Mens rea only requires that the wrong was intended and known to be wrong rather than unintended (unforeseeable). Unlike premeditation, *mens rea* does not require the act to be planned beforehand. Whereas intention is inferred when a competent person does something (e.g., stabbing you) with foreseeable effects, premeditation must be shown.

Mens rea is not always required. "Strict liability" may hold a business

The law often ranks justice—what is felt to be deserved—
above the useful effect the severity of punishment can have by
reducing the frequency of the prohibited conduct. It is the
possible conflict between the demands of justice and of utility
that prompts H. L. A. Hart to lament: "It is not clear what, as
between the objective harm caused by a crime and the subjective evil intention inspiring it, is to be the measure. . . . Is
negligently causing the destruction of a city worse than the in-
tentional wounding of a single policeman?" [11]

The strength of our desire for justice is readily underes-
timated because justice is a moral concept and suspect, as all
moral concepts have become. They have lost so much prestige
that we may wonder uneasily: could it be that "justice" is a
disguise for unconscionable murky feelings such as vindic-
tiveness or jealousy? Tangible utilitarian explanations of punishment are readily accepted; justice is not. Yet, though un-
derestimated in the abstract, the idea of justice persists. Its
strength becomes apparent when cases are considered
concretely.

Justice above all demands punishment of the guilty, not the
innocent. Consider an imaginary situation. Suppose it were
shown to be socially useful to make some innocent person suffer whenever a crime has been committed and to reward the
criminal. Suppose it were advantageous (say it would reduce
homicide rates) for murderers to be rewarded, and innocent

---

responsible for faults, or an offender for offenses, which cannot be shown to
have been produced by his intent or neglect. Since it punishes the offense
without showing the guilt of the offender who is held liable, strict liability is
always unjust. It may be useful, though, and sometimes the only practical way
to minimize the evil to be controlled by the threat of punishment. Thus, when
it is impossible to determine individual responsibility and the control of an
evil is imperative, the reduction of it through strict liability may have desirable effects for the group that are sufficient to outweigh the injustice to individuals. At least, so most groups have felt. But for those who believe in justice, in
accordance with what the individual deserves, the case for strict liability is
always uneasy. It involves punishment without a show of individual cul-
pability. For those who do not believe in individual responsibility, the case
for *mens rea* is as uneasy, for it makes punishment depend on a subjective
state of mind that is hard to ascertain and even to define.

people to be deliberately executed each time a murder is committed. Would we want to do so? To ask the question is to answer it. We would reject such a distribution of punishments and rewards. For our desire to see justice done according to desert—to see a just distribution of punishments to the guilty, not the innocent—is at least as strong as our desire to achieve socially useful results. Fortunately, the two desires clash only rarely and not as starkly as in this wholly imaginary illustration. But marginal tradeoffs are frequent. It would be foolish to underestimate the desire for justice simply because it is not as fashionable among philosophers as it once was, because the desire for utility is more widely accepted now.

Our sense of justice is still so strong that many of us hope, or fear, that even the natural suffering we see around us through misfortune, or painful disease, is retribution, deserved by previous offenses. Many religions suggest that suffering is imposed by an inscrutable divine authority according to what is deserved (however difficult it is to understand why), or that offsetting punishments and rewards will be distributed ultimately:

> *judex ergo cum sedebit*
> *nihil inultum remanebit.**

Retributive and Distributive Justice

The sense of justice which demands that punishments be deserved also expects rewards to be deserved. *Suum cuique tribue* ("give to everyone what he deserves") is part of Ulpian's †
definition of a just order. But unlike punishments (retribu-

---

* In Thomas a Celano's hymn about the day of reckoning, *Dies Irae* (Day of Wrath): [God] will sit as judge/to whom nothing will remain hidden. (If the poet was right, those who banished his language from church rituals have little to look forward to.)

† Domitius Ulpianus was a diligent compiler of Roman law who wrote during the reign of Caracalla.

tion), rewards (distribution), such as monetary earnings, are not dispensed by court decisions. Given the distribution of property, an automatic market distributes incomes. It distributes unequally, so that some people are and stay poor while others are and stay rich. The unequal distribution is explainable, even justifiable, on economic grounds, but morally it appears unjust. The needy may not get all they need, the rich far more than they need. While persons of undoubted moral merit remain poor, others of little moral merit may become or remain rich because of luck, cunning, or other morally irrelevant abilities. The lack of moral justification for the existing income distribution—the discrepancy between what people are felt to deserve morally and what they get—is the main source of opposition to the market economy.*

Once the system of distributive justice is regarded as less than fair, it is easily surmised that offenders violate laws and are punished because they have been deprived of the minimal gratification of needs that would have kept them law-abiding. In other words, maldistribution forces them into crimes by depriving them of essentials. Other citizens remain law-abiding because they have not been so deprived. Maldistribution—society, the system—thus becomes the real culprit, the offender the victim, the law-abiding citizen the beneficiary.

* The notion of moral desert is altogether deserted by John Rawls' "justice as fairness" (A Theory of Justice, [Cambridge: Harvard University Press, 1971]). Rawls suggests that "desert," whatever merit it is based on, is a product of character and position, both inherited or at least not meritorious and, therefore, not deserving either retribution or reward. The moral notion of desert is thus dissolved, and justice becomes equality, independent of merit, with only such deviations as are justified by increases in welfare (and some principled qualifications). Rawls does not dwell on retributive (penal), but mainly on distributive justice, which has indeed become fashionable among philosophers, whereas retributive justice is often regarded as old-fashioned. The former stresses the rights of members, the duties of society; the latter, the duties of members, the rights of society. This may be part of the explanation. Applied to penalties rather than rewards, Rawls' views probably imply a weakening of the principle of retribution according to what the offense deserves and greater stress on the utilitarian functions of penalties (op. cit., p. 240). The best criticism of Rawls is found in Robert Nozick, Anarchy, State and Utopia (Basic Books, 1974).

In the form in which it is often stated, this argument proves too much. It denies the individual responsibility of all the deprived. Yet only some of the deprived become offenders. If unjust deprivation were the only, or major, cause of crime, how can we explain that some do, and others, as deprived, do not, rape and rob and burglarize? In a more qualified form, however, the argument makes a great deal of sense (see Chapters VIII and IX).

A variant of this argument maintains that the deprived do not commit more crimes than those who are better off, they commit different crimes and, above all, are caught and convicted more often, and therefore appear to commit more crimes.* If true, the failure to catch and to punish an equal proportion of offenders from among the well-to-do and the poor would indicate that punishments are distributed unfairly among classes. But an unfair distribution among classes would not make the punishment of guilty individuals unjust, whatever class they belong to. The injustice to the deprived would consist only in the ability of others to escape. It is corrected not by conferring that ability on the deprived, too, but by taking it from the well-to-do.

To assuage the feeling of social injustice, jurists have from time to time proposed that courts hand out rewards to the deserving as well as punishments to the guilty. It has not been found practical to do so.† In turn, other reformers and many revolutionaries have proposed that income be distributed by a political system that would replace the market and distribute in accordance with moral merit or material need. However,

---

* The statistical data on which this hypothesis rests are questioned by Nigel Walker (*Crimes, Courts and Figures*, [Baltimore: Penguin, 1971], p. 37). Further, since the data are usually gathered from adolescents, they may reflect the fairly universal and classless adolescent tendency to minor law defiance, without casting much light on class differences in crime frequency among adults. The data may also reflect adolescent bragging.

† Such rewards may well be distributed by other institutions. High honors and rewards to those who help fellow citizens or law officers to arrest offenders or who help persons attacked by criminals are desirable and might help to counteract the too frequent indifference of the public.

this is not likely to be achieved. Distribution by a political system would amount to distribution in accordance with political ability and would produce a different, but certainly not a more equal or a morally more acceptable, distribution of income than is now provided by the market: political ability is no more identical with moral merit than is the economic ability that wins in the marketplace. Political abilities—such as pleasing one's superiors; or getting oneself elected; or gaining power in some other way—are as unequally distributed and as morally irrelevant as economic abilities. Distribution of income by a political or bureaucratic system—e.g., a planning agency—merely would replace the discrepancy between the economic and the moral with a discrepancy between the political and the moral. There is no reason to believe that there would be less distributive injustice. An equal distribution, on the other hand, which would give the same income to a loafer and to a diligent worker, would offend our sense of justice. A distribution "according to need" would put political authorities in charge of defining *need*. The latter two distributions also would leave us bereft of any incentive to perform. They would be impractical as long as incentives are needed. A formula for "justice" is not easy to find. Distributive justice seems as elusive as happiness.

Yet, if the social system as a whole is thought to produce an unjust distribution of rewards, of the good things of life, our feeling about the justice of the legal order and of its distribution of punishments to offenders turns sour. However just in applying its rules, retributive justice cannot be ultimately just unless distributive justice is. For retributive justice necessarily defends and sanctions the distributive order in its major political and economic aspects. Legal justice never can do less, though it can do more. Marxists have been quite correct in pointing this out. They go wrong mainly when they imply that the defense of the status quo is more characteristic of capitalist justice than of justice in the socialist order. Yet courts and laws always interpret, articulate, and defend the social order of which they are part. Any economic and political system, whether socialist or capitalist, run by planners or by the market, sanctions itself by laws and courts that distribute punishments to those who violate its rules. The Marxist systems now existing actually seem to require more frequent and severe punishment of offenders than the non-Marxist systems.[12] There is indeed no *a priori* reason why a more equal income distribution should require fewer legal defenses than a less equal one, and there is no *a posteriori* evidence that it does. A feeling of distributive injustice can be generated by any distributive system. Some individuals and groups always are, or feel, deprived in relation to others. No society will perfectly embody the elusive and inherently ambiguous idea of social justice debated among philosophers since Aristotle first attempted to define it.

IV

Justice, Order, Charity

Some philosophers have denied that one can conceive of justice separately from law, since the laws are "the rules of just and unjust" (Thomas Hobbes).* Which would leave lawmaking bereft of justice or, for that matter, injustice. Indeed, *within* the legal system justice must be done according to law. Law is meant to be the concretization of justice. But this does not help us to decide about the legal system itself or on what particular laws to make. As citizens and legislators, we cannot escape the duty of defining and developing the social order we want to have. Our idea of justice thus must be prior to, and independent of, the laws we make in accordance with it.

Penal laws are meant (1) to articulate, sustain, and develop the social order by penalizing forbidden acts; (2) to do justice to offenders and non-offenders alike; and (3) to be charitable. These three precepts may demand divergent laws, practices, and penalties. Nothing harms lawmaking and law enforcement more than the common failure to distinguish the conflicting injunctions implied in the desire (1) to defend the social order, (2) to do justice to individuals, and (3) to be chari-

* A similar (though more limited) view was introduced into English jurisprudence by John Austin (1790–1859) and has been independently elaborated in the late Hans Kelsen's *Pure Theory of Law*. (Berkeley: University of California Press, 1970.)

table, each of which the criminal justice system must accommodate.

Order

"Order is heaven's first law," Alexander Pope wrote. It certainly is the first law of society; societies require a stable organization of their institutions into a functioning whole, as well as rules that minimize violence, restrict each person for the sake of others, regulate conduct, and punish offenders.

Order is indispensable to justice because justice can be achieved only by means of a social and legal order. Though justice may reside in an alternative order, it never can be an alternative to order. Nonetheless, order and justice can clash in at least two ways. First, more justice may be found in an alternative order established by demolishing the prevailing one: order can be impaired, albeit temporarily, for the sake of more justice. Secondly, whether itself just or unjust, any order may require injustice to be done to individuals for its defense: justice can be impaired for the sake of order.

Governments usually give priority to order over justice, although they rarely admit as much. Even governments firmly committed to do justice to each individual convince themselves that in the end more justice is done to all individuals by sustaining the social order than is lost by doing, or allowing, injustice to some individuals for the sake of order—by letting some of the guilty go, for instance, or even making some of the innocent suffer. It certainly is arguable that justice to more persons—not quite the same thing as more justice—can be achieved at this price at times. By and large, this is the justification for the priority of order.

Apart from injustices that may be involved in the process of defending even a just social order, some distributive injustice, some unequal and morally unjustified distribution of benefits—income, power, prestige—is observed in every known order and seems unavoidable despite, or because of, equality of opportunity. All societies are likely to reward some activities more than others; wherefore, some persons are likely to have higher incomes. The most intelligent, or talented, or ruthless, or inventive, may be more rewarded than others if their activities are socially more useful, or more appreciated, or merely more apt to gain rewards. Inequality follows from unequal talents, abilities, and inclinations and unequal valuations placed on them. The pattern of inequality can be changed; but it is hard to conceive of a society that can reward equally every talent, or lack of it, every inclination and every degree of diligence, and it is as difficult to conceive of a moral justification for any distribution of inequalities.*

Whether it be just or not, the enforcement of the social order in which they govern has always been the paramount duty of governments; † other duties, even the duty to do justice, are subordinate to it. Governments are ultimately entrusted with the safety of all the institutions, values, and individuals of society. Justice is only one value within the social order, albeit of peculiar importance. Other values, such as survival or freedom, are no less important. Preservation of any of these values (or of the social order as a whole) may require a course of action which may slight other values. Thus, justice may be impaired to preserve or enhance another value, or the social order as a whole.‡

Courts are only one arm of the government. They are responsible for justice and can take as their motto *fiat justitia ruat coelum* or, more directly, *pereat mundus*. ("Let there be

---

* For a contrary view see Nozick *op. cit.*, footnote 4, p. 30.

† In the case of a revolutionary government the social order defended may be in the process of establishment.

‡ When John Rawls writes "Justice is the first virtue of social institutions as truth is of systems of thought," meaning that justice cannot be "outweighed by the larger sum of advantages enjoyed by many" (*A Theory of Justice*, p. 34), he expresses a sentiment more noble than sensible. Empirically, it is not so, and normatively, it would surely be immoral to sacrifice all social advantages to "justice" when justice is conceived (as it should be) as something other than social advantage.

justice even if the heavens fall," or "if the world perish.") In theory at least courts are responsible *only* for justice. Governments cannot so limit themselves, not even in theory. They are responsible for everything else as well. Their directive must be *salus publica suprema lex* ("the public welfare" or, directly, *salus populi,* "the welfare of the people," is "the highest law"). Whenever the public welfare—order—is in conflict with justice to individuals, it is the duty of governments to make the public welfare prevail, whereas it is the more restricted duty of courts to provide justice.

How Much?

Actually, history seldom presents stark conflicts between justice and order. Additional ideas and interests usually are involved, and the choice is not either justice or order, as though one could altogether exclude the other. Quantitative judgments invariably are needed: how much justice to individuals is to be sacrificed to how much social order? Nobody would favor the sacrifice of any amount of justice, however much, to any amount of order, however little; nor would anyone trade all order for some justice. Even if one favors a general priority for justice or order (or, as politicians do in public speeches, for both), it is hard to reach agreement on the value question: how much of one *ought* to be sacrificed to the other? About the practical question it is even harder to reach agreement: how much of one value *must* be sacrificed to obtain more of the other?

This dilemma usually comes shrouded in layers of rhetoric. Often, moral and constitutional principles are used to hide the quantitative nature of the lurking conflict. They are invoked as though their mere assertion could decide how much of one principle must be sacrificed to the other in each specific instance. To decide if and when the police should be allowed to "stop and frisk," or to listen in, or to detain without warrant, is to decide *how much* of the privacy of suspects, or of their freedom, should be sacrificed to *how much* public safety. Such questions are decided by balancing the danger presented by the suspects against the sacrifice of justice involved in infringing on their freedom or privacy when they are only suspects or have as yet violated no law. The two putative quantities are balanced against each other, and some of one must be traded for some of the other.

Occasionally, the law itself may sacrifice justice to other social values or needs. "Strict liability" does, since it punishes offenses regardless of the ability or intention of the offender to avoid them.* Indeterminate sentences also are justifiable, if at all, not by being just but only by the social benefits they are expected to produce—the reform or the incapacitation of the offender. An offense must have been committed, and, within the outer limits of punishment established by law, authorities other than judges decide on grounds other than justice—other than what is deserved by the offense—if the offender is to be released after one year or twenty. The penalty actually served depends on an estimate of the future behavior of the offender, of the social usefulness of keeping him in prison or out. In some foreign countries similar practices have been codified. The Italian *Codice Penale* (Art. 108) recognizes a *delinquente per tendenza*—an offender found to have persistent criminal leanings. Unlike the *delinquente abituale* (Art. 102–103) or *professionale* (Art. 105)—the habitual or professional offender—the *delinquente per tendenza* need not be a recidivist to be confined beyond the term deserved by his actual offense.

The Gospels, Melville, and Adam Smith

The demands of justice (retribution) and order (security or welfare) often clash. The trade-off is seldom satisfactory. A world where justice is perfect and order is always in harmony

* See footnote, pp. 27–28.

with it would be better; we never cease to clamor, *aperite mihi portas justitiae* ("open the gates of justice to me"), but we clamor because the world of perfect justice is not the world we live in.

The Gospels present us with perhaps the most famous instance of conflict between order and justice. Pontius Pilatus felt in duty bound to sentence to death one he probably thought innocent when, on reasonable evidence, he thought that the maintenance of law and order required no less. Justice was slighted in favor of order. Herman Melville poignantly affirmed the governor's painful duty when, writing toward the end of his life, he had the guiltless Billy Budd * accept the death sentence imposed by Captain Vere—who knew him innocent but plausibly believed that Billy had to die, to daunt incipient mutiny. The ship of state sailed on, its ropes and pulleys groaning but its crew safe. Justice to the individual gave way to law and order, the paramount need of society, which governments exist to satisfy. For on law and order depend the rights "governments are instituted among men" to secure.

Fortunately, the maintenance of social order rarely demands so clearcut a sacrifice of innocents. Most often the person punished is guilty of some offense, though an exemplary punishment, which exceeds retribution proportioned to past guilt, may have to be imposed for the sake of order, not justice.† When the crime committed is socially most dangerous order demands the harshest punishment—often harsher than what charity, and sometimes justice, would dictate. If a hungry man steals, and his temptation is shared by others whose stealing would endanger the social order—be it the rationing of scarce food on a becalmed ship, or in a country suffering from famine—he will have to be severely punished because others similarly situated might do what he did. This is

---

* In the homonymous novel. Legally, Billy could never be guilty of murder though he may have been guilty of some degree of manslaughter.

† Thus Moses was kept from the Promised Land for one moment of disobedience.

certainly uncharitable, and unjust: the penalty applied to deter may exceed what seems just, proportionate to the wickedness of the crime. Punishments required to maintain order often can be justified only on that ground, and not on grounds of justice, let alone compassion.

Adam Smith well realized that the requirements of order may be inconsistent with those of justice. "When the preservation of an individual is inconsistent with safety of the multitude, nothing can be more just than that the many should be preferred to the one. Yet this punishment, how necessary soever, always appears excessively severe." [13] Smith illustrates the matter by the case of "a sentinel who falls asleep upon his watch and suffers death by the laws of war." The spectator "looks upon the sentinel as an unfortunate victim . . . whom still, in his heart, he would be glad to save; and he is only sorry that the interest of the many should oppose it." [14] Death surely is a punishment disproportionate to the minor negligence involved. Falling asleep is not motivated by wickedness nor intended to damage the army. For a willful murder, execution may be just. But for falling asleep? Yet, Smith reasons, "the safety of the multitude" requires no less. The army must depend on sentries keeping awake. Order necessitates a punishment far above what justice would countenance.*

Severe and uncharitable, even intrinsically unjust and disproportionate punishments become more acceptable if distributed justly, i.e., equally to all those guilty of the same offense. If the maintenance of social order requires hardships or injustice (disproportion)—as in war, or famine—they will be more readily accepted if distributed impersonally and equally, without "discrimination." Justice will be redefined: if the innocent are to sacrificed they must be equally or at least

---

* Smith did not separate order from justice, but opposed charity to both in his formulation. Actually, what I have called "order" could be called, following Smith's usage, "justice to the multitude" of those who would be harmed if it were impaired, as distinguished from justice to the individuals who suffer for the sake of the "multitude." (My "order" here would include self-preservation, as does Smith's "justice to the multitude.")

impersonally sacrificed.* If punishments are to be disproportionate to the offense, the disproportion must be the same for all. Justice requires equality of sacrifice beyond and apart from what is needed to overcome the difficulty. Famine can be mitigated by any restriction of food consumption, however distributed, provided it is orderly. Wars can be won by putting enough soldiers into the field—it does not matter who is drafted. But justice requires that sacrifices and dangers be equally shared and distributed. Thus, the severe punishment of the hungry thief is accepted, if it is felt that the governing elite, which inflicts it, suffers hardships equal to those inflicted on the governed and is equally subjected to the harsh law: *dura lex, sed lex* ("harsh law, but the law") means that the law, however harsh, must be accepted because all are subjected to it.†

Justice is needed by any social order, then, even if occasionally restricted, redefined, or subordinated to other values. Unless those living within it feel that the social order is reasonably just (however they define justice), that order can last only if they are deprived of freedom. And, however different they are, all notions of justice have certain elements in common—notably the demand that people felt to be equals be dealt with in ways felt to be equal.

Justice, Order, and "the Revolution"

Mankind has made great material progress since Rome ruled and Melville wrote. There has been some social progress, too,

* In some circumstances impersonal distribution may be accepted as just instead of equal distribution. Thus, distribution by lottery may be more acceptable than an equally irrational distribution by personal preference of the distributing authority.

† The nature of the hardships to which different groups are exposed may vary according to the status of each group, as long as it is felt that the groups are subjected to equivalent hardship.

so that the episodes described in the Gospels or in *Billy Budd* have become rare. Not as rare, though, as one might wish. In 1887 Lenin's older brother Alexander was executed upon being convicted of plotting the assassination of the czar. It did not occur to the government of Imperial Russia to execute other members of his family (who were innocent of wrongdoing) because they might constitute a future danger. Lenin himself was unmolested and later permitted to enroll in the University of Kazan. He soon began to plot against the regime but suffered only mild punishment (exile which, under the czar, was inconvenient but not a hardship).

When Lenin came to power, the Bolsheviks executed the czar, as well as his wife, without a trial. Though it is not easy to justify these killings, it is not impossible. However, the Bolsheviks also had a firing squad shoot all available relatives of the imperial family and all the children. They were too young to have done anything that could remotely justify their being killed. The Bolsheviks feared that these children— merely by existing—might constitute, or become, a danger to the new social order. Justice, which never allows the deliberate killing of known innocents, was denied for the sake of protecting the new social order from a danger neither clear nor present. The motive of revenge may have played a role, although in violation of the sensible injunction (Deuteronomy 24:16): "The fathers shall not be put to death for the children, neither shall the children be put to death for the fathers: every man shall be put to death for his own sin."

At its second congress (Brussels–London, 1903), the majority of delegates of the clandestine Russian Socialist Party (Bolsheviki) had decided to give priority to their revolution over individual justice and individual rights. The highly respected "Father of Russian Marxism," G. V. Plekhanov, elaborating on a statement of another participant, proclaimed "*Salus revolutiae suprema lex,*" a proclamation remarkable not only for its grotesque Latin but also for its (in the context) quite explicit willingness to subordinate every other principle

—liberty, individual rights, justice, decency, democracy—to the revolution. "There are absolutely no democratic principles which we ought not to subordinate to the needs of our party," Plekhanov added.[15] He later retreated from his position when he saw his pupils take it literally. But Lenin thought his revolutionary ends justified any means. (Stalin and Hitler went further still: their concentration camps cannot be explained, let alone justified, as necessary for the defense of the social order they were imposing. They were irrationally cruel, immoral even as seen from Plekhanov's original standpoint.)

In America, fortunately, the subordination of justice to the defense of the social order takes place, when it does, on a more modest scale. Those who wish otherwise—either for the sake of revolution or, on the contrary, for the sake of a more militant defense of the status quo—are not likely to gain the power necessary to fulfill their wish in the foreseeable future. The general public is understandably unwilling to let them. Indeed, the public sees a subordination of justice in many attempted reforms and, therefore, is slow to enact them. Despite a remarkably high crime rate, little is done to make it easier to apprehend suspects and convict the guilty, or to expedite the general work of the criminal justice system. The rights of individuals are so highly valued at present that suspects often seem favored while the need for social defense is slighted.

Justice and Unequal Conditions

People differ, and so do the situations in which nature or society places them. So do, therefore, the degrees and kinds of opportunity, of temptation, of need, or stimulation to violate laws to which different people are exposed or by nature inclined. These disparities loom large in the modern mind, particularly the disparities generated by different social environments and locations. Often it is urged that justice would be more perfect if it were to pay more heed to the different living conditions, the different environments, of the rich and the poor, the white and the black, the educated and the uneducated, the suburbanites and the slum-dwellers. Such differences are real and immensely important, and they do lead to different temptations, of different intensity, and to different opportunities for crime.

Yet the penal law can attend to dissimilarities of condition and personality only when the purpose of making the law—to restrain people from doing what is forbidden—and of applying the law—to do justice—can be neglected in favor of charity. For, if the law is to restrain anyone at all, those who are tempted to do what it prohibits must be restrained as much as those who are not. They must be restrained even if the conditions in which they are constrained to live tempt them to break the law. More motivation for criminal conduct, or stimulation to wrongdoing, or more opportunity for it, or greater deprivation of legitimate opportunities, cannot justify or excuse doing what is wrong. Temptation is precisely what the law must restrain, however well the difference in the degree of temptation explains why an offense was committed by one person rather than another. Different intensities of temptation were assumed when the act was prohibited, and equal punishment prescribed for those who commit it. When the border between temptation (he could have done otherwise) and compulsion (he could not have done otherwise) is demonstrably crossed, justice pays heed by not blaming the offender. If the offender could not have restrained himself, he cannot be punished for his failure to do so. Otherwise, different needs and situations may be considered as aggravating or mitigating, but not as excusing, the offense.

It is easy, though unfashionable, to see why justice must disregard the different needs which generate disparities of temptation among persons and groups. A frustrated man rejected as repulsive by the sexual partners he craves may be more tempted to rape than another person better endowed or situated; * an irritable person is more disposed to assault than a phlegmatic one; a poor and deprived man may be more tempted to steal than a wealthy one. But the prohibition against rape must be applied equally to repulsive (and frustrated) individuals and to attractive (and unfrustrated) ones; the prohibition against assault to the ill- and to the even-tempered; and the prohibition against stealing to rich and poor alike. Else the forbidden act would be prohibited only to those not inclined or tempted to commit it. Which won't help. The purpose of the law is to forbid what some people are tempted to do, by character or by circumstance. The threat of punishment is meant to discourage those who are tempted, rather than those who are not, regardless of whether the temptation comes from within (motivation, inclination) or from without (opportunity, stimulation, deprivation).

Class Justice?

Since the law quite deliberately restricts the tempted as well as the untempted, there is a kernel of truth in the belief, held by revolutionaries of various persuasions (most elaborately by Marxists), that the law is a device of the rich and powerful to keep the poor and powerless in check. The threats of the law are meant to restrain those who would do what the law prohibits. Obviously, the poor and powerless are more tempted to take what is not theirs, or to rebel, than the powerful and wealthy, who need not take what they already have.

However, the discovery that the penal law restrains the poor and powerless more than the wealthy and powerful who are less pressed, or tempted, to do what it forbids is about as revealing as the disclosure that the Prohibition laws were meant to restrain drinkers more than the teetotalers who imposed

---

* Actually, most rapists seem more hostile than frustrated, and frustrated, if at all, only because hostile. But whether it be anger or frustration, they have a strong motive to rape, which is what is relevant: having a motive is an explanation, not a justification or an excuse.

them. Obviously, the law restrains some groups more than others and is violated by some groups more often than by others. This does not make the law unjust, contrary to what Anatole France implied when he ridiculed "the law [which] in its majestic equality forbids rich and poor alike to sleep under bridges . . . and to steal bread." That his sarcasm is quoted often and with approval, even by people learned in the law, suggests that charity is a more appealing concept than justice. Yet the heart cannot replace the mind. Any body, including the body social, wants both.

So, because the temptation to break the laws is unequally distributed, because of different personalities and different living conditions, the laws—and the punishments for violating them—must weigh or fall more heavily on some persons and groups. Those less favored by nature or society are more tempted to violate laws and therefore suffer punishment for doing so more often. Unless society consists of identical personalities living in identical conditions, it cannot be otherwise.* Inequality of condition cannot be an objection to equal laws and punishments as long as it is possible—though it may be more or less difficult—to act lawfully. However, compassion for the victims of unequal temptations, for the offender who suffers punishment, if not for the offense for which he suffers it, remains a virtue.

Justitia Dulcore Misericordiae Temperata †

Unlike justice, charity stresses the "need" (a word too often used for wish) of the individual criminal, his motivation, and the intensity of the temptation to which he is exposed. The

---

* Objections to inequality of condition are objections to the system of distributive justice, unless they are objections to God.

† Justice tempered by mercy (literally by the sweetness of compassion) was urged, if not realized, as Roman law became colored by the Christian spirit.

greater his need, or the temptation, the more readily charity can forgive one's yielding. Justice requires distribution, or retribution, according to what the act deserves, and equal treatment where desert is equal. But charity will give most when the need of the individual, independent of his merit, is greatest. And charity will mitigate punishment most when the guilty person was most needy, motivated, deprived of other gratifications, or tempted to commit the offense. Charity (from *caritas*, Latin for "love"), then, will stress the individual and social differences that justice must ignore. The charitable person loves the offender, regardless of his offense, because he is a fellow human in need. Compassion rests on the realization that we, too, could have done what the offender did, that, in Tolstoy's words, "The seeds of every crime are in each of us," that only "by the grace of God" were we placed in circumstances which tempted us less than the offender or made us less responsive to temptation. The act remains odious and deserving of punishment. But compassion may be felt for the actor who suffers it. Deserved suffering is suffering still. And we may have deserved no less, except that fate was kinder to us.

Justice can be tempered by mercy but cannot be replaced by it. Justice requires that offenses be punished as such without regard to the offender, that the law differentiate among offenders only in terms of their offenses. We may feel charity, mercy, or compassion for offenders as persons brought to their offenses by individual circumstances, pressures, and misfortunes. This leads us to attend to their individual needs, to do what can help them rather than what is deserved by their acts. The impulse is generous and needed. But distribution of punishments (or rewards) by charity cannot take the place of distribution by justice, according to what is deserved.*

* Pardons, amnesties, and acts of executive clemency are meant to blunt or thwart justice occasionally for the sake of tempering it with charity or of better achieving political goals, such as social harmony or order. A pardon thus may be justified, but it is not intended to be just. Its purpose is to thwart legal justice for the sake of political or charitable ends.

Accommodation: Order, Justice, Charity

Raison d'état ("reason of state," the preservation of the social order) may require a punishment beyond or below what is deserved by the degree of guilt (as Adam Smith's sleeping sentry, reminds us). Justice according to law demands punishment according to what the crime deserves, regardless of the individual need to commit it, or on the other hand, of the social need to restrain others: justice requires a legal "tariff" for crimes. Charity, finally, responds in compassion to the individual's needs, defects, deprivations, and disabilities. Usually, but not always, *raison d'état* demands more punishment than justice, and charity less. The demands of *salus publica* (deterrence, prevention, order), of justice (individual desert according to law), and of charity (compassion with individual need) often differ. But though principles and theoretical categories be divergent and discontinuous, life is continuous. In practice, each time a sentence is imposed the criminal justice system must try to accommodate all three principles.

Differences in Temptation

Accommodation is easier, of course, the less disparate the social circumstances which make it comfortable for some and hard for others to resist temptation. If there are no hungry people, the temptation to steal bread is both reduced and equalized. Can we, then, reduce the intrinsic and extrinsic disparities which produce different temptations for different groups? Could we thereby decrease the crime rate and the need for punishments which, if just, still are uncharitable? With less frustration, poverty, inequality, resentment, or ill temper, there might be altogether less crime. We shall turn to this possibility in Chapters VIII–XI.

At any rate, we must realize that some temptations to violate them will be with us as long as there are laws. Otherwise they would not be needed. Whatever we can do to equalize it, the distribution of opportunities, appetites, and achievements among people is likely to remain somewhat unequal. Major material differences can be reduced. But the frustrations and resentments produced by minor inequalities actually may become more intense. Perhaps greater economic equality merely shifts our jealousies and our feelings of deprivation to different objects. We do not know how great a reduction—if any—of frustration and crime a radically egalitarian society would bring; and more equality is not easy to achieve without losses in productivity, creativity, ambition, diversity, and liberty, not to speak of intensive individual relations, notably love, which by their nature lead to unequal degrees of frustration and temptation.* With less of these there may be more boredom, which itself easily enough becomes a cause of crime. Still, each proposal for more equality must be accepted or rejected on its individual merits. Quite possibly, some proposals can avoid the disadvantages I anticipate and in time can reduce even the need for punishment. But the experience of mankind gives no grounds for optimism.

A Brief Summary

It may help to summarize briefly what has been said about punishment so far.

If laws are needed to restrict conduct for the sake of social welfare; if threats of punishment are needed to control violations by those tempted to break the law; and if threats remain credible only if carried out when violations do occur—then retribution must be inflicted as threatened on those guilty of

---

* By definition so, if love is defined as a preference.

crime. Retribution will be useful, if the laws are, by making the laws effective; and just, if the laws are, when inflicted only on the guilty according to what is deserved by their guilt.

Charity weighs individual needs, motives, and temptations; justice weighs what is deserved by guilt. The preservation of society and of the social order, finally, may require that we subordinate charity, and sometimes even justice, to punish most severely what most endangers society and the social order, even when there is little guilt, or none.

When laws are made and punishments prescribed, the requirements of order (utility) must prevail; when laws are applied, justice according to law should prevail, tempered by charity. All three principles must ultimately coalesce in the criminal justice system.

V

Utilitarian Functions of Punishment

The threat of punishment is useful inasmuch as it controls crime. When the threat has not been effective—when an offense has been committed despite it—the punishment imposed meets the obligation society undertook when threatening it and is morally justified if undertaking the obligation was. However, retribution is useful beyond being a moral obligation—above all, by making the threat of the law credible (as discussed in Chap. II); and in three additional ways: (1) by incapacitating offenders, (2) by reforming them through intimidation or rehabilitation, and (3) by deterring others from committing offenses.*

Incapacitation

For as long as it lasts, the incapacitation of detained offenders protects society from them.

The only total, permanent, and irrevocable incapacitation is

---

* Threats are meant to deter. Carrying them out, against someone they did not deter, adds credibility indispensable to the deterrent effect. However, de-

execution. Other punishments, such as imprisonment, produce partial, revocable, and usually temporary incapacitation.* Although some convicts commit crimes in prison, or
direct extramural criminal activity from there, most do not. Imprisonment reduces the number of offenses they commit over
their lifespan—if they would have continued illegal activities
had they been free, and if, once out of prison, they do not
make up for lost time. Two general points should be noted
about this reduction of offenses. To consider these points, the
incapacitating functions of imprisonment must be analytically
separated from the retributive, rehabilitative, and deterrent
ones. Thus isolated, the effects of incapacitation are the same
whether caused by incarceration or by hospitalization.

Incapacitation does not decrease the offenses of convicts
who would not have committed additional offenses anyway—
e.g., of generally law-abiding citizens who commited a "crime
of passion" in a specific, nonrecurrent situation. As for others,
incarceration reduces their criminal activity only for the duration, unless it also affects their conduct upon release—unless
prisoners are reformed. Some are. Others are criminalized,
i.e., led more thoroughly into a criminal career. Most seem
unaffected either way upon release; but the effects of imprisonment on criminal careers are difficult to gauge.

Whatever the effects of incapacitation on the number of
crimes a prisoner commits over his lifetime, they must not be
confused with effects on the crime rate: the crimes committed
annually per 100,000 persons. The temporary or even the permanent incapacitation of convicts reduces the crime rate only
if there is no compensating increase of crime by others. Often
there is.

---

terrence does not depend on credibility alone and therefore is best listed independently. Note also that threats always deter marginally: not all, but some
offenses are deterred by effective threats.

* Some punishments, such as fines, are not incapacitating at all; others,
such as denying a license to practice a profession or to engage in an activity
(e.g., driving), are partially incapacitating.

When illegal activities are produced as legal ones are, when crimes are produced like wheat or shoes or advertising, such an offsetting increase must be expected. When some farmers or shoemakers or ad men are incapacitated by disease, the rate of wheat or shoe or ad production hardly decreases. Nor does the rate of crime when some criminals are incapacitated—if their crimes are produced as wheat or shoes or ads are. The criminal population—or that of wheat farmers—is what it is because some are normally expected to be incapacitated. The number of farmers or criminals producing the current output would be smaller if some were not ordinarily incapacitated by various misfortunes, such as illness or imprisonment. If the rate of incapacitation increases temporarily, because of an epidemic of pneumonia or of convictions, production suffers temporarily. But the total number of persons engaged in producing shoes, or crimes, soon adjusts to produce the output determined by profitability. Hence, incapacitation will have little effect. Incapacitation is effective mainly when the forces that determine the production of crime cannot be compared with the forces that determine the supply of shoes or wheat. When is that the case?

Some crimes are produced exclusively by exceptional people, as some commodities are. If some of these people are incapacitated, production is reduced. Offenses committed almost exclusively by persons with uncommon psychological characteristics, such as psychotics, can be reduced by incapacitation: there is, at any time, only a limited and reasonably fixed supply of psychotics. Child molesting, for example, is done by offenders with an uncommon psychology (though they need not be psychotics). Incapacitating all of them would eradicate the offense. Since it is impossible to identify and incapacitate these offenders before they commit the offense, child molesting cannot be eliminated. However, incapacitating convicted child molesters reduces the rate of child molesting if, left free, they would have continued to commit the offense. Such offenders are not likely to be replaced.* The "Boston Strangler" also produced the kind of crime that can be reduced by incapacitating the criminal. Whenever the crime depends on a fixed and limited supply of persons exclusively capable of committing it, and when many of these can be convicted, the crime rate can be affected by incapacitating them. The incapacitation of multiple rapists—likely to have developed a sort of addiction to raping—will reduce the rate of rape produced by them. On the other hand, increases in legal costs—punishments—are more decisive in deterring non-addicted rapists from joining the ranks or continuing. The total rape rate is affected by both incapacitation and by the deterrent effect of punishment.

Many offenses, however, are committed by a range of fairly ordinary persons. If the psychological characteristics needed to commit the offense are not rare, those incapacitated may be easily replaced. The supply cannot be depleted by incapacitation and the crime rate is not affected by it (except temporarily), whether incapacitation is caused by an epidemic or by incarceration. The time lag for replacement differs according to the attractiveness of the offense, the skill required to commit it, etc. But when crimes depend mostly on the benefit expected by reasonably rational offenders, the crime rate depends on varying that benefit through varying the cost to offenders and not simply on incapacitation of those who are caught. Punishment (cost), whether imprisonment or a fine, will affect the crime rate by deterring. But by and large crime rates will be independent of incapacitation by imprisonment, natural death, execution, or sickness of any number of easily replaceable offenders.

An imprisoned Mafia "soldier," or "capo," is prevented from committing crimes. But he is readily replaced. The total

---

* Others may engage in similar offenses. But they do not replace those who have been incapacitated in the sense of having been attracted to the activity by their absence, which made a profitable situation available.

of Mafia crimes is not reduced by incapacitating Mafiosi. Or, to take a different case, when a "normal" proportion of all practicing prostitutes is incapacitated by disease or imprisonment, the rate of prostitution is "normal." If the proportion incapacitated is temporarily higher than "normal," owing to a police "crackdown," there may be a temporary decline of the activity. But if the proportion incapacitated remains permanently higher than before, the rate of prostitution will be unaffected once more: more prostitutes will be needed to provide the same level of service; more will be recruited if providing the service continues to be attractive. (We are considering here only the incapacitating effect of imprisonment, not its deterrent effect, which may make supplying the service less attractive and thus more costly to customers.) The rate of prostitution depends on factors that make the occupation attractive, not on depleting the supply of practitioners by incapacitation, unless uncommon qualifications are needed. They are not. Nor are the qualifications of car thieves, heroin dealers, muggers, or ordinary robbers and burglars rare enough for incapacitation to make much difference. (There are exceptions to which we will turn.)

A Restatement

The foregoing may appear a little too sweeping to some readers. The following restatement is more qualified and unavoidably more technical.

The crime rate is fairly independent of the incapacitation of actual offenders as long as an unlimited number of potential offenders is willing to replace them as soon as net benefits suffice—when the supply of offenders is elastic. In that case more people would engage in crime than do presently if the net benefit were higher (compared to legitimate opportunities);

fewer, if the net were lower; and as many as do now (regardless of incapacitation) as long as the comparative net benefit
does not change.

To assume an elastic supply of potential offenders is to assume that all or most "normal" people will yield to the attrac-
tion of an illicit gain, if the net benefit—the positive difference
between cost and gross benefit—suffices compared to the net
benefit from licit activities. This assumption may seem extreme. One may question whether people who are quite "normal," who are not deviant, who do not have something wrong
with them, will engage in an illegitimate activity, even when
it holds out net benefits over and above legitimate activities.
We need not decide this question. Whether or not those who
commit offenses when there is a net benefit have something
wrong with them, there are too many to expect that the crime
rate can be reduced by incapacitating some. Instead, it must
be reduced in the first place by reducing the comparative net
benefit from offenses, by making them less profitable.

In most cases changes in comparative cost-benefit ratios that
significantly affect the crime rate depend on changes in the
legal costs imposed for offenses: higher costs (punishments)
reduce the comparative attractiveness of crime. However,
when legal costs are held constant, net benefits also can be affected by the crime rate itself. This is the case when opportunities for crime are limited. Additional crime then requires the
utilization of less good (marginal) opportunities and becomes
less profitable. Bank robbing may be an instance. And the
value of illegitimately obtained items, or of illegitimate services, declines as more come on the market. Thus the resale
value of stolen cars and hijacked or stolen goods will decline
when the supply rises.[16] The profitability of various rackets
also is affected by the availability of opportunities and the
presence of competing rackets. In all such cases, crime can
be made less profitable by reducing opportunities for it still
further. Better burglar alarms, more guards, traveler's checks
instead of cash, better lighting, and unpickable car locks all

help. But the most important thing is to increase the legal cost of the offense to the offender and to those whose offense consists of merchandising the illegitimate activity or its fruits, or in buying either. All three cost increases would reduce the benefit from crime (to the original offender, to the merchandiser, and to the ultimate purchaser, respectively), thereby reducing both the supply and the demand for it.

When money is taken rather than goods, and when the opportunity to do so is unlimited—as in mugging, but not in bank robbing—the legal cost to the offender must be increased to reduce the rate at which the offense is committed. It is hard to reduce the opportunity for mugging and impossible to reduce the resale value of money.

All this is not to discount incapacitation entirely. Incapacitation plays an independent role (in the short run) when the offense requires skills that take time to acquire; or, even in the long run, when the offense has an expressive as well as an instrumental function. An unknown number of offenders may become sufficiently addicted to the expressive thrill of crime so that they will habitually continue even when the net benefit from their offenses has become quite low. Others habitually continue for other reasons, e.g., alcoholism, or ignorance of legitimate gainful activities, or inability to utilize them. To illustrate: the rate of gambling can be increased or decreased by varying the net benefit to gamblers. But some people will gamble however low the benefits are. If gambling is already unattractive to those not addicted to it, incapacitating those addicted to it would reduce the rate of gambling. So with other expressive crimes, such as rape or—in an unknown proportion of cases—robbery, often a pseudo-instrumental crime. In sum: the crime rate can be reduced by incapacitation whenever the nature of the crime, or of the criminals, is such that any part of the supply of people attracted to the crime is inelastic.

The first line of social defense is the cost imposed for criminal activity. Cost-benefit ratios are decisive for the part of the supply of offenders that is elastic. Incapacitation remains of value once the cost imposed for an offense is high enough to deter most people. Incapacitation, then, will reduce the number of professionals who have become addicted to a particular crime and who continue even when the net benefit becomes very low, and generally of those who commit it for nonrational reasons. These are mostly multiple offenders. Their number is limited, but they commit a disproportionate number of crimes—half of all those committed in certain categories.*

Reform

The intimidation, or rehabilitation, of the convict is expected to lead him to law-abiding conduct upon his release.

"Rehabilitation" is meant to change the offender's intent, motivation, or even character toward law-abiding conduct. "Intimidation" causes avoidance of offenses because of fear of punishment. Whereas rehabilitation affects the offender's wish, intimidation leaves the wish unchanged—only it is not carried out because of fear. To wit: one may no longer wish to cheat, or one may wish to but control that wish for moral reasons (rehabilitation); or one may still wish to cheat but control the wish for fear of punishment (intimidation). Since internal motivations and restraints are not directly observable, the distinction between rehabilitation and intimidation cannot easily be made on the basis of statistical data. Sometimes, too, it is impossible to tell what has produced law-abiding behavior in an individual: an offender released after the age of thirty-five may become law-abiding simply because he is older—perhaps his age is a lasting form of incapacitation; perhaps he has been rehabilitated or intimidated.† Nonetheless, the distinction is

* See Chapter XXI.
† Both incapacitation and reform can reduce the crime rate. It requires careful scrutiny of the statistical data to separate the causes of reduction.

of some importance in penology: policies aimed at intimidation differ from policies attempting rehabilitation or merely incapacitation.

Reform, and particularly rehabilitation, assumes that the convict committed offenses because of some personality disorder that can be corrected by treatment. (As will be seen in Chapters XI and XVI, there is no evidence for this view, which confuses deviation from moral norms with psychic disease.) If the treatment succeeds he will become rational enough to see that "crime does not pay," that it is irrational. He will be reformed.

However, if a given offender's offenses are rational in the situation in which he lives—if what he can gain exceeds the likely cost to him by more than the gain from legitimate activities does—there is little that can be "corrected" in the offender. Reform will fail. It often fails for this reason. What has to be changed is not the personality of the offender, but the cost-benefit ratio which makes his offense rational. That ratio can be changed by improving and multiplying his opportunities for legitimate activity and the benefits they yield, or by decreasing his opportunity for illegitimate activities, or by increasing their cost to him, including punishment.

Replacement

If successful, rehabilitation or intimidation, though keeping the released prisoner law-abiding, still may not affect the crime rate if the rehabilitated or intimidated former prisoner is replaced. People who have committed crimes can be prevented from committing more, temporarily or permanently. But rehabilitation, intimidation, or incapactitation are unlikely to affect many crime rates as long as those incapacitated or reformed are readily and fully replaced, as they will be if their offenses are attractive enough to new recruits. In this re-

spect, crime does not differ from dentistry. If the average
working life of dentists or lawyers were shortened by fifteen
years by early retirement, there would be no long-run effects
if dentistry or the law remained sufficiently attractive to new
recruits. So with most criminal activities. Not that the supply
of prospective lawyers, or offenders, is infinite. Not everybody
qualifies for either activity. But the supply is great enough for
replacement rates to be unaffected by depletion.

Incapacitation and reforms are meant to affect the behavior
of individual convicts. They are the most direct and tangible
effects, actual or desired, of incarceration in "correctional institutions," as prisons are euphemistically called. But they are
not the primary goals of punishment. And at least some offenders require neither incapacitation nor reform: they will
not commit further crimes anyway. The man who kills his wife
during a jealous quarrel may never marry or kill again. He
needs neither reform nor incapacitation. Other offenders cannot be reformed by any known means. If incapacitation or
reform were primary goals, nonreformable offenders would be
imprisoned permanently, even if their offenses were trivial,
while many murderers might be released upon pleading
guilty. Punishment would depend on an assessment of the offender's future behavior. It would be independent of his offense. However, this would defeat not only justice but also the
main utilitarian purpose of punishing offenders: deterrence.

Deterrence

Unlike incapacitation and reform, deterrence is not concerned
with the convict. It is a message addressed to the public at
large. The punishment of the offender deters others by telling
them: "This will happen to you if you violate the law." Deterrence protects the social order by restraining not the actual offender, who, *eo ipso*, has not been deterred, but other

members of society, potential offenders, who still can be deterred. As an English judge succinctly remarked: "Men are not hanged for stealing horses, but that horses may not be stolen."

What is needed for intimidation may differ from what is needed for rehabilitation; and incapacitation is needed as long as neither works. Each requires different treatment and each must be tailored to the individual offender: the length of his imprisonment ideally depends on his progress, on his current or expected future conduct, rather than on his past offense. Indeed, if the law or the court ignores the individual character and prospect of an offender, there are disadvantages: rehabilitation might be missed; imprisonment not needed to reform or incapacitate him may be imposed; or unreformed convicts may be released. On the other hand, unless the future behavior of individual offenders can be objectively predicted, individualized treatment easily becomes capricious and unhelpful—as it has become in our system.

Unlike reform, retribution depends only on the past offense of the offender; and deterrence depends only on what is expected to restrain not him but others from committing the offense in the future. Since retribution and deterrence are not addressed to the individual offender, neither depends on his current or his future conduct. The punishment required by either purpose then does not depend at all on the individual offender. It is the same for all those guilty of the same offense. Disregarding the personality of the offender has advantages. Punishment is predictable and impersonal, and arbitrary differences in penalization are minimized. Indeed, if the punishment, or its size, depends on what the judge, or parole board, thinks about the chances that the offender will be law-abiding in the future, the threat may become too uncertain to deter others readily. Deterrent effects largely depend on punishment being meted out according to the crime, so that a prospective offender can know the likely cost of the offense and be deterred by it.

Subsidiary Meanings

Deterrence has a number of subsidiary meanings more relevant to crime prevention in general than to punishment as a specific means thereto. Thus "deterrence" may refer (a) to the fear of apprehension rather than of punishment: a police patrol, or a visible burglar alarm, deters. But apprehension probably is feared more, the more punishment is feared. "Deterrence" can also refer (b) to fear of dangers other than punishment—fear of falling off the wall one scales, or of being bitten by watchdogs, or shot by the intended victim. Further "deterrence" may refer (c) to foreclosing opportunities for crime, to the effect of protective devices, such as locks, which make it harder for the offender to accomplish his purpose. In short, one may be deterred by the difficulties and dangers involved in committing an offense, as well as by the fear of punishment.

Circumstances that deter by making it more difficult to commit crimes explain why crime rates differ among neighborhoods, and why, although it seems paradoxical, many crimes victimize the poor more often than the rich: the poor usually are easier to victimize. The rich have more to be stolen, but often they also have better locks, or guards, or dogs, or higher walls, all of which deter. Neighborhood grocers are robbed more often than banks are; the punishment might be the same and the loot greater in banks, but banks are watched better and the F.B.I. pursues bank robbers, whereas grocery robbers need fear only the local police. The number of burglaries may be reduced by stronger locks or brighter lights, as well as by more deterrent punishment; and robberies may decrease either because shopkeepers arm themselves, or because more robbers are caught and punished. However, I shall focus here on deterrence defined as the restraining effect the punishment of criminals has on others.

VI

Some Indirect Effects of Punishment

For what mortal is righteous if he has nothing to fear?
Aeschylus, *Eumenides*

Stigma

The deterrent effect of punishment depends on stigmatization as well as on material suffering. Punishment removes from the community, temporarily or permanently, those who violate its laws. Whatever the tangible effects, that removal has a symbolic meaning of surpassing importance. It vindicates the social order by branding crime as antisocial, the criminal as outcast. The moral solidarity of those who live within the law is reaffirmed by casting out those who break it.* Punishment not only proclaims wrong the acts the law forbids, it also marks as odious, as "criminal," the violation of the law and the violator.† This symbolic effect of punishment helps form the all im-

---

* Among social psychologists, this idea has been stressed by George Herbert Mead; among criminologists, by Leon Duguit; among sociologists, by Émile Durkheim.

† H. L. A. Hart calls stress on this aspect of criminal law the denunciatory theory of punishment. Joel Feinberg analyzes it subtly in "The Expressive Function of Punishment," reprinted in *Doing and Deserving* (Princeton: Princeton University Press, 1970).

portant internal barriers which restrain most of us from law
violations without conscious thought, let alone calculation.
The fear, however inchoate, of the stigma of punishment is as
powerful a restraining force as the fear of material suffering or
deprivation. Only with persons who have little to lose will the
denunciatory effects of punishment not be deterrent. Nor will
the material effects, unless quite severe. As Herbert L. Packer
writes: [17] "Deterrence does not threaten those whose lot in
life is already miserable beyond the point of hope."

The stigmatizing effect of conviction is greater and more deterrent the higher the status of the convict: conviction may
cause a painful loss of reputation and end the career, or bar
from his profession a lawyer, accountant, physician, politi-
cian, or executive. The stigmatizing effect also depends on the
attitude of one's social group. The mere contact with the criminal justice system brings disgrace in some societies or groups;
in others, even a conviction is shrugged off. An arrest record is
easily available to prospective employers in some societies; in
others, even a conviction record is hard to discover. In highly
mobile societies, such as ours, the stigmatizing effect of punishment is minimized. Offenders find it easier to escape from
their past than in less mobile and more highly bureaucratized
societies. Reformed offenders have opportunities for a fresh
start—an advantage; and unreformed offenders have fresh opportunities for offenses—a disadvantage. By reducing the stigmatizing effect of punishment, mobility also reduces its deterrent effect; both are likely to be weaker the less closeknit and
stable the community in which the punishment occurs and the
more easily the punished person can leave his stigma behind
by moving into circles where he is not known.

The stigmatizing effect of legal punishment is at a low ebb
now. Some reasons may be suggested. (1) Criminal careers are
romanticized and glorified quite often now. In the past they
were not—think of Shakespeare or Dostoyevsky. (2) Social scientists and intellectuals generally tend to explain offenders as
victims and to neglect their role as victimizers. The explanation frequently is treated as a justification. (3) Some educa-

tional institutions—mainly those attended by middle class off-spring—stress "creative" individual attitudes and "self fulfillment." They avoid general rules or treat violators leniently. Their alumni, in turn, find it hard to apply strict rules to law violators or to see them as anything but victims of society. (4) Respect for law and the stigmatizing effect of punishment are bound to decline as social authority does. Social authority is declining, in part a reaction to its assertion by the likes of Stalin and Hitler, in part probably a long-run trend.[18]

Can Legal Threats Be Effective?

Despite punishment, crime persists. Not everybody is deterred. And not everybody can be, however certain and severe the punishment threatened. Those who for some reason are bent on self-destruction, or who seek to be punished, obviously cannot be deterred by the threat of punishment.* Nor can those who are unable to grasp threats, or dangers, or to regulate their conduct in accordance with them. Threats must be ineffective, then, with those whose (unconscious) intentions are met by them, or who suffer from relevant defects of cognition or volition. Finally, persons who are excited by gambling with threats, or by defying them, are deterred only when the odds are very much against them. They may perceive minor threats and threats unlikely to be carried out as invitations.

Still, the overwhelming majority of people are deterrable in most situations most of the time. There could be no legal order if the proportion of altogether nondeterrable persons in the general population was not quite small. Even among con-

---

* Some persons commit crimes so as to suffer punishment, which relieves them of unconscious guilt feelings produced by prior experiences. There is no evidence to indicate that this is decisive in causing a significant number of offenses. Even if they have a desire for punishment most offenders appear to control it, despite occasional ambivalence, for they do their best to avoid punishment.

victed offenders the nondeterrable proportion is small.* Most offenders are deterrable, even though they have not been deterred by the actual practices of the criminal justice system. Professor Herbert L. Packer remarks: "People who commit crimes appear to share the prevalent impression that punishment is an unpleasantness best avoided. They ordinarily take care to avoid being caught. If arrested, they ordinarily deny their guilt . . . if brought to trial, they . . . resist being convicted." [19] People who do not want to be punished can be deterred in principle by the threat of punishment. Whether deterrable people actually are deterred depends on three things, which combine in various proportions.

Internal Restraints and External Stimuli

Whether or not a crime is committed depends on external stimuli, pressures, opportunities, and threats; and, on the other hand, on internal dispositions to respond to these or to restrain oneself. Different personalities respond differently to the same external situation—that is what marks personalities as different. Hence, in the same situation crimes will be committed by some and not by others. However, the same individuals will commit offenses in some situations but not in others. Thus, given the personality, the situation can determine whether or not a crime is committed.

Whether any given threat of punishment (part of the external situation) suffices as a deterrent will depend on internal dispositions and on the external situation which makes the offense more or less tempting. Even the threat of very severe and certain punishment will not deter some people whose character leads them to underestimate threats, or people very strongly motivated by hate or love, or people who have only weak internal restraints. On the other hand, there are external pressures or temptations that will bring even people with

* The proportion of nondeterrables among repeated offenders, particularly youthful ones, is greater than in the general population. And the proportion of all offenses that can be attributed to multiple recidivists is quite high (see Chapter XXI).

strong internal restraints to commit offenses despite the threat of harsh punishment. That threat is only one of many variables, internal and external, which jointly determine whether or not someone will commit a crime. But it is an important variable.

It need hardly be said that no exclusively psychological theory of crime causation can be exhaustive any more than an exclusively social one. Crimes are committed by individuals who have different personalities and respond to different social environments. Any theory must take into account both differences in environment and in personality, though it may focus primarily on either.

The Habit-forming Effect of Legal Threats

"The existence of a 'threat' helps to create patterns of conforming behavior and thereby to reduce the number of occasions on which the choice of a criminal act presents itself. Every one of us is confronted daily by situations in which criminal behavior is a possible alternative. Sometimes the presentation is sufficiently vivid that we think about it and reject the criminal alternative. More frequently and more significantly, we automatically and without conscious cognition follow a pattern of learned behavior that excludes the criminal alternative without our even thinking about it." [20] Self-restraint, as Herbert L. Packer here points out, may involve either not even experiencing the possible criminal opportunity consciously, or a conscious rejection of it as immoral or dangerous. The threatened punishment, even when it does not overtly and directly affect the decision, may well form, or at least reinforce, the restraining elements in the character of the person which lead him, consciously or unconsciously, to avoid committing offenses.

Cost and Benefit Perceived by the Prospective Offender

External difficulties and credible legal threats increase its cost to those tempted to commit a crime. If the cost rises high enough, compared to the advantage expected, the crime can be discouraged. But the fact that the crime is too costly, relative to the gain and to other opportunities to achieve one's aims, need not be directly present in the mind of the person who is deterred by the cost. The man who drinks a glass of beer with his lunch is not usually considering the comparative price of *Haut-Brion* 1948. He may not know the price; he may never have heard of the wine. Nonetheless, it seems fair to say that he formed the habit of drinking beer because *Haut-Brion* 1948 (and other things of the kind) was too costly for him. And this may be true of many of his behavior patterns, including the habit of law-abiding behavior. However indirectly, deterrence depends on whether the difficulties and legal threats which increase the cost of crime to the criminal suffice to discourage him when compared to the benefits he expects. Offenders are discouraged when the *net* gain from illegitimate opportunities is below the net gain from the available legitimate activities. A total lack of legitimate opportunities always makes crime attractive; so does the presence of extraordinary criminal opportunities. Most of the time a comparative edge will suffice to attract at least some people to offenses. Their number depends on the size of that edge over what they can expect, given the situation, from legitimate activities.*

Internal and External Threats

Costs, habit-forming threats, and the internal restraints they reinforce coalesce to control the crime rate. J. F. Stephen strikingly summarized the effects: "Some men, probably, abstain from murder because they fear that if they committed murder they would be hanged [cost]. Hundreds of thousands abstain from it because they regard it with horror [internal restraint].

---

* It is likely that the perception of legitimite opportunities and of legal threats differs from group to group and may in part account for different crime rates. But no data are available on the role this variable may play.

One great reason why they regard it with horror is that murderers are hanged [habit-forming threat]." [21]

Although it is usually helped by habit and by moral restraint, the threat of punishment by itself can effectively deter if it is severe and credible enough. In enemy-occupied territories, in prisoner of war camps, or in penal institutions, the population often does not respect as legitimate the laws or regulations imposed to keep it subdued. There may be no moral allegiance to these laws; in some cases a moral and patriotic duty is felt to violate them. Yet experience shows that the threat of punishment (particularly of execution) is enough to deter most people from breaking despised laws regarded as immoral and illegitimate and imposed by despised authorities.[22] It is an interesting question—which invites experimental answer—whether in such cases deterrence is produced primarily by fear of punishment, or by the habit of obeying authority, which may persist even when the authority is morally repudiated. The habit may rest on the ability of authority to punish those who do not obey, but it may survive in the absence of either punishment or legitimacy.

Unquestionably, it is morally preferable, and less costly, to create conditions that reduce provocations to law-breaking. Enforcement is easier when laws are accepted and people feel morally obligated to obey them. Less punishment is needed and what is needed seems morally more acceptable. But this is no reason to underestimate the efficacy, as distinguished from the morality, of deterrent threats even in the absence of moral acceptance of the laws.

Most people are law-abiding quite apart from any fear of external punishment because they feel it is wrong to commit crimes. They have been taught to do right and to avoid wrong, which includes crime. Even if they were tempted—and many people are sufficiently socialized not to feel temptation in normal circumstances—they fear the punishment their own conscience will impose. They have internalized what originally was, and still remains, an external threat. Psychoanalysts refer to this process as the creation of the super ego; sociologists, as socialization. The success of this process is decisive: when it fails with most people, society cannot function well. Once a person actually calculates and weighs dangers, or the risk of punishment, society probably has lost the war against crime within that person, even if it still wins battles here and there. Calculators will commit crimes when they feel the risk is low enough, or the stakes high enough; and once they start calculating, people usually find situations in which they think crimes pay. However, most people do not calculate. They are not tempted, or they shrink from serious crime, because the tradition of punishment has created and perpetuated a feeling that crime is wrong beyond any calculation of the risk of being caught and punished. That feeling will last as long as punishment does—as long as it is frequent and severe enough to be dimly expected, if not precisely calculated.

When punishment is not only uncertain but altogether improbable, crime rises precipitously. Johannes Andenaes [22a] noted that crime rose (e.g., robbery increased tenfold) when in 1944 the Germans arrested the entire police force of occupied Denmark. Francis Russell [23b] notes how crime rose during the Boston and Liverpool police strikes (1919) and during the Montreal police strike (1968). In every large population there are elements restrained from violence and crime only by the threat of punishment which the presence of the police vouchsafes. If the punishment is unlikely, crime surges. But indirectly the threat of punishment restrains everybody.

PART TWO

CONTROLLING CRIME

VII

What Causes Crime?

There are no fewer causes and explanations of criminal than of noncriminal behavior. Why, after all, do some of us become editors or dentists while others don't? Why do some of us drink or climb mountains while others don't? Dentists or editors, drinkers or climbers differ from others mostly by their vocation or avocation. The possibility of becoming a dentist or editor, a mountain climber or a beer drinker inheres in many a person for whom it never becomes an actuality. Internal and environmental factors may drive the person to become a salesman instead, or a steamfitter or an advertising executive, and avocationally to become a baseball player or milk drinker. So with the possibility of becoming a criminal or a law-abiding citizen. Most of us could become either; what we do become depends on the same sort of combination of internal and external stimuli that may produce a teacher instead of a truck driver. Let me set down a general classification of the causes that are likely to influence the choice. It is not meant to do more than to suggest possibilities and probabilities.

Tarde, Sutherland, and Merton

The French magistrate and sociologist Gabriel Tarde explained the spread of social behavior, law-abiding or criminal, as a process of social "imitation." Later, the American criminologist Edwin Sutherland refined Tarde's notion of imitation. According to Sutherland, some persons imitate one thing and others something else, such as crime, owing to "differential association":

> The hypothesis of differential association is that criminal behavior is learned in association with those who define such behavior favorably and in isolation from those who define it unfavorably, and that a person in an appropriate situation engages in such criminal behavior if, and only if, the weight of the favorable definitions exceeds the weight of the unfavorable definitions.[23]

The term "weight" is more explanatory in physics, from which the metaphor is taken, than in sociology. Yet Tarde and Sutherland suggest a direction in which an explanation—of contagion rather than origin—must be sought. Though a little less formal, Mom held the same theory when she said her "boy got into trouble because he ran around with the wrong bunch." She did not explain what made the bunch go wrong. Nor does Sutherland. Infection is indeed transmitted by contact: we learn much of our behavior from others who serve as models. But associations with others are selective at least at some points. And one also selects what one is predisposed to imitate in their behavior. The interpersonal transmission of behavior, criminal or otherwise, thus does not exclude an intrapersonal contribution to its genesis. Neither Sutherland nor Mom explains individual immunity or receptivity to contagion, which surely is as important in the analysis of imitative behavior as it is in that of the infectious disease—particularly if we are interested in immunization.* Finally, even when

---

* See John Stuart Mill quoted on p. 107.

sources of infection are equally present in two groups living in quite similar conditions, infection may grow in one group and not in the other. Obviously, historical factors must account for different group receptivity as well as current social circumstances. But we have no fully satisfactory explanation.

Plato (and two thousand years later Emile Durkheim) referred to rulelessness and social disintegration as "anomie." Robert Merton, giving a somewhat different sense to it, uses that concept to explain the social causation of criminal behavior.[24] When a society holds out goals (such as wealth) with the suggestion that all could and should attain them, yet does not make them equally available, those unable to attain these goals by legitimate means may be driven to use illegitimate means. This happens in highly mobile class societies, such as ours, the more the attainment of the goals is felt to be possible or necessary for everyone, so that non-attainment signifies failure. It happens less often in more traditional societies, where the ambition to rise is less widespread and success is not measured by the individual achievement of wealth. If true, Merton's concept would help explain the comparatively high crime rates in the U.S.

Following Travis Hirschi's [25] classification, Merton's is a *strain* theory: it explains delinquency by the strain between available means and the goals for which the delinquent is strongly motivated by his society. Sutherland's theory is one of many *cultural deviance* theories. These hold that offenders deviate from norms accepted and enforced by society as a whole by following deviant norms prevailing in their subgroup. Finally, the original Plato-Durkheim notion of anomie can be called a *control* theory. It stresses the bonds that tie individuals to society and to the social order and control their actions. "We are moral beings to the extent that we are social beings," Émile Durkheim said. Rapid change (particularly when it occurs at a different pace in different parts of society), the imposition of different norms from the outside, crosscultural contacts, and various conflicts all can weaken social organization and the attachment of individuals to society. For social bonds to be created, models, "significant others," must be available inside and outside families. Else social norms are unlikely to be firmly internalized and followed. In a highly mobile society such models become scarce as relationships become transitory and casual. Control theory helps explain why crime rates are high among those whose ties with the social environment have become undone (drifters or outsiders). On the other hand, Mafia members may be closely tied to one another and not alienated at all; cultural deviance is a more fitting description of their behavior.

Although often formulated as an exclusive universal explanation, and although contributing to the explanation of some kinds of crime and of criminals, each of the three types of theory helps little with other kinds. Surely, some offenses are caused mainly by cultural deviance (Sutherland), others by strain (Merton's anomie), and still others by a weakening of social ties and controls (Durkheim's anomie). And various combinations are possible. As for the differences in crime frequency among social groups, they may be explained by the different opportunities different groups have by "differential association" or cultural deviance (which is really implied in the concept of "social group") and, finally, by the prevalence of anomie in some areas, in the form of resentment (Merton) or detachment and alienation (Durkheim). Many other variables combine to produce crime. Finally, properly understood social explanations are consistent with explanations of crime based on individual personality. One may catch a disease by infection in an environment which multiplies bacilli. This is equivalent to the environment of some social groups. But not all individuals do catch the infection: individual disposition, or vulnerability, is needed as well. So with criminality. This explains why within the group some persons do, and others do not, become offenders. Society contributes to the formation of different personalities, to the way in which they seek expression, and to the situations in which they express themselves legitimately or unlawfully. When the same persons act differently in different—socially created—situations, the difference must be social. When different persons act differently in the same situation, the difference must be psychological. The environmental explanation is needed in the first case, the psychological in the last.

Changes in the rates for particular types of crime do not depend much on changes in the criminal inclinations of individuals and on whatever causes them. Such inclinations, and their causes, are likely to be fairly constant. Changes in the frequency of any given crime more often depend on changes in the opportunity to commit the crime (at a risk acceptable to the criminal) and on variations of the benefit derived from it. Thus, the rate of auto theft will depend mainly on (a) the total automobile population; (b) the supply of easily stolen cars; (c) the (legal) cost of stealing cars; and (d) the demand for stolen cars. Clearly (d) depends on social attitudes toward buying goods of dubious origin.[26] This attitude depends on the likelihood and size of punishments. Given (a), (b), and (c), the rate of auto theft is readily influenced by (d) which can be influenced in turn by varying the penalties for the purchase of automobiles of uncertain origin. Since property, other than money, is stolen for resale, chances are that the rate at which it is stolen is analogously determined and can be similarly influenced: punishment for purchasing goods of doubtful origin will reduce the demand for them; therefore, their value and the benefit derived from the crime will be reduced. Increasing the direct cost to the thief, his punishment, is another way of curbing the offense. But even if that legal cost remains constant, the cost-benefit ratio can be changed by increasing the chances for, or the severity of, punishment for purchasing stolen goods.

Fascinating as they are, there is little need here to go further into theories of crime causation. They do help to make the occurrence and frequency of criminal conduct intelligible. But none promises to tell much that can be applied to crime control now or that suggests modification of its instruments, such as punishment. The more general the theory is the less it helps in policy decisions. How would we reduce strain, change subcultures, strengthen the ties of individuals to others? Not that these theories are useless. They can help negatively by warning us of criminogenic developments. And, as they are elaborated, they may give us clues to concrete measures to be taken, particularly when, as in the case of property crimes, quantitative tests can be conceived. Meanwhile, consider some of the shaping influences on professional and occasional offenders.

Crime as a Career

When crime is a career, the occupational choice of the criminal is influenced by the factors that usually influence occupational choice, whether it ends in urology, banking, bookkeeping, bookmaking, or burglary. Parental models; the expectations one learns to place on oneself; opportunities restricted in one respect and enlarged in another by traditions, by family connections, or by local conditions; the influence of friends and acquaintances or of the whole milieu in which one moves; all these and innumerable other things contribute to the choice of career and to the shaping of the character of the professional bookmaker, lawyer, or racketeer. Thus, the career of the *mafioso* from a family of *mafiosi*, or of the prostitute born to a prostitute, of the petty thief who comes from a family of drifters involved in shady activities.

Some criminals differ from noncriminals: their internalized restraints are slightly weaker in some directions, or their impulses (which when unrestrained lead to unlawful acts) are slightly stronger. But there need be no such psychological difference to produce an offender. External temptations or opportunities for crime may have been greater, or legitimate opportunities fewer, for the offender than for others. Or the offender may have learned to accept as legitimate some activities the law prohibits because people around him did, just as some social environments make liquor or drugs acceptable, while others lead one to reject them as toxic or sinful.

The idea that "crime does not pay" and is therefore always irrational does not seem to be borne out. Crime does "pay" in many cases and can be quite rational for the person engaged in it. In Gary Becker's words: "Some persons become criminals therefore, not because their basic motivation differs from that of other persons, but because their benefits and costs differ." [27] Four important propositions can be inferred from this.

1. Although some crime can be explained by the persistence of irrationality, some must be explained by the persistence of rationality.

2. No society can weed out all irrational people. Moreover, irrational acts occasionally are committed by ordinarily quite rational people. Who has never done anything irrational? Thus, some offenses would be committed even if they were irrational and the offenders rational. Others are committed because the offenders are irrational, and still others because the offenders are rational.

3. Rational crime is as unlikely to be eradicated altogether as irrational crime. No society is likely to succeed in making all crime disadvantageous (irrational) to everybody. However, societies can reduce rational crime by increasing the comparative cost and reducing the comparative benefit of crime wherever possible so that fewer offenders can rationally hope to achieve a greater gain from crime than from legitimate activity. Basically, this means two things: first, to make the opportunities for legitimate gain greater or more available, thereby reducing the comparative benefit of illegitimate activities; and second, to increase the chances of apprehension and conviction and the severity of punishments for illegal activities, thereby adding to the costs of crime compared to legitimate activity, as well as reducing net benefits.

4. Rehabilitation of those for whom crime is rational is not likely to be effective. If they are rational, they cannot be cured of irrationality or sickness or exceptional character dispositions they do not possess. What must be "rehabilitated" are the circumstances that made crime rational.*

Nonprofessional Offenders

What about nonprofessionals? Some nonprofessional offenders do not differ significantly from nonoffenders. Why, then, do they commit crimes? The old saying about the condemned man, "There but for the grace of God go I," points toward an explanation. The occasional offender may have found himself in a situation in which many other persons also would have violated the law. Perhaps many more did than were caught—the chances for occasional offenders to be caught are small in most cases. But consider those who did not commit offenses. Perhaps they did not merely because they never were in the situation of the actual offender. Had they been in that same situation, they might have acted as the offender did. The offender's personality (internal motivation) may not be different from theirs at all. Deterrent threats may be as effective with him as with others, but the (external) temptation may have been stronger or different from the temptations or opportunities to which other persons were exposed.

The wife murdered by her husband may be a wife most other husbands would have murdered. They were lucky enough not to have married her. She—the external stimulus— was different, not her husband. The million dollars the embezzler stole might have been stolen by others had they had the chance he had. The gas station the robber held up might

---

* Rehabilitation of convicts—of which punishment may be the major instrument—still may play a role. The mere fact of law violation calls for it. It may be habit-forming. Ordinarily, citizens should not violate the law even when it is rational to do so. (See Chapters XI and XVI on rehabilitation.)

have been held up by others, except they never had a chance to fall in with robbers. To take an extreme instance: in 1846–47 the Donner party, consisting of ordinary people on their way to California, was snowed in on a Nevada pass. They acted in extraordinary ways—as cannibals—because they were in an extraordinary situation. They were no more inclined to cannibalism than others lucky enough not to be snowed in. In not so obvious and radical a fashion, external rather than personality differences may produce other crimes. They are committed by ordinary people in extraordinary, though not necessarily extreme, situations, which press or tempt them to act unlawfully. Offenders may commit offenses, then, because they find themselves in situations in which most persons would—except that most other persons "by the grace of God" never found themselves in these situations.

To be sure, not all crimes are committed by "ordinary" people. Most offenders are not psychopaths, but some are. Psychopaths, by definition, differ from ordinary people in that they do not experience guilt feelings. They find it psychologically easier to commit crimes. (They may be few, but their crimes are all the more striking.) Certain types of neurotics and psychotics also commit crimes. (Most do not.) Ordinarily, however, crimes are committed by persons within the range of the psychologically "normal." Most commonly, a slightly unusual situation comes together with a slightly deviant personality; neither need be extreme, but the combination can produce a crime. If the person's resistance to ordinary temptation is just a little less than average, or his motivations—e.g., greed—just a little more than ordinary, there is no reason to assume a wholly "different" criminal or sick personality. "Average" by definition means that about half the population is above and half is below the mid-point, and that most people are quite near to it. An impulse stronger than average, or a resistance to the impulse slightly weaker than average, may lead one to react excessively to what are otherwise common temptations. The murdered wife was a nuisance. Someone else might have shrugged her off, but she was too much for the husband who murdered her. Someone else might have resisted the opportunity to steal $10,000 (although not, perhaps, the opportunity to steal $100,000?). But for the embezzler, $10,000 proved too much. Others might have resisted most or even all of the temptations the offender succumbed to. Still, the line between the offender and the nonoffender is as blurred as is the line between ordinary and extraordinary temptation. The polar extremes are clear. But most people fall somewhere between them.

Two Types of Offenders

In many cases it would not be easy to find out which individual offender belongs to which offender group, but it is useful analytically to distinguish at least two groups. One group of offenders is propelled decisively by *intrapsychic* forces, by traits of character, however they were acquired. These persons would be likely to commit crimes in most situations in which they find themselves. This group may be subdivided into those only *temporarily* disposed to offenses (e.g., some adolescents going through an assertive and defiant stage in their development) and those *permanently* so disposed for persistent characterological reasons. (The latter subgroup must be permanently incapacitated whenever possible.)

A second group of offenders is quite different. As far as their character goes, they are no more criminally inclined than nonoffenders. But they have been placed in some kind of *situation* (e.g., marital or economic) in which the average person would commit an offense. The offenses committed by persons who fall into this second group are primarily due to *extrapsychic* (or *interpsychic*) stimuli, in the absence of which the offenses might not have occurred. Offenders who respond to external stimuli rather than being driven intrapsychically also fall into two subgroups: those whose environment makes crime rational in terms of costs and benefits, and those who find themselves, temporarily at least, in a situation where crime is a psychologically normal, though not necessarily rational, reaction (e.g., a number of Shakespeare's tragic heroes). Although each offender in the first (intrapsychic) group commits more offenses, most offenders probably are in the second (extrapsychic) group.

The intra- and extrapsychic groups overlap. Here again they can be distinguished at the extreme poles. But most offenders fall in between, although either the external or the internal may preponderate. Nonetheless, the distinction has relevance when we are concerned with rehabilitation or incapacitation. Little of either is needed for the group that offends merely because of extraordinary external provocations. Punishment is exacted for the sake of retribution and of deterrence. For the group that is characterologically disposed to committing offenses, rehabilitation is needed, although we don't really know how to provide it. For at least some members of this group, rehabilitation may be impossible. Incapacitation may be the only way of protecting society.

Differences in situation, personality, or milieu, then, may explain why some offenders were not deterred while others were. But they do not exonerate offenders or make all offenders nondeterrable. The differences help explain why an offender was not deterred while others in similar situations or with similar motivations were deterred. The offender himself might also have been deterred if circumstances, including the threat of punishment, had been different. And he remains responsible for his acts. The temptations to commit crimes are many; we are all surrounded by them and apt, in some degree, to yield, for "the spirit is willing but the flesh is weak." Most people sooner or later find themselves in situations which may tempt them. Because most offenders are not significantly different from the rest of the population, society must reinforce resistance to temptation by punishment and by stigmatizing crime as odious, so that most people will not yield to the temptations no society can eliminate.

VIII

Poverty

Ferri and the Social Environment

One of the most seminal thinkers on crime causation and control was the Italian lawyer Enrico Ferri,* the leader of what came to be called "the positive school of law." Ferri discounted punishment as retribution and as a means of crime control. He strikingly related the frequency of crime to the environment: "Just as in a given volume of water, at a given temperature, we find the solution of a fixed quantity of any chemical substance . . . so in a given social environment . . . we find the commission of a fixed number of crimes." [28] Ferri's view that crime rates differ according to cultures, subcultures, and economic environments is borne out by statistics. Now so generally accepted as to appear to be common sense, Ferri's view raises three questions. If the crime rate depends on the environment, does that (1) exonerate individual offenders from responsibility and (2) make it impossible to deter them by the threat of punishment? Finally, regardless of punish-

---

* Ferri's (1856–1929) views directly and, more often, indirectly have influenced theories of punishment the world over; they have certainly influenced the American criminal justice system, although Ferri is seldom acknowledged and might not have approved of the development of his ideas.

ment, (3) what can be done to change environments so as to reduce crime rates?

What Ferri says about the relation of the social environment to crime can be said less strikingly, but as truly, about the relation of the social environment to art, chess, or baseball. In the "given social environment" of Florence in the Renaissance, art flourished; of Detroit in the twentieth century, crime; of Tokyo, neither; of Russia, chess; of the American heartland, baseball. To grant the influence of the environment does not usually lead us to deny the responsibility, the merit, or demerit, of the individual artist baseball, or chess player. Why should offenders be thought of differently? Are they less responsible, or deterrable, than artists or baseball players, who prosper in some but not in other environments?

If the costs and benefits of crime were uniform throughout all environments, so would the crime rate be. It is not. Different environments produce a different cost-benefit ratio for crime, and therefore different crime rates. Ferri is quite right about this. The cost (punishment) may be the same in all environments. (Actually, if one considers stigmatization as part of it, the cost is lower in the most criminogenic environments.) But the benefit may not be. Therefore, the cost-benefit *ratio* differs and with it the crime rate, even if the cost of crime is the same for all offenders. Further, different environments shape character differently. This too helps explain the variance in crime rates among social groups, for it leads to different subjective sensitivity to the advantages and disadvantages of criminal conduct.

A poor person usually stands to gain more from crime and is likely to have fewer legitimate alternatives than a wealthy person. The subjective costs to the poor may be lower, too: people living in slums see more crime and internalize law-abiding behavior less than middle-class persons. Since both the objective and the subjective cost-benefit ratios favor crime more, crime rates are higher in the slums. It does not follow, however, that legal sanctions cannot influence crime rates, or the variance among them; that deterrence cannot work; or that offenders lack the ability to refrain from offenses and are not responsible for them. To use Ferri's analogy, the legal cost of crime (punishment) must be considered part of the "temperature" (environment) that causes more or less of the "chemical substance" (crime) to be dissolved in a given "volume of water" (population). Changing the cost of crime can change the crime rate by changing the cost-benefit ratio. By making it less favorable to crime, the crime rate is reduced. This actually follows from Ferri's argument, although he does not acknowledge it.

Ferri, and most of his followers, to this day reject the threat of punishment as a deterrent in favor of opening legitimate opportunities to the poor and of individualized "treatment" which is to rehabilitate or incapacitate criminals. This rejection is not logically entailed by the stress on the environment and, if one looks closely, not altogether consistent with it.* Besides, to compare the criminal to an inert "chemical substance" is to beg the question of responsibility and retribution, not to answer it. Still, although wrong in excluding the threat of punishment as a variable in the offender's environment, Ferri has the considerable merit of drawing attention to other variables that had been neglected.

Social Conditions and Legal Sanctions

The incidence of crime in various groups, characterized by age, sex, income, race, subculture and education, varies greatly. Quite possibly, the living conditions of groups with

---

* Ferri, a defense lawyer as well as a professor of law, was inclined to stress the causal importance of the environment to the exclusion of individual responsibility and deterrability. He never saw the threat of punishment as an environmental variable; or, perhaps, he did not think of it as an important variable in deterring crime. He preferred to take the legal punishment for granted and study other changes in the social environment which might reduce crime.

high crime frequency are a cause of it. Some of these conditions can be changed; others cannot be. Violent crime is highest among young males, but we cannot abolish youth or maleness. Nor is it likely that much can be done about the cultural influences which forge, or intensify, the links between youth, maleness, and comparatively high rates of violence. However, some conditions are exclusively social, and in principle they could be changed to reduce the crime rate. However, social conditions and customs respond only reluctantly to governmental intervention. They do change. They can even be changed deliberately. But not easily. No effective way has been found to predict, let alone direct, historical change. Dictatorships have tried but have seldom achieved what they intended. The results achieved by democratic reformers are not very promising either.

Apart from any intrinsic merit they may have, social changes would be quite worthwhile even if the conditions to be changed merely invited a high crime rate without being so compelling as to make criminals not deterrable or not responsible. Poverty is usually regarded as a prime suspect among crime-causing conditions. If poverty, or the slums in which it dwells, abets a high incidence of crime, then a change of income distribution to alleviate the condition of the poor, or decent housing for slum-dwellers, might reduce crime. Perhaps social change could do so more effectively than deterrent punishment. But the claim that social reform would reduce crime "more effectively" than the threat of punishment remains somewhat gratuitous as long as no one has tested the comparative effectiveness (and cost) of changes in social conditions against the effectiveness (and cost) of changes in deterrent punishments. Chances are that either change would be costly and could be effective. Both may help, as in the following illustration, in which "littering" stands for "offenses." If one wishes to reduce littering, one can do so by

---

He could as well have taken the rest of the environment for granted and the threatened punishment as a variable.

a.   increasing the fine for litterers;
b.   increasing the likelihood of paying it (a and b constitute the cost of littering to the litterers);
c.   providing more litter baskets (i.e., making legitimate opportunities available as an alternative to the offense);
d.   educating, or exhorting people to avoid littering (i.e., trying directly to intensify internal restraints);
e.   reducing the amount of wrapping paper and other materials that people are likely to throw away (reducing the opportunity for offenses).

It can be seen readily that it would be silly to insist *a priori* that any one of these measures is superior to the others. Each can play a role. The effectiveness of each depends on the conditions in which it is applied, and on the combination of crime-causing and -controlling factors to which it is added. One must compare the cost-effectiveness ratio of each of these crime-reducing measures to that of the available alternative measures. There is no principle that opposes environmental change to legal threats of punishment. Both can reduce crime. Relative to cost, each is more effective than the other in some circumstances and less in others. The question is always: Which change at the particular time, in the particular situation, will be most effective in reducing crime, per unit of cost? ("Cost," here, is to be understood as including anything valued that must be foregone to make the change, such as money, or privacy, or the freedom of the convicted.) Since the reduction of crime is the benefit expected, the analysis can proceed on cost-benefit lines. But far more factual data are needed than are now available: how much is crime reduced (under given circumstances) by additional arrests, convictions, and prison years—which cost X—or by higher wages or better dwelling space—which cost Y? (See Chapter XIII for some of the data currently available.)

By changing opportunities, changes in social conditions can change the motivations and temptations which influence crime rates, together with internal restraints and legal threats. So far, however, many of the social changes expected to reduce crime rates, such as higher incomes for the "underprivileged" or a decrease in their proportion in the population, have not been effective. Perhaps they point in the right direction but are insufficient or incomplete. It also might be that the direction of the change proposed is too vague or even irrelevant.

Most property crimes are instrumental and at least quasi-rational in motivation. They spring from a desire to get something one does not have enough of. The offender believes that he might not get what he wants by legitimate means or easily enough. He expects, rightly or wrongly, that he will get it through his offense, that his crime will pay. Such instrumental crimes can be reduced by making them costly enough, by seeing to it that they do not pay. Environmental changes that open legitimate opportunities, or close illegitimate ones, also will reduce offenses, unless ambition rises faster than (legitimate) opportunity.

Crimes against the person—e.g., killing someone in a brawl—often are expressive rather than instrumental; they express a current feeling rather than serve as a means to future results. Differences in the frequency of purely expressive crimes among social groups may depend on different subcultures, as does some of the variance in the frequency of instrumental crimes. In one subculture a person sues when insulted; in another he assaults and is expected to do so. In one subculture a poor person steals and is expected to steal; in another he is expected to accept unpleasant work or to starve. Expressive crimes are probably a little less deterrable than instrumental crimes since they are more affected by cultural and emotional factors. (The distinction cannot always be made easily. Burglary is more often instrumental than murder. But some burglaries are expressive and some murders are instrumental.)

Money certainly is one of the things for the sake of which crimes are committed, if only because it buys so many other things. Yet the willingness to get money illegally is neither confined to the poor, who by definition have the least money, nor shared by all of them. Wealthy people, though seldom engaged in muggings or burglaries, may commit embezzlements or frauds or engage in corrupt activities. Crime is not confined to any group, although each group has its own typical set of crimes. "The greatest crimes are committed not for the sake of basic necessities but for the sake of superfluities," Aristotle thought. Surely some crimes are—most, if not all, sexual crimes; most, if not all, organized crime activities, rackets, political crimes, and corruptions (including high treason); most, if not all, frauds. All of these crimes gratify greed, passion, or the wish for power, rather than assuage poverty. But reduction of poverty still promises to reduce some crimes most frequently committed by the poor—e.g., muggings, burglaries, theft, robberies, assaults. This promise has not been kept.

Poverty in the United States

In the last fifty years, poverty has been greatly reduced in the U.S. According to present government standards and statistics, measured in dollars of constant purchasing power, poverty was the condition of one-half of all our families in 1920; of one-fifth in 1962; and of less than one-sixth in 1966. In 1967, 5.3 million families out of 49.8 million were poor—one-ninth of all families in the U.S. The proportion has decreased a little further since. If crime has been reduced as much as poverty, it is a well-kept secret.

More poverty, then, cannot be the cause of the higher crime rates we experience, because fewer people are poor and they are less poor than in the past. Perhaps more relative poverty could be the cause: the distance between those who have remained poor and the non-poor can increase even when there are fewer poor and when both poor and non-poor are better off. This has not happened. On the contrary, the distance between those who have more and those who have less has decreased. Between 1936 and 1950 the income of the top 5 percent of all recipients rose by 14 percent, and the income of the highest quintile of all income recipients rose by 32 percent. But the income of the lowest quintile rose by 125 percent—four times as much as the income of the highest quintile. The trend toward equalization has pervaded the income structure as a whole, although its steepness has varied in different periods and in different segments of the structure. There is less relative poverty, less poverty, and a smaller proportion of poor than twenty, fifty, or a hundred years ago.

Resentment

A different explanation of the failure of crime rates to decline with poverty seems plausible. It stresses not objective poverty but subjective resentment of it. This, too, is at best a partial explanation: no single factor can explain the worldwide rise in crime rates which is most striking in the U.S. But at least this explanation is not inconsistent with the facts.

It is possible that in a society in which advancement is expected from everybody the poor are drawn to crime by resentment. If they are still poor they have not advanced enough—however much they did advance. They may have found few legitimate ways of advancing further, perhaps because of lack of opportunities and education (this idea is popular, though unproven); or, owing to low intelligence * and insufficient per-

---

* Richard Herrnstein's *I.Q. in the Meritocracy* (Boston: Atlantic Monthly Press, 1973) reasons that equality of opportunity produces, or will produce, low intelligence among the poor, since, with equal opportunity, the more intelligent will not stay poor. If intelligence is hereditary and opportunity equal, intelligence will be drained from the lower into the upper classes. But low intelligence would not prevent high resentment in a society where self-esteem depends largely on success measured by increases in income.

sistence or to excessive "present-mindedness" * (this idea is unpopular and also unproven).

Contrary to expectations shared by revolutionaries (who fear contentment) and by reformers (who hope for it), the resentment of the poor may have been increased by shortening the distance between them and others. A contemporary rival of Karl Marx, Ferdinand Lasalle, spoke of the "damned wantlessness of the poor." He no longer could. When rich and poor were as "two nations," † the resentment of the poor was vague and unfocused; they experienced and envied each other more than the remote rich. No longer isolated by vast and apparently insurmountable distances in education and living conditions, the poor now share much of the common outlook. They share, above all, the consuming ambitions of the non-poor, brought home to them more than ever by TV. But they still lack the means to fulfill them, and they resent what they now feel is not just poverty but deprivation. Further, while the habitual is regarded as inevitable and the inevitable is tolerated, the inadequate is resented. Improvement as a process is always felt to be inadequate—it can never keep pace with the rise in expectations it generates; at least temporarily it sharpens dissatisfaction. This may have happened and may contribute to the motivation which, in some circumstances, produces crime.‡

Thus, less, rather than more, poverty might help to explain high crime rates and the high variance among social groups, if the remaining inequality is resented more. Resentment might

* The concept of present-mindedness is lucidly expounded in Edward Banfield's *The Unheavenly City* (New York: Little, Brown, 1970), it seems certain to play some role in the distribution of income as does, probably, Christopher Jencks's concept of luck (*Inequality* [New York: Basic Books, 1973]).

† A phrase used by the British Prime Minister Disraeli in his novel *Sybil* to describe the nineteenth-century situation in England.

‡ Perhaps this helps explain why no decreases in delinquency have occurred, even though Belton Fleisher, in *The Economics of Delinquency* (Chicago: Quadrangle Books, 1966), has estimated that "a 10 percent rise in incomes might well result in a 20 percent decline in delinquency."

justify offenses emotionally and reduce moral restraints. There are many indications of intensified resentment (though there is no conclusive proof). But contentment cannot be manufactured. It does not altogether depend on circumstances any government can control.

The proportion of the poor in society was so great in the past that they saw their condition as natural. So did everybody else. Nobody any longer can. They are comparatively few now, and the social perception, including the self-perception of the poor, has changed. A small minority, the poor feel isolated from the great majority and passed by. In turn, the rich feel guilty for having left them behind. No one—rich or poor— any longer believes that poverty is an individual responsibility or fault of the poor, let alone part of a divinely sanctioned, just, or even tolerable social order. No longer accepted as part of the physiology of the body social, poverty has come to be regarded as social pathology. It is now seen as an injustice committed by the rich, who are held responsible for depriving the poor.* In many minds this injustice legitimizes the offenses the poor commit, absolves them from responsibility, and makes deterrent measures unjust and somehow also ineffective.

---

* The indignant reaction to the work of Herrnstein, Banfield, and Arthur Jensen suggests no less. These scholars have sinned by ascribing poverty to causes other than the injustice of the rich or of "the system."

IX

Black and White

> "Environment is the root of all evil—and nothing else! A
> favourite phrase. And the direct consequence of it is that if
> society is organized on normal lines, all crimes will vanish
> at once, for there will be nothing to protest against, and all
> men will become righteous in the twinkling of an eye."
> Dostoyevsky: *Crime and Punishment* *

Ghettos and "Political Prisoners"

Except in narrowly specifiable conditions, the law does not
see offenders as victims of conditions beyond their control.
But criminologists often do.† Paul Bator describes views
shared by many: ". . . that the criminal law's notion of just
condemnation is a cruel hypocrisy visited by a smug society on
the psychologically and economically crippled; that its prem-
ise of a morally autonomous will with at least some measure

---

* Dostoyevsky's novel is directed against this notion, which he puts in the
mouth of one of Raskolnikov's friends. The notion itself is still around. Thus,
Alex Thio in *The American Sociologist* (9 [February 1974] n.48): ". . . laws
benefit the powerful, for it is much easier and less costly for them to punish
the powerless criminals than to eradicate the cause of the crimes by changing
the basic structure of society . . . laws, by virtue of enabling the powerful to
perpetuate the social-structural causes of murder, rape, arson and burglary,
ensure the perpetuation of those crimes."

† To legally excuse an offense, it must be shown that external conditions
were such that a reasonable person acting with normal diligence could not
have avoided his act—unless it is shown that the offender lacked the mental
competence to know what he was doing or that what he was doing was wrong.

of choice whether to comply with the values expressed in a penal code is unscientific and outmoded; that its reliance on punishment as an educational and deterrent agent is misplaced, particularly in the case of the very members of society most likely to engage in criminal conduct; and that its failure to provide for individualized and humane rehabilitation of offenders is inhuman and wasteful." [29]

Most criminologists are not that explicit. But S. I. Shuman, professor of law and psychiatry at Wayne State University goes further. He maintains that "if the ghetto victim does what for many such persons is inevitable and is then incarcerated . . . he is in a real sense a political prisoner," because he is punished for "the inevitable consequences of a certain sociopolitical status." * If these consequences were indeed "inevitable," the punishment would be unjust, as Prof. Shuman argues. Why, however, would the (unjustly) punished offender become a "political prisoner," as Prof. Shuman also claims?

All punishments are imposed, or sanctioned, by the political order which the law articulates. Are all convicts, then, political prisoners? or all those unjustly punished? or all convicts who come from severely disadvantaged groups? If such a definition were adopted, every convict or all disadvantaged convicts or everyone unjustly punished would be a "political prisoner." "Political prisoner" would become a synonym for "convicted," for "disadvantaged," or for "unjustly punished."

If we want to distinguish between political and other prisoners, a "political prisoner" must be defined as someone imprisoned because he tried to change the political system. The aim of his crime determines whether or not the criminal is "political"; the offender who intended personal enrichment cannot become a political criminal independently of his actual intent simply because a penalty is imposed for "the inevitable consequences of a socio-political status," which led him to try

* *Wayne L. Rev.* (March 1973), pp. 853–54. Prof. Shuman's argument is more intelligent than most, but otherwise prototypical.

to enrich himself illegally. If any unlawful attempt to improve one's personal situation within the existing order "because of the inevitable consequences of a certain socio-political status" is a political crime, then all crime committed by severely deprived persons are "political." But is the ghetto dweller who becomes a pimp, heroin dealer, or mugger a "political criminal" just as the one who becomes a violent revolutionary? Ordinarily, an offender who did not address the political order is not regarded as a political criminal (whether he is a victim of politics or not), whereas an offender whose crime did address the political order is a political criminal (even if he is not a victim of politics). This usage permits a meaningful distinction, which Prof. Shuman obliterates, by making "political" refer to (presumptive) causes rather than to overt intentions.

Inevitable Crimes?

Prof. Shuman goes on to claim that "arguing that inevitability is too strong a connection between crime and poverty or ghetto existence because not all such persons commit crimes, is rather like arguing that epilepsy or heart attack ought not to excuse because not all epileptics or persons with weak hearts are involved in a chain of events which results in injury." He adds that "those poverty or ghetto victims who do not commit crimes are extraordinary."

Surely "extraordinary" is wrong here as a statistical generalization. Most poor people do not commit crimes; those who do are extraordinary, not those who don't. Perhaps Prof. Shuman means that it is more difficult within the "ghetto" than it is outside not to commit crimes. Quite likely. But "inevitability"? Here, the analogy with epilepsy or heart conditions is unpersuasive. Such diseases serve as legal excuses only because they produce seizures beyond the control of the person affected. These seizures are legal excuses when they are the cause of the crime or injury, or of the failure to control it. Otherwise, a weak heart (or an epileptic condition) is not an excuse. Thus, poverty could not be an excuse, unless it can be shown to produce seizures beyond the control of the poor which cause them to commit crimes. Poverty does not produce such seizures. Nor would poverty deprive the victim, if he were to experience a seizure (of criminality?) of control in the way an epileptic seizure does. Poverty does affect motivation and increase temptation. So does sexual frustration or, sometimes, marriage. But these are conditions, not uncontrollable seizures inevitably leading to crime. To have little or no money makes it tempting to steal; the poor are more tempted than the rich. But a poor person is not shorn of his ability to control temptation. Indeed, it is to him that the legal threat is addressed. He is able to respond to it * unless he suffers from a specific individual defect or disease that makes him incompetent.

There is a generous and strong moral bias in Prof. Shuman's argument, although he does not seem fully aware of it. That bias was already noted by Friedrich Nietzsche when he wrote in *Beyond Good and Evil:* "[writers] are in the habit of taking the side of criminals." Stated in undisguised moral terms, the argument goes: the poor are entitled to rob or rape because of the injustice they suffer—poverty. The moral nature of the argument is concealed by an erroneous factual claim: poor offenders can't help committing crimes and, therefore, should not be held responsible. The nonfactual, moral nature or bias of the argument is easily revealed if "power" is substituted for "poverty."

Suppose one were to credit fully Lord Acton's famous "Power tends to corrupt and absolute power corrupts absolutely." Those who hold power could then be held responsible for criminal acts only to some degree, since they live in conditions which tend to corrupt them. Those who hold "ab-

* See Chapter IV.

solute power" could not be held responsible for criminal acts
at all. They would be "power victims," just as ghetto dwellers
are "ghetto victims." Their rapes would be political acts, and
they would be political prisoners when punished for them.
Power would become a legal excuse. "Absolute power" would
become an absolute excuse. This does not appear to be what
Prof. Shuman advocates. Yet he urges that poverty (or slums)
should be an excuse since—like power—it leads to crime.*
Prof. Shuman wants to excuse the poor and not the wealthy
and powerful not because as he suggests, poverty is causally
more related to crime than wealth but because, he sees deprivation as morally unjust and painful and power and wealth as
morally undeserved and pleasant. This is why he wants to excuse the poor and punish the wealthy. He is morally preju-
diced against those corrupted by undeserved wealth—whom
he gives no sign of excusing—and in favor of those corrupted
by unjust deprivation.

The generosity of his prejudice leads Prof. Shuman to over-
look a logical error in his argument. In some sense everybody
is what he is, and does what he does, as a result of his genetic
inheritance and of the influence of his environment—poverty,
wealth, or power—which interacted with his genetic inheritance to produce him and his conduct. This is no more the case
for the poor than for the rich, for criminals than for noncriminals. However, there is no reason to believe that, except in individual cases (which require specific demonstration), genetics or the environment so compel actions that the actor must
be excused because he could not be expected to control them.
Unless none of us is responsible for what he does (an idea
dealt with in the next chapter), it would have to be shown why
criminals, or why poor criminals, are less able to control their

---

* To take a more concrete instance: what are the psychological reasons (the
scientific or causal as distinguished from the moral ones they rationalize) for
excusing the slum-dwelling robber (who wishes to support his habit or girlfriend) and not the embezzler (who wishes to take his girlfriend to Acapulco)?
Wherein is the latter's ambition, greed, wish for prestige, or sexual desire less
strong or predetermined by his character and experience than the former's?

conduct and therefore less responsible than others. This cannot be shown by saying that they are a product of the conditions in which they live. We all are. Nor can nonresponsibility be claimed by showing that their living conditions are more criminogenic than others. Greater temptation does not excuse from responsibility or make punishment unjust. The law, in attempting to mete out equal punishment, cannot and does not assume equal temptation.*

When it is used to excuse crime in the way advocated by Prof. Shuman, moral indignation about squalor, however well justified, may have the paradoxical effect of contributing to high crime rates—which do not reduce squalor or poverty. Crime becomes less odious if moral disapproval of poverty, slums, or ghettos becomes intense, pervasive, and exculpatory enough to suggest to the "underprivileged" that they are entitled to take revenge through crime, and when they do, to be spared punishment. Those inclined to offenses will perceive the reduced certainty and severity of punishment in such a moral climate as a failure of society to defend its social order. Offenders, not unreasonably, will attribute this failure to doubts abut the justification of the social order and to guilt feelings about those deprived by it, who are believed to be "driven to crime" and, when caught, to be unjustly punished "political prisoners."

Black Crime Rates

Crime among blacks occurs at a rate about ten times higher than among whites when blacks and whites are compared as groups. Most crimes are intraracial. The victims of violent crimes are almost as often black as the criminals. (The victims of property crimes committed by blacks and of assaultive

* See Chapter IV.

crimes concerned with property, such as robbery, are more often white.) Some figures may give an idea of the gross difference. In 1970 blacks in the United States accounted for about 60 percent of all arrests for murder and, according to the F.B.I.'s figures, for 65 percent of the arrests for robbery.[30] (Blacks constitute about 12 percent of the population.) The difference between black and white crime rates may well be explained by different environments. What has been said in the preceding section should prevent confusion of such an explanation with a justification for individual offenses.

However, simple comparisons of black and white crime rates are misleading. They ignore the fact that a greater proportion of blacks are young and poor, and that the young and poor of any race display the highest crime rates. In other words, age- and income-related variances must not be attributed to race. The age-specific crime rates of blacks are only slightly higher than those of whites on the same socioeconomic level.[31] The remaining difference cannot be attributed to racially discriminating law enforcement.[32] What discrimination there is may lead in the opposite direction. Crime is less often reported in black communities, and police are less inclined to arrest blacks for crimes against blacks than to arrest whites for crimes against whites.

The difference in crime rates should not come as a surprise. Blacks have been oppressed for a long time. Many are recent migrants from rural to urban areas who have the usual difficulties of acculturation faced by most immigrants. Their access to the labor market was and still is limited because of lack of training due to past discrimination. All this has some effect on the legitimate opportunities available to them and, as importantly perhaps, on the ability of individuals to utilize what opportunities there are.

Thus, we should expect a somewhat higher crime rate for blacks, and no explanation in *current* economic terms is needed. Such an explanation would not be supported by the available data. Between 1960 and 1970 the median income of white families went up 69 percent; that of black families doubled. Whereas only 3 percent of black families earned more than $10,000 a year in 1951, 13 percent did so in 1971.* The disparity between the income (and the social status) of blacks and whites, though it remains considerable, has been diminished even faster than the difference between white poor and non-poor. The difference between black and white crime rates has not decreased. Clearly, the crude economic explanation—poverty—won't do. Possibly, resentment of the remaining disparities has not decreased, although they have become fewer and less considerable. Resentment then could have prevented the black crime rates from falling as blacks became less deprived and the black-white difference in economic and social status became smaller.†

Continuing cultural differences, created by historical circumstances, probably contribute to the difference in crime rates of blacks and whites as well, but we know too little as yet to usefully describe, let alone explain, these cultural differences. Phrases such as "the culture of violence" merely describe what is yet to be understood.‡ Surely crime is largely produced by the lifestyles generated by the subcultures characteristic of those who commit it. But does this tell us more than that crime is produced by a crime-producing subculture?

---

* The figures used are in dollars of constant purchasing power, i.e., they exclude the effects of inflation; they are taken from Ben J. Wattenberg and Richard M. Scammon "Black Progress and Liberal Rhetoric," (*Commentary*, April 1973).

† For teenagers the economic picture is much darker. (And teenagers account for much crime.) One-third of black teenagers were unemployed in 1971 against 15 percent of white teenagers. The high unemployment rate probably contributed to high crime rates in both cases, and the difference in the unemployment rate of white and black teenagers contributed to the difference in crime rates. The high teenage unemployment rates may be caused at least in part by minimum wage legislation, which requires that teenagers be paid a minimum that often exceeds what their production is worth to employers. (The minimum wage rate for most other workers rarely is above what they are worth to employers.)

‡ Ghettoization does not explain much, for, except for black "ghettos," the incidence of crime in "ghettos" (ethnically segregated slums) is low. In Chinese or Jewish "ghettos" there was little crime. On the other hand, variances in crime rates everywhere are associated with ethnic differences.

Environment and Personality

What are we to conclude? Many people, black and white, living in the conditions ordinarily associated with high crime rates—such as poverty or inequality—do not commit crimes, whereas many people not living in these conditions do. It follows that these conditions are neither necessary nor sufficient to cause crime. Crime rates have risen as poverty and inequality have declined. It follows that high crime rates need not depend on more poverty or inequality, and are not remedied by less. More resentment may increase crime rates even when there is less poverty; but resentment is hard to measure and may increase with improving conditions, as was pointed out by Alexis de Tocqueville.*

Since the incidence of crime among the poor is higher than among the non-poor, it is quite likely that when combined with other ingredients—not always easily discernible (possibly inequality?)—poverty produces high crime rates probably by affecting motivations and temptations. Thus, poverty may be an important element—though neither indispensable nor sufficient by itself—in the combination that produces high crime rates and explains the variance among groups. But recognition of the importance of poverty as a criminogenic condition should not lead us to neglect individual differences. Enrico Ferri, unlike some of his latter-day followers, did not neglect them. He wrote:

If you regard the general condition of misery as the sole source of criminality, then you cannot get around the difficulty that out of the one thousand individuals living in misery from the day of their birth to that of their death, only one hundred or two hundred become crim-

---

* *Democracy in America*, e.g.:

It is natural that the love of equality should constantly increase together with equality itself, and that it should grow by what it feeds on. . . .

. . . The mere fact that certain abuses have been remedied draws attention to the others and they now appear more galling; people may suffer less, but their sensibility is exacerbated. . . .

inals. . . . If poverty were the sole determining cause, one thousand out of one thousand poor ought to become criminals. If only two hundred become criminals, while one hundred commit suicide, one hundred end as maniacs, the other six hundred remain honest in their social condition, then poverty alone is not sufficient to explain criminality.[33]

The Legal and the Social Approach

Surely it is futile to contrast environmental (social) with individual (psychological) causation as though mutually exclusive alternatives. Instead, we might ask in quantitative terms

1. How much of the variance in crime rates—among social groups, or between two time periods—is controlled by specific differences in social conditions?
2. Which of these (a) can be changed and (b) at what cost, monetary and non-monetary?
3. At what cost can we then reduce the crime rate in general, or the variance, by changing social conditions? What specific social change is likely to bring about what specific change in crime rates and in variances?

To illustrate: if we assume that X percent of the variance between black and white crime rates is explained by the lower employment rates of black males, then we might be able to predict that a rise of X percent in the employment rate of black males would lead to a decline of X percent in the crime rate, or in the variance. There are all kinds of pitfalls in such a simplified model. Employment rates, for instance, are determined by a variety of factors. Richard Cloward came to grief by assuming that employment rates are determined exclusively by employment opportunities.*

Still, in the apt words of Enrico Ferri: "Certain discreet shelters arranged in convenient places contribute more to the

* See Daniel Patrick Moynihan's *Maximum Feasible Misunderstanding* (New York: The Free Press, 1969) for an analysis of these pitfalls.

cleanliness of cities than fines or arrests." [34] Ferri meant public urinals. But the principle applies to any change in the social or physical environment, and the questions it poses are always (1) what is the ratio of the cost of the change in social conditions to the benefit (the reduction in crime rates) compared to the ratio of a change in other variables (e.g., expenditures on police; higher or more regular punishments) compared to the benefit (the reduction in crime rates); and (2) given these ratios, which change is preferable in view of other merits or demerits?

Parking violations can be reduced by better policing, higher fines, and more public garages. Very high fines would help but may not be tolerable. More public garages will help but may be too costly. Without some punishment for violation there would be no incentive to use public garages, and without some legitimate opportunity it is likely that the law will be violated unless punishments are extremely severe and certain. The alternatives "improve social conditions" and "increase punishment" are not mutually exclusive. They are cumulative. The question is which combination promises the greatest benefits at the least cost.

X

Free Will, Responsibility, Rationality, Deterrability

Angelo: I will not do it.
Isabella: But you can if you would.
Angelo: What I will not, that I cannot do.
Shakespeare, *Measure for Measure*, Act II

The Insanity Defense

In modern times the law distinguishes between "sane" and "insane" offenders. People are not held responsible for unlawful acts if it is shown that they were unable to understand the unlawfulness of their conduct, or to restrain it, because of a disease or defect which existed at the time of the crime. A person incapable of understanding that his act was unlawful could not have been deterred by the threat of punishment, nor would he deserve retribution. Thus, pathological cognitive incompetence which prevents one from realizing the wrongness, or the harmful effects, of one's acts is a legal excuse that exonerates people suffering from gross delusions, or an incapacity to perceive reality or to deal with it rationally.*

---

* Such persons are usually deemed dangerous once they have engaged in unlawful acts. They may be committed to a psychiatric institution. Though not intended to be punitive, such a commitment may not differ much from incar-

There are people quite lucid and aware of the wrongness of their acts but unable to avoid them because they are driven by an "irresistible impulse." Some court decisions have made this condition, which is real enough, a legal excuse. However, despite its psychiatric validity, the legal usefulness of the concept of compulsive behavior seems questionable. It is unlikely that psychiatry will ever be able to ascertain whether an otherwise competent person who does not resist an impulse fails to do so because he cannot or because he will not. The issue hinges on the philosophical meanings of "will" and "can" as much as on clinical findings. It also is quite conceivable that impulses will be resisted less often when they are not regarded as resistible.

Neither the philosophical nor the clinical determination is of great significance for psychiatric practice. Psychiatrists need not decide to what extent a patient was "compelled" to or willed a given act. But for legal purposes that question must be decided clearly. Because it cannot be, the legal usefulness of the concept of "irresistible impulse" is questionable. So is the "Durham rule," which holds an accused not criminally responsible if his unlawful act was the product of mental disease or mental defect.*

---

ceration, except that (1) the procedure establishing that an unlawful act was done by the person to be committed is often not as rigorous as it would be with a defendant found sane; (2) the duration of the institutionalization is not proportioned to the gravity of the act committed but determined by psychiatric judgment of the patient's mental health and dangerousness—which can be quite capricious; (3) while institutionalized, the patient is deprived effectively of rights that he would have retained if he had been incarcerated as a sane convict; and (4) the patient may be subjected to involuntary treatment beyond being held in custody. Thomas Szasz' many crusading books illustrate the horrors of involuntary commitment (e.g. his *The Age of Madness* [Garden City: Doubleday, 1973]).

* The basic precedent for the insanity defense is still the M'Naghten case (1843), which in eighteen states and in federal jurisdictions is supplemented by the irresistible impulse test. The Durham rule—*Durham* v. *U.S.* (1954)—is too vague for use. What is a "mental defect" or "disease"? Anything a psychiatrist says? Is the crime evidence for it? What else is? Does an addict have a mental disease? a rapist? a sadist? How does one know that the unlawful act was "the product" of the disease and not of the sane part of the personality?

General Determinism and Punishment

The factual proof required for intellectual incompetence or psychic incapacity is not needed if nonresponsibility is allowed to rest on "general determinism"; it holds that criminals are *never* responsible because crimes are *always* determined by the environment and the genetic makeup of the criminal. They produce personality and behavior, including all specific acts, criminal or otherwise. Logically, they must, if the words "personality" and "environment" are used, as they often are, to include all determinants of behavior, deviant or not. However, the point at issue is the nature and quality of the factors, within and without, which cause, or compel, behavior. John Stuart Mill suggests some of the problems involved:

Our character is formed by us as well as for us; but the wish which induces us to attempt to form it is formed for us, and how? Not, in general, by our organization, nor wholly by our education, but by our experience—of the painful consequences of the character we previously had—or by some strong feeling of admiration or aspiration accidentally aroused. But to think that we have no power of altering our character, and to think that we shall not use our power unless we desire to use it, are very different things, and have a very different effect on the mind. . . . It is of no consequence what we think forms our character, when we have no desire of our own about forming it, but it is of great consequence that we should not be prevented from forming such a desire by thinking the attainment impracticable, and that if we have the desire, we should know that the work is not so irrevocably done as to be incapable of being altered. . . . We are exactly as capable of making our own character, *if we will*, as others are of making it for us.[35]

Mill here concurs with Aristotle:

You may say that very likely he could not help it, he is just that sort of man . . . he can [not] stop being unjust or dissolute merely by wishing it. Yet the illness may be voluntary . . . nobody blames a man for being born ugly, but we do blame those who lose their looks from want of exercise and neglect of hygiene.[36]

Whether or not it correctly describes the human predicament, "general determinism" is irrelevant to punishment. "General determinism" does not claim that criminals are the product of their genes and of their environment and that noncriminals are not. But, unless offenders are more "determined" than others, there is no reason why they should be less responsible for their acts than the general population. No reason, then, to exempt them from the means used to guide conduct in general, such as punishment for misconduct.

Further, if responsibility is discarded on grounds of general determinism, responsibility must be discarded not just for criminals but for legislators, judges, and wardens—i.e., for the general population. There is no more reason to blame them (or, for that matter, "society," the product of its history as are its members, including criminals) for punishing the criminal than to blame the criminal for committing the crime. Both are equally determined. Neither can help what he does.

Just as nothing follows about retributive justice from general determinism, so nothing follows about deterrability either: the threat of punishment is part of the environment, one of the forces that "determine" actions. Deterministic views of all kinds are entirely consistent with theories of deterrence, which actually require a causal (though not necessarily "deterministic") view of human behavior.

Causation and Compulsion

Barnes and Teeters [37] write: "If a criminal does what he must do in the light of his background and his hereditary equipment, it is obviously both futile and unjust to punish him as if he could go straight and had deliberately chosen to do otherwise. It would be as foolish to punish him for having contracted tuberculosis. This consideration entirely destroys whatever logic there was in social revenge * as a basis for

* See Chapter II on the confusion between retribution and revenge.

punishment." Barnes and Teeters are wrong in suggesting (1) that causal determination—by background and hereditary equipment—extends only to offenders, while the rest of society is free to choose and therefore responsible, and (2) that a causal view implies compulsion, and therefore nonresponsibility. These errors are found frequently in textbooks and in the minds of many students who were taught from them. Besides being irrelevant to punishment, general determinism also rests on confused reasoning. A brief comment on its validity, as distinguished from its relevance, may not be amiss.

General determinism is used to explain crime because of an insufficient distinction between "causation" in general and "compulsion," a special kind of causation. It is as though one confused "weather" and "rainstorm" and concluded that all weather is a rainstorm. Causation of one's choice of behavior does not deprive it of its character as free choice or relieve the actor of responsibility for it—unless the causation is compulsion, internal or external. To illustrate: I cause you to come to the forbidden place by asking you to—but you decide to let yourself be persuaded. Though it was caused (by my asking), you are responsible for your decision. My asking you is rather different from compelling by threatening to shoot you if you don't come; and the compelling threat is almost, but not quite, the same as forcing you by dragging you there without giving you any choice. Only in the last two cases are you not responsible—you were not free. To be persuaded also is different from an internal compulsion: internal compulsion differs from internal causation just as external compulsion differs from external causation. Unless these distinctions are made, the point most relevant to legal judgments—the difference between the person who could have done otherwise and the person who could not—is obscured.*

* Causation (simply being affected by one's own experiences) and compulsion are notably confused by Barnes and Teeters (italics supplied): ". . . the argument for deterrence cannot be logically squared with the doctrine of the free moral agent, upon which the whole notion of punishment is based. If a man is free to decide as to his conduct, *and is not affected by his experiences*, he cannot be deterred from crime by the administration of any punishment,

Deterministic views would be inconsistent with our notions of guilt, justice, and deterrability only if the criminal's actions were entirely (or, at least, to a greater degree) produced by environment and genetics and the noncriminal's actions were not. One must hold that the criminal never, and the non-criminal always has "freedom of will," * that non-criminals are caused while criminals are compelled. Such a doctrine could be justified only by holding that offenders are compelled by "sickness" or by "social conditions" whereas nonoffenders are not.

If criminals were so different from the general population, so unlike it—owing either to their genes or to the conditions in which they live—as to be altogether insensitive to threats, and thus not deterrable, or altogether incapable of rational choice, and thus not responsible, they could be dealt with, if at all, only by changing the conditions in which they live or their genetic character. Deterrence and retribution would be futile and unjust. On the other hand, law-abiding persons, also produced by genetic and environmental forces, albeit different ones, would not need deterrence; they would lack the differential characteristics that lead to crime. There would be no need for retribution against them either, since they would not commit crimes. Thus, deterrence would become either ineffective or unnecessary; and retribution could never be justified when a crime has been committed and, of course, would not be justified otherwise. However, there is no evidence to indicate that society consists of these two distinct and nonoverlapping groups. (This matter will be discussed in the next two chapters.)

---

however severe." (*New Horizons in Criminology,* pp. 337–8.) Why should "the free moral agent" not be "affected by his experiences"? He is affected causally (but not compelled) which is why he can be influenced (deterred by punishment).

  * "Freedom of the will" is contingent on, not inconsistent with, causation by prior experience, environment, and inheritance. Nor is free will inconsistent with an observer's prediction of the use the possessor will make of it, as St. Augustine already pointed out (*De Libero Arbitrio*).

Does Deterrence Assume Rationality?

I have suggested throughout that deterrence is the most important of the utilitarian functions of punishment, though it has been fashionable to discount it. Now I'd better take up some objections to this view.

Many humanitarian thinkers spurn deterrence because they perceive it as sheer hypocrisy, merely an excuse for revenge. In turn, popular moralists, and the social scientists they popularize, frequently write as though crimes were always bred by poverty, by deprivation, and by injustice, or committed mostly by aberrantly motivated and improperly conditioned personalities, who need help and not punishment. A letter in the *New York Times* (July 16, 1972) expresses the sentiment: ". . . to the hijacker the hijacking seems to represent a last, desperate effort for personal integrity in times that make this basic human feeling so hard to realize. It saddens me to hear these frightened, despondent men sentenced to more of the same despondency for 20 years."

Attempts to control crime by means of punishment are regarded widely as not only cruel but intellectually disreputable. Though more outspoken than other writers, Barnes and Teeters are not untypical *:

An additional purpose of punishment is to deter potential wrongdoers from the commission of similar or worse crimes. This is simply a derived rationalization of revenge. Though social revenge is the actual psychological basis for punishment today, the apologists for the punitive regime are likely to bring forward in their argument the more sophisticated, but equally futile, contention that punishment deters from crime. . . . The claim for deterrence is belied by both history and logic.[38]

* "Punishment does not . . . prevent crime," Walter Reckless writes in *The Crime Problem* (N.Y.: Appleton Century Crofts, 1967, p. 508). The opinions of criminologists readily become progressive dogma. Thus Garry Wills (*N.Y. Review of Books*, May 29, 1975, p. 13) flatly states, "Prisons . . . demonstrably do not deter."

The equation of punishment and revenge has been dealt with in Chapter II. What about the theoretical arguments which seek to show that deterrence cannot be effective because people would have to be more rational than they are in order to be deterred by threats?

Jeremy Bentham and Cesare di Beccaria, the most effective theoreticians of deterrence, associated it with the rationalistic psychology which prevailed in their lifetime and has since been discredited. Because of this original association, objectors often claim that those who believe punishment can deter must imagine the prospective criminal sitting down to work out the ratio of costs to benefits of his crime before he commits it. It is not likely that many prospective offenders do; and, therefore, threats of legal punishment are thought unlikely to deter. Thus R. M. Gardiner:

> The belief in the value of deterrence rests on the assumption that we are rational beings who always think before we act, and that we base our actions on a careful calculation of the gains and losses involved. These assumptions, dear to many lawyers, have long since been abandoned in the social sciences." [39]

Or Paul B. Horton and Gerald R. Leslie:

> . . . misplaced faith in punishment may rest upon the unrealistic assumption that people *consciously decide* whether to be criminals— that they consider a criminal career, rationally balance its dangers against its rewards, and arrive at a decision based upon such pleasure pain calculations. It supposedly follows that if the pain element is increased by severe punishments, people will turn from crime to righteousness. A little reflection reveals the absurdity of this notion. [40]

True, our actions rarely are calculated consciously. Emotions and other nonrational factors play a great role. Yet, contrary to what is asserted in the passages quoted above, deterrence does not depend on a rationalistic psychology or on the calculations attributed by it to prospective criminals. The behavior of each of us is influenced by the actions of other people. They produce both emotional and material incentives and disincentives for us. People come to work because they are paid and quit, or change, if paid better elsewhere or if they find it more rewarding in some other way. They do avoid unrewarding or painful work or work that pays less than other work they can get. The theory of deterrence rests on these simple observations and not on calculations by its subjects. Punishment is a disincentive by means of which legislators attempt to structure the situation so that people will avoid unlawful actions. It is not necessary that the people who are to be deterred calculate, but only that the legislators who want to deter them do. Those who are to be deterred need only respond in predictable ways. People ordinarily do—or else social life would be impossible.

Prospective offenders need be no more rational than rats are when taught by means of rewards or punishments to run a maze. Experimenters must calculate the effects they desire and the means appropriate to achieve them. So must legislators. But the rats do not calculate, nor do the subjects of legislation need to. Admittedly, there are differences between people and rats, in some cases major ones. However, neither people nor rats *need* rational calculations to respond to incentives or disincentives, although people, unlike rats, *can* calculate if they wish to. Legal threats are effective if those subjected to them are capable of responding to threats (whether or not capable of grasping them intellectually), of learning from each other, and of forming habits. Deterrence depends on the likelihood and on the regularity of human responses to danger, and not on rationality. Experience shows that human beings are better at responding to threats, and much better at learning from each other, than animals are.*

As long as human responses are regular, a rational, even an economic, analysis of crime and punishment is possible, whether or not its subjects calculate their responses rationally. Crime can be conceived of as a product of offenders whose production depends on the net benefit (total benefit less cost)

---

* See also Chapter V.

to them; and the criminal justice system can be conceived as a product of society intent on a net benefit (crime control) purchased at a cost. We then can ask how much greater or smaller the social benefit would be if we expended less (in money, or by granting wider civil liberties to suspects) on crime control and tolerated more crime, or if we expended more and reduced the crime rate. The answer—based on the quantitative data that experience alone can produce—should help us to decide on policies. (The necessary political, ethical, and sociological considerations must be attended to separately. Though immensely helpful, the economic model of crime and crime control is not exhaustive.)

Economists would have been unrealistic to abandon the idea, confirmed daily by experience, that production and sales, supply and demand, are greatly influenced by prices (costs, from the purchaser's point of view) and that lower prices tend to encourage and higher prices tend to discourage purchases. Moviegoers, no more than offenders, calculate rationally and expertly to balance the expected pleasure from the movie against the cost of seeing it and against the cost of alternative pleasures. Still, however attractive the feature, movie theaters that charge $500 for admission, would not find many customers. Prospective offenders can be discouraged just as moviegoers can be. If the costs of offenses to offenders—the punishments—go up, crime is reduced. Price increases do not eliminate purchases, but they do reduce them. Increases in the cost of crime (the price charged by society) reduce it—but not to zero.* Indeed, some people will not be deterred despite the increased cost. But others will be.

Gardiner may be right when he writes: "Amongst criminals foresight and prudent calculation is . . . conspicuous in its absence" and that "[many] prisoners cannot learn from the threat of it." † That may be why they became criminals in the

* To avoid misleading implications of the term price, the reader is referred to Chapter II, pp. 17–18.

† ["it" being punishment] *loc. cit.* n. 39. Note that those who discount deterrence (of others) sooner or later almost invariably mix it up with reform (of convicts).

first place and are now prisoners. Some people would pay $500 to go to the movies. But most people would not. Nor do the great majority of people become criminals. They are deterred—they learn from the punishment of others and are restrained by the fear of suffering it. Incentives and disincentives are effective throughout social and economic life. Human behavior is sufficiently responsive to credible threats and promises to make punishment deterrent.

Certainty and Severity

Bentham and Beccaria thought that the certainty of punishment (of paying) is most important if the punishment (the price) is to deter. This stress on certainty is sometimes used to question the comparative effectiveness of severity. But Bentham and Beccaria meant to correct a contemporary situation: in the eighteenth century penalties were still extremely severe, but they were, perhaps for this reason, haphazardly applied and therefore uncertain. Uncertainty reduced or even nullified the deterrent effect. No doubt, severity by itself cannot replace certainty. But the reverse holds equally true. What the prospective criminal is certain of—the size of the punishment—matters if being certain of it does: being certain of punishment deters from crime only if the punishment is sizable. Being certain of no punishment or of a mild one would not deter much. The stigmatizing effect of conviction (Chap. VI) can take the place of punishment only with some offenses— not with traffic violations, for instance—and only with some persons—e.g., politicians, professionals, or executives, but not with gangsters, con men, or muggers.

Although neither certainty nor severity of punishment can substitute for the other, they can reinforce each other synergistically. That "any deterrent impact from severity depends on the level of certainty" [41] is as true as that any deterrent impact of certainty depends on the level of severity. George

Stigler argues correctly that the expected punishment for an offense is "the probability of punishment times the punishment—$100 if the probability is one-tenth and the fine $1,000. Hence, increasing the punishment would seem always to increase the deterrence." * He would also have been correct had he said "increasing the probability of conviction would seem always to increase the deterrence of punishment."

Severity and certainty can be varied independently. Hence, legislators often must decide whether to change one or the other. The costs differ and so do the returns. The marginal substitutability of certainty and severity still must be considered as an open question. The deterrent effect of punishment is maximized when the two ingredients are optimally proportioned; otherwise the mixture may be more costly and still yield less deterrence. But the optimal combination can be determined only by empirical observation. Psychologists have found that "sufficiently severe punishment will suppress behavior effectively even if it is only occasional, whereas mild punishment [will not] even if it is administered every time." [42] But we do not know when this is the case, and when mild but certain punishment is more effective. Much more must be learned to reach definite conclusions. Possibly there are several equally effective combinations of certainty and severity; and it seems likely that punishment becomes ineffective if either falls below a minimal level. The situation is isomorphic to a lottery. Purchasers may be attracted by increasing the size of prizes, or their number, or the frequency of distribution. The managers will have to find the optimum combination.

---

* "The Optimum Enforcement of Laws," (*J. of Pol. Econ.*, 78, 1970). Stigler's "always" assumes that those threatened can know (at least vaguely) the size of the threat, i.e., are not altogether irrational. People who are could not be responsible for their crimes under our legal rules.

XI

Are They Sick?

"She can't help herself, I'm afraid. It's her character, you
see."

Dostoyevsky: *Crime and Punishment*

By definition, punishment could not deter at all if actual and
potential offenders alike were not deterrable. Incapacitation
and reform would become society's main protection, for punishment is useless if the population falls into two separate
groups: potential or actual offenders who are not deterrable,
and others who are not potential offenders and need not be deterred. Is this a realistic picture?

The Image of the Sick Offender

Although seldom so explicit, some such dichotomous image is
suggested when it is claimed that general deterrence cannot
ever be effective, or punishment just, wherefore rehabilitation
or incapacitation should replace them. This has been the message of social science as it is popularly understood. "The behavioral sciences have helped shift the load of responsibility
from individuals to environments. Their message allocates responsibility for conduct to causes beyond the control of the

actor. He is seen as a *product*. . . . Modern morality . . . converts sin to sickness and erases fault. Its working hypothesis is that if behavior is caused its agent is not culpable." [43]

The shifting of "the load of responsibility" has psychological advantages. The image of the sick offender is comforting. Offenders would be different from ourselves, they would be abnormalities, if not monsters. Since they are not responsible, we would not have to worry about guilt, punishment, and justice, only about treatment or incapacitation. Moral choices would be needed no more. After all, there are few moral problems about hospitalizing the sick. Nor need one worry about one's own rectitude: if I did something wrong, it shows, *ipso facto*, that I was sick and am not to be blamed. How nice. As Ramsey Clark puts it with the guilelessness for which he is so widely admired: "healthy, rational people will not injure others. . . . Rehabilitated, an individual will not have the capacity . . . to injure or to take or destroy property." [44] Since "rehabilitated" means "law-abiding," the rehabilitated convict certainly would have to be. But it does not follow that lawbreakers are sick or irrational. "Healthy, rational people" can "injure, or take, or destroy property," just as sick people can be law-abiding. Clark's identification of health and morality, sickness and criminality, is not based on any known clinical findings.*

Deterrence and Deterrability

For the most part, offenders are not sick. They are like us. Worse, we are like them. Potentially, we could all be or become criminals. Which is why deterrence is necessary. The population cannot be neatly split into two disconnected

* Theoretically, attempts to reduce "right" or "wrong" to "healthy" or "unhealthy" merely disguise and shift moral problems from one forum to another without solving them.

groups—potential offenders and untempted citizens. Beginning with Adam, people have been temptable—mankind seems never to have been "rehabilitated" in Mr. Clark's sense—even though most people do not commit crimes. They do not, not because they are "healthy" but because they are deterrable and deterred when credible threats are made. Actually most of the time, internal restraints are strong enough for most people to avoid the need to confront the external threats of the law. But these internal restraints are by no means independent of external threats (as has been pointed out already in Chap. VI). The deterrent punishment of offenders is needed, then, to keep nonoffenders law-abiding.

To be sure, criminals would not have been criminals if they had been deterred. However, the question is: could they have been deterred? And above all, will *others* be deterred by the punishment of those who have not been? The ever-popular reports of prison wardens, social workers, ministers, or psychiatrists, whose experiences have taught them that punishment has not deterred convicts, are true. But they miss the point (the fallacy is called *ignoratio elenchi*). Prison psychiatrists or wardens *ex officio* only deal with those who have not been deterred. The issue is whether others can be or have been deterred, and secondarily, whether or not the convicts themselves could have been deterred. The threat of punishment never can deter everybody. There would be no criminals if it did. Not even the most extravagant threat could deter all at all times. It is enough if most people are deterred most of the time.

Convict Populations

In the past criminologists such as Cesare Lombroso believed that criminality is genetically inherited. His theories were discarded (rightly) to be replaced by theories holding that social influences produce criminality as though it were a psychic disease. Yet convict populations do not seem to differ significantly from the non-convict groups (comparable in sex, age, race, income, education) from which they are recruited. Nigel Walker [45] found that histories of mental disorder in England were no more frequent among "primary recidivists" than among comparable non-convicts; he found a slightly higher frequency only among "repeated recidivists." Now, absence of a "history of mental disorder" need not mean absence of mental disorder; but there is no reason to suppose that mental disorder is more often present among convicts than among others in the same socioeconomic group when its history is not. Studies in the U.S. and elsewhere also have found no significantly higher frequency of psychic disorders among recidivists, let alone first offenders, than among the general population.[46]

Some authors have found "sociopathy," alcoholism, or drug dependence frequent among recidivists.* This is not surprising. "Sociopathy" is a description of a type of behavior that often includes criminal conduct, not an explanation or an etiology. "Sociopathy" is almost as likely to be found among repeated offenders as blondeness is among blondes, and it is as helpful in explaining crime as "somnolence" is in explaining sleepiness. Whether called "sociopathy" or criminality, antisocial behavior may be part of many psychological disturbances; it also may be a trait of healthy personalities.

Drug dependence is found among many recidivists because addicts must engage in illegal activity in order to stay addicts. Drug dependence is a cause of their crimes only in the unhelpful sense in which crime is caused by criminality. Alcoholism is a different matter; it can play a precipitating and contributing role when it combines with crime. Yet most alcoholics are not criminals, and most criminals are not alcoholics. If the statistical correlation of criminality to cigarette smoking

---

* None of this is a legal excuse for crime.

turns out to be higher than to drinking, I would not recommend relying on smoking as a cause of crime any more than relying on alcoholism.

Sickness as a Moral Term

If offenders are not clinically sick more often than nonoffenders in their socio-economic group, why are they so often believed to be? Besides being comforting, the belief rests on some equivocation about what is meant by "sick." Often, "sick" is used as used as though synonymous with "caused." Yet if causal factors in the personality of the actor produced offensive acts, offenders would be no more sick than others. All acts can be conceived of as effects of antecedent internal causes. Sickness is neither more nor less produced by causal factors than is health, criminal no more than law-abiding conduct. Sick and healthy behavior patterns differ, when they do, because the specific causes and effects of each do, not because one is caused (determined) and the other is not. So with criminal and law-abiding behavior.

Just as it is consistent with health, so causality is consistent with responsibility and deterrability. Indeed, responsibility and deterrability both require that behavior be influenced by external and internal causes. Responsibility assumes that some causes are within the control of the actor; deterrability assumes that the threat of punishment can cause him to obey the law. If acts were uncaused one could not be responsible, for one could not control one's acts—to "control" is to "cause"—nor could threats deter, for to deter is to cause to refrain.

If indeed sickness, and not just crime, were to differentiate criminals from others, then offenders would have to display symptoms of disease other than the offense itself (otherwise the explanandum becomes the explanation). To be relevant, the disease indicated by these symptoms must render offenders less deterrable and less responsible than others. Causal factors must not just be shown to lead to crime—as others do to law-abiding conduct—but they must be shown, independently of the crime, to be pathological; and the pathology must be shown, independently of the actual nondeterrence, to produce nondeterrability and to deprive the criminal of control over his own conduct and, therefore, of responsibility for it.

All too often crimes themselves are used as diagnostic tests to yield a circular definition: "Whatever produces crime must be pathological [sick] because it produces crime." When so used, the term "pathological" expresses moral disapproval disguised as clinical diagnosis and adds nothing to "criminal." But if "sick" and "criminal" are defined independently of each other, sick persons are found to act criminally no more often than others, or healthy persons less often. Immorality, including criminality, no more is illness than illness is immorality.* Neither can be inferred from the other.

The reduction of moral to clinical judgments is seductive to the modern mind. Because science is associated with demonstrability, it has gained the prestige lost by religion, historically the main source of morality. However, here the language of science is used to misrepresent the nature of moral judgments, to make them appear to inhere in the facts. H. A. Overstreet illustrates this use of clinical (scientific) diagnosis as a disguised moral judgment: "A man . . . may be angrily against racial equality, public housing, the TVA [Tennessee Valley Authority], financial and technical aid to backward countries, organized labor, and the preaching of social rather than salvational religion. . . . Such people may appear 'normal' in the sense that they may be able to hold a job and

* The first is today's fallacy; the second, that of the past. (I have discussed this matter at some length in my introduction to Krafft-Ebing's *Psychopathia Sexualis* [N.Y.: Putnam, 1965].) Note also that sickness is a quality of actors, not actions, and can produce a wide range of "moral" or "immoral" actions, while reducing the actors' responsibility for either.

otherwise maintain their status as members of society; but they are, we now recognize, well along the road toward mental illness." [47] Prof. Overstreet does not say whether disagreement with him on all, or on any, of these questions puts one "well along the road toward mental illness." No matter. There is no independent evidence showing that those who do not share his views on these moral, political, or religious issues are further "along the road toward mental illness" than those who do.*

* The notion that to be morally wrong, in the view of the observer, is to be sick, has not been generated by modern social science although it has been popularized by it. It is as old as Plato, who contended that vice is ignorance, a sort of psychological disease. Indeed, according to Anthony Kenny, "the concept of mental health was Plato's invention" ("Mental Health in Plato's *Republic*," in *Proceedings of the British Academy*, 1969). Unlike his modern followers, Plato thought of punishment as curative. Nonetheless, many "correctional institutions" seem like malicious caricatures of his *Republic*.

XII

Addiction

Decriminalization?

Even writers who do not overextend the notion of disease to include all criminal behavior usually regard drug addicts and alcoholics as sick people who need to be cured rather than punished. It is certainly true that punishment does not stop addiction, and this appears to bolster the case against regarding it as a crime. Either way, what, is the role of addiction in *causing* crime—and what can be done to control it?

Reluctant to treat it as a crime, many authors consider addiction a disease—as though that were the only alternative. This view has been generally accepted and has entered the law.* Thus, William F. Hyland, attorney general of New Jersey, stated, according to the *New York Times* (Sept. 27, 1974): "Prison terms for addicts have failed and my feeling is that we must get the drug user out of the system of criminal justice and get him the medical help he requires." The idea seems to be that if the prison does not rehabilitate, medicine can. Logi-

---

* *Robinson* v. *Cal.* 370 U.S. 660 (1962) declared it "cruel and unusual" to punish persons who suffer from "the illness of addiction." (Whereas "addiction" thus is no longer a crime, sale or possession of narcotics can be.) Some courts have declared that statutes making drunkenness a crime are unconstitutional for the same reason.

cally this is a *non sequitur,* and factually it is unfortunately untrue.

However, one need not regard either crime or disease as the only fitting description of addiction. Habit would do—it did until recently for alcoholism, which traditionally has been disapproved of, though tolerated, without being thought a disease. (It becomes a legal offense only when public and a nuisance: "drunk and disorderly.") Yet one may question whether the social harm justifies treating drug addicts as criminals, or whether addiction necessarily leads to other offenses. Does addiction produce the high crime rates among addicts, or does the high price of drugs and the difficulty of obtaining them cause addicts to support their habit by crime? Since it is the legal prohibition which makes the otherwise cheap habit costly, decriminalization, by reducing the cost of drugs, would weaken the addict's motives for committing crimes. True, addictions usually erode the internal restraints that keep people law-abiding. And many addicts committed offenses before they were addicts and probably would have continued anyway, even if they had not become addicted or if their drugs were cheap. Addiction and criminality may have a common cause, but although they may reinforce they need not produce each other. Still, a case can be made for legalization of drugs as a crime-reducing measure, even though the effects are not easy to predict. In England legal drug maintenance works reasonably well.* It does not follow that the same policy would work in the U.S. High penalties for addiction are quite effective in some foreign countries; they are not in the U.S. Chances are that the effectiveness of either strategy depends on circumstances which differ from country to country and which have not all been identified.

---

* In the past all physicians could prescribe drugs for addicts in England. When abuses occurred, special drug clinics were licensed to do so.

Addiction and Disease

If the reasons for defining it as a crime are questionable, the reasons for regarding addiction to anything—alcohol, drugs, cigarettes, or food—as a disease are no less so. Usually, three things are confused to produce the label "disease."

1. The *process* of *becoming* addicted. This is as voluntary as getting married—and no more a disease. Either process is generated by some combination of impulses and personality, the attractiveness, or promise, of the object (spouse or drug), and the pressure of the environment.

2. The *state* of *being* addicted. Like smoking, overeating, being a bachelor, or being married, being addicted to drugs or alcohol is a habit hard to shake. A bad habit with bad effects. But bad effects make it a disease only if smoking or sunbathing is. That the habit is hard to stop makes it a disease only if being married or being in love is. A hard-to-stop habit, whether "constructive" or "destructive" is a hard-to-stop habit, not a disease.

3. The *effects* of *being* addicted to drugs, food, alcohol, or cigarettes. They are much worse than the usual effects of sunbathing, or of being married or single. They may include cirrhosis of the liver, obesity, emphysema, cancer, hepatitis, and, with drugs, almost always impaired general volition and cognition. These effects are diseases, protodiseases, or symptoms of diseases. An intense, often overpowering craving for more drugs (or drinks, or food) and a reduced resistance to the craving are among the most frequent effects; which makes it hard to discontinue addictions, even when they become quite self-destructive.* These effects often are pathological, but the addiction that leads to them is not itself a disease.

Doing something which leads to bad effects or even to disease—eating unhealthy foods, smoking, continuously taking drugs, or playing too much tennis (which produces "tennis

---

* Withdrawal produces painful symptoms of its own which are partly somatic in origin and partly psychogenetic. (They have been remedied by placebos. Yet there is some physiological basis as well.) Both anxiety and the purely physical effect of withdrawal increase the reluctance to give up addiction.

elbow")—is not itself a disease. A bad or exaggerated habit which feeds on itself and which, when continued, can lead to diseases, is not itself a disease. The person who exposes himself to pneumonia may catch it. But exposing oneself is not a disease. Both the cigarette addict who gets cancer and the heroin addict who as a result of his initial voluntary exposure contracts an overpowering craving have exposed themselves to what they eventually contracted, but the exposure is no more a disease than sexual intercourse is when it exposes one to syphilis. Even the overpowering craving itself, once acquired, and the inability to rid oneself of it, share only some features of disease.

Actual diseases neither start nor stop because one wants them to. One does not volunteer for psychosis or cancer. One does volunteer for addiction—few persons become addicted unless they volunteer *—and no one stops being addicted unless he wants to.† Unfortunately, one cannot decide to stop having cancer no matter how staunchly one sticks to one's decision. One can give up addiction by deciding to. To call an admittedly pernicious and debilitating habit a disease is a metaphor—sometimes a pernicious and debilitating metaphor. Above all, people cannot be deterred from getting a disease by the threat of punishment: if we threaten to punish anyone who develops cancer, or catches the flu, no fewer persons will contract either. Threats do not prevent people from contracting diseases. But if we punish becoming addicted, fewer persons do become addicted. This is possible only because, at the least, *becoming* addicted is not a disease. It is not beyond the control of the person who becomes addicted, even if *being* addicted were a disease.

---

* There are exceptions to the voluntariness of becoming addicted. Babies born addicted do not volunteer, nor do people who become addicted because they had to take drugs to control disease or pain. These cases are numerically insignificant.

† When the drug is withdrawn, the part of the craving which was induced by taking it ceases but not the inclination to start the habit again. Only if the addict wants to change can he be helped to do so.

Note that physicians have extremely high addiction rates. This suggests that (1) high socioeconomic status does not protect against addiction and (2) complete information does not protect against addiction. The most popular "cause" of addiction (poverty) and the most popular remedy (education) thus seem largely irrelevant. On the other hand, the high addiction rate among physicians suggests that (3) easy availability of drugs and low likelihood of punishment for illegitimate use do contribute to high addiction rates.

Psychic Disturbance and Disease

Some of the widespread confusion about addiction arises from the use of the word "compulsion" to describe a force that comes from within the person compelled. Such a person may indeed feel "forced" (on pain of anxiety or physical symptoms) to do what seems irrational to the rest of his personality, as though it were imposed from the outside (ego-dystonic). No one has described this syndrome more persuasively than Freud: ". . . the patient's mind is occupied with thoughts that do not really interest him, he feels impulses which seem alien to him, and he is impelled to perform actions which not only afford him no pleasure but from which he is powerless to desist . . . he is perfectly aware of his condition . . . only he simply cannot help himself." Surely the patient suffers against his wishes, as he does when he is physically ill. One part of his personality compels the other and is destructive to it. His thoughts or, in compulsions, his behavior become involuntary to a major degree. There is a severe psychological problem.* But most psychic (internal) compulsions still differ signifi-

* When the whole psyche is affected (as in many psychoses) so that it cannot be guided from within, and does not perceive or interpret external threats, there is convincing similarity to physical disease. The effectiveness of the treatment no longer depends on the patient's will, and punishment does not significantly deter either potential or actual psychotics.

cantly from compulsions by force or physical disease. The patient can exercise some control and can refrain from yielding to his compulsion. Pedophiliacs or exhibitionists do not act according to their compulsion when they think policemen are watching. In contrast, the symptoms of cancer are not controlled by the presence of policemen or physicians. Still, such internal compulsions do resemble diseases, or symptoms of diseases, in major respects; and they are not voluntarily contracted. Addictions are contracted voluntarily, however much they may *become* compulsive once they are present.

Habits

Habits can be as injurious as diseases. Even if the habits to be changed are not diseases, one can benefit from psychological help if one wishes to change them. Once acquired, addictions, more than other habits, control the individual who has acquired them. So, however, may one's wife once one has married her. In both cases, treatment may be needed. Yet the habit is self-inflicted, the loss of control a natural consequence for which the individual is liable. Addicts, or husbands, or wives, have volunteered for a relationship which, in some cases, becomes controlling and destructive. Neither the volunteering nor the relationship it produces are diseases. The result, destructive control (by the drug or the spouse), shares some features of disease. It won't do to say that the habit, addictive or uxorious, is a product of personality and environment. So are all habits. We remain responsible for them.

Sigmund Freud was trained as a physician. His patients were referred to him by other physicians. Naturally, he thought of his treatment as curing a disease. His training (and his dignity) required no less. Any alternative conception of what he treated would have encouraged a return to the hortatory, moralistic, judgmental—and ineffective—treatment given in the past. Things have changed since Freud invented psychoanalysis. Psychoanalysis now is best described as a process by means of which personality can be partially reshaped and reintegrated through the cooperation of an analyst and a patient. There is no need to assume the presence of a disease requiring cure. After all, it is possible to restructure the body, to change the shape of the nose or eyes, although the cosmetic surgeon does not presume that he has cured a disease or dysfunction. His treatment is simply to bring about a desired change. Perhaps the analogy seems frivolous—"cosmetic" has that connotation. Can we say that aborting or delivering a baby—both medical tasks—are curing a disease? If not, why must the psychoanalyst be thought of as treating a disease? Sometimes he does, but at other times he may merely help the patient to lead a happier or more productive life or to achieve his aims. That is indeed what—sometimes—he can do for the addict even though addiction is not a disease.

Addiction and Deterrence: Statistical Evidence

Wilson et al. defined the "expected costs" of an illegal act as "the probability of being arrested, multiplied by the probability of being sentenced to prison and the length of the average prison sentence," [48] and found that "when the cost declined sharply in 1961–1970 . . . the number of addicts in Boston increased about tenfold . . . the largest increases in the number of addicts tended to follow years in which the certainty and severity of law enforcement were the lowest." The relationship between "expected costs" and the spread of addiction confirms that being addicted shares only some characteristics of disease and that becoming addicted shares none. Since the transmission of addiction responds to threats of punishment, unlike the transmission of infection, becoming addicted shares the relevant characteristics of healthy behavior.

If people can be deterred from becoming addicted by the threat of punishment, the tactic usually advocated by "progressive" or "sophisticated" politicians and supported by public opinion—"go after the big guys, the wholesalers, and leave the poor addict victims alone"—is not the best, though it appeals most to our sense of justice. Addiction is not caused by importing heroin but by buying and injecting it. Buying it causes the heroin to be imported. Without a market—demand—there would be no imports or wholesalers. They do not create the demand; they profit from it. If sent to prison, they are easily replaced. Profits are high enough to attract new wholesalers despite the most severe punishments, even at the risk of death. On the other hand, severe enough criminal sanctions regularly applied might reduce the rate of new addictions to near zero. This would reduce the profitability of importing and wholesaling drugs. Thus, although punishing wholesalers can do no harm, if one wishes to do good by deterring new addicts, it is necessary to punish severely the kid who wanted to try it once.

Deterrence Possible, Rehabilitation Hard

With respect to addiction—and to all self-inflicted "diseases"—it is very important to keep general deterrence (of others) clearly apart from reform (sometimes confusingly called "special deterrence") of the persons punished. Punishment can effectively deter (others) from taking drugs and therefore from becoming addicted. But punishment does not reform. It does not restrain most of the already addicted from continuing or resuming the drug habit. The fully habituated addict is indifferent to most of the unpleasantness of punishment other than the unavailability of the drug, which has become paramount in his life. He is likely to be a member of a group in which drug addiction is approved of and punishment is not felt to be stigmatizing. Addiction—whether to alcohol, heroin, or cigarettes—is largely a psycho-cultural phenomenon, thriving with social support and wilting without it. If addiction were a purely physical matter caused exclusively by taking the drug, the craving would stop upon withdrawal. But the psychic craving remains, either because of psychic predisposition or habituation, even after the physical need disappears. Prison does not diminish the addict's psychic craving or his willingness to yield to it. All this makes addiction to drugs no more a "disease" than romantic love, but also makes it no more easy to "cure" (and much more noxious).

If the punishment of the addict is unlikely to rehabilitate him, it might be noted that hardly anything else does either. It is popular to advocate "medical treatment" for addiction, instead of prison, but there is no medical treatment for addiction, although prisons can be (and often are) disguised as hospitals. Some authors [49] have reported successful behavior modification of chronic alcoholics, including reduction of drinking habits to nonalcoholic proportions, by means of withholding privileges in hospital wards. It is too early to say whether or not the results achieved would last outside the hospital setting, and at what cost. Groups such as Alcoholics Anonymous can be quite helpful if the addict wishes to be helped. But these groups must be voluntary to be effective.

XIII

Does Punishment Deter? Statistical and Experimental Evidence

The Data

Until quite recently, ideologists were given their head in criminology, for statistical or experimental evidence to prove or disprove theories about deterrence was hard to come by. Thus, Gregory Zilboorg could write: "No realistic results can be brought forward to support the claims of the principle of the deterrent effect. We have only our inalienable faith that man can frighten man into decency, goodness, or at least moral neutrality." [50] And Lawrence S. Kubie wrote: "We know it is a fantasy that punishment deters others." [51] The prevailing intellectual climate led all too many criminologists to accept the arguments against responsibility and deterrence already discussed. Perhaps a "deterministic" view of criminologists—and of their nondeterrability from error—should be taken.

There are only a few experiments in the literature purporting to show the effectiveness or ineffectiveness of general deterrence. The light they cast is still diffuse, fitful, and by turns arbitrarily focused. Yet, they shed some light. Consider the following.

An Experiment [52]

Multiple choice "quizzes" were given to groups of students who were then asked to calculate their own grades by checking to see if they had given the correct answers. They cheated (by changing their original answers) about one-third of the time. This level of cheating remained unchanged throughout the experiment in a control group which was neither exhorted to honesty nor threatened with punishment.

When students were morally exhorted to be honest, the rate of cheating was not reduced. On the contrary, it rose: students took 41 percent of all opportunities to cheat instead of the previous 34 percent. The rise is puzzling. "Educating, or exhorting people" * is often favored as a means of reducing offenses: it costs the least, morally and financially. It also is ineffective and, here, counterproductive.

When a threat was made, and was made credible, to punish cheaters, the cheating level was reduced from 34 percent to 12 percent. The reduction—nearly two-thirds—was somewhat less when the threat was made less credible.

It was also found that cheating was most frequent, and threats of punishment least effective, with students whose actual performance fell most below the grades they expected or needed. They had the most to gain from cheating.

This experiment supports three tentative conclusions.

---

* Among the measures listed on p. 88 in Chapter VIII. This result is inconsistent with the effectiveness of exhortation to taxpayers reported by Schwartz and Orleans (*U. of Chicago Law Rev.* 1967, Vol. 34, pp. 247 ff.). Perhaps students felt the exhortations excluded sanctions, whereas taxpayers felt threatened by exhortations.

1. Moral exhortation can be useless or counterproductive even in a population presumed to have internalized the moral norms it is exhorted to follow.
2. Threats of punishment can be very effective, the more so the more credible they are.
3. Temptation is least resisted by those who have most to gain from offenses. The threat of punishment is least effective with them. The greater the advantage the offender can expect from the offense, the greater the threat needed to deter him. By and large, then, the needy are more tempted and less easily deterred than the prosperous; the ambitious, than the satisfied.*

As the experimenters were the first to point out, much more knowledge is needed about the effectiveness of threats under various conditions with different populations when compared to other crime-reducing measures. Still, if not conclusive, the experiment suggests that threats can be effective and are needed the more the greater the prospective gain from offenses, the greater the "need" to commit them.

In the last ten years there also have been several sophisticated statistical investigations of deterrence. They support the conclusion that punishment does deter. No critical analysis of these factual investigations have been published to invalidate them. The preponderance of evidence—as distinguished from assumptions and guesses—now points to the effectiveness of general deterrence. "Special deterrence"— rehabilitative treatment of the offender—does not work: those who are punished because they already have committed crimes are quite likely to commit more, and perhaps no fewer than they would have without punishment. But this is irrelevant to the deterrence of others.

Experimental evidence indicates that punishment deters others with respect to infractions of parking regulations as well as of college rules.[53] If higher parking fines deter more than lower ones, longer jail terms should deter more than shorter ones; if students are deterred by threats of punishment

* Wherefore Shakespeare has Caesar say: "Let me have men about me that are fat."

but not by moral appeals, so might other people be. But we cannot be altogether certain, since the populations to be deterred, the circumstances, the punishment threatened, and the offense from which it is to deter all differ. The average parking violator does not engage in serious crime. The temptations, too, are of a different kind. Deterrence from trivial offenses may not tell us enough about serious crimes and criminals.

Statistical studies of the deterrent effect of punishment on serious crimes are based on data from the FBI's annual *Uniform Crime Reports,* which define and report on seven "Index Crimes": burglary, larceny, auto theft, robbery, rape, aggravated assault, and murder (including non-negligent manslaughter). The *Uniform Crime Reports* present the most reliable national data available for study. However, the sad truth is that all our crime data are remarkably inexact. There is a gap between reported crime and crime actually committed, for the size of which we lack reliable estimates. The unreported offenses are usually referred to as "dark figures." We can only guess how much the size of the gap changes from place to place and time to time; therefore, comparisons are hazardous. There are also great variations in the differences between crime reported *to* the police and crime reported *by* the police, so as to enter the FBI statistics. Police like high clearance rates, defined as the proportion of crimes solved to crime reported. These can be increased by clearing more, or by reporting less, crime. Differences in crime rates thus may be due to differences in reporting to, or by, the police. Reporting rates to the police are more predictable than reporting rates by the police, which may vary with commanders. But even the former introduce an element of uncertainty, which differs according to the nature of the crime.

It is hard to ignore murder, and the reporting rates are high.* Crimes of violence are likely to be reported if someone

---

* But not complete. The unidentified body found in the river could be a victim of murder or suicide. The police looks better with "suicide" (case closed) than with murder (case not closed).

is hospitalized, but if not, a sizable though unknown proportion goes unreported. Burglaries are usually reported in affluent areas because insurance companies do not pay otherwise. Since the poor are not insured, they often do not report burglaries—the police rarely are able to clear them up, so reporting is a waste of time. Muggings that do not lead to injury often go unreported, too, and so do rapes that do not lead to injuries. For none of these crimes do we really know the unreported proportion. But it is not unreasonable to estimate that only 50 percent of all offenses enter the statistics—that the rate of crime is 100 percent higher than it appears from the official data.* Finally, acts which were crimes may be reclassified as legal (e.g., abortions), and generally the definition of crime varies from place to place and over time. All this can contribute to misreadings of crime statistics. There are many other difficulties. However, the statistical investigations to be considered are not likely to be greatly affected by them.

The Results

Jack Gibbs [54] studied the FBI data for 1959 and 1960 with reference to homicide only.† He concluded that the greater the certainty and the severity of the punishment in the forty-eight states, the lower the homicide rate; therefore, one must "question the common assertion that no evidence exists of a relationship between legal reactions to crime and the crime rate." Louis Gray and J. Martin,[55] after making their own analysis of the same data on homicide, concluded that: "certainty and severity of punishment have a demonstrable impact on the ho-

* Comparison of the crime rates projected from questionnaires answered by a sample of the population of possible victims with crimes actually reported to the police lead us to estimate that actual crime rates may be more than double, perhaps even three times as high, as those reported by the FBI.

† Capital punishment, thought too rare and uncertain to be of statistical importance in the period studied, was excluded.

micide rate. . . ." So did Frank Bean and R. Cushing: [56] "the variable measuring legal reaction to crime retained its association with criminal homicide rates in a direction consistent with the deterrence hypothesis." Each of these authors used analytical techniques to eliminate methodological weaknesses suspected in the work of the others. There was no significant difference in results. Since homicide, often committed in the heat of anger, is thought to be less affected by the size of the punishment threatened than most crimes, these results are surprising.

George Antunes and A. Lee Hunt [57] applied a more elaborate statistical technique to data for 1960. They analyzed not just homicide but all seven Index Crimes in forty-nine states, concluding "the hypothesis that penal sanctions act as a general deterrent of crime finds support in our data." *

Perhaps the most sophisticated and pathbreaking analysis of variations in crimes across states in the U.S. has been published by Isaac Ehrlich.[58] His work concerns all Index Crimes in the years 1940, 1950, and 1960. The 1940 data include—depending on the crime—from thirty-six to forty-three states; the 1950 data, forty-six states; and the 1960 data, forty-nine states. Ehrlich used an elaborate simultaneous equation model for a regression analysis that included the following variables: [59]

1. current and one-year lagged crime rate: the number of offenses known per capita
2. estimator of the probability of apprehension and imprisonment; the number of offenders imprisoned per offenses known
3. average time served by offenders in state prisons
4. median income of families
5. percentage of families below one-half of median income
6. percentage of nonwhites in the population
7. percentage of all males in the age group 14–24
8. unemployment rate of civilian urban males ages 14–24 and 25–39

* Attention is drawn once more to the excellent summary by Tittle and Logan in *Law and Society Review* (Spring 1973) (Sec. n. 53).

9. labor-force participation rate for civilian urban males ages 24–34
10. mean number of years of schooling of population 25 years old and over
11. percentage of population in standard metropolitan statistical areas
12. per capita expenditure on police in fiscal 1960, 1959
13. number of males per 100 females
14. dummy variable distinguishing northern from southern states (South = 1)

Note that numbers 4–14 refer to variables other than punishment that can influence the crime rate.* The list suggests that the author has taken into consideration the factors known or likely to influence crime rates. These vary from state to state and over time. So do certainty and severity of punishment. By separating the effects of other factors that may influence crime rates from the effects of punishment, it is possible to isolate the statistical relationship between crime rates and punishment: deterrence. Since Ehrlich did not bother with legally prescribed punishment but only with actual punishment rates, he measured the effect not of the legal threat but of the *credible* legal threat of punishment.

Ehrlich found that some factors he separated from the effects of punishment do play an important role. Independently of punishment, property crimes rise with income inequality (resentment?), whereas murder and rape are little affected by it. All crimes rise with the percentage of nonwhites in the population; all decline with higher expenditures on law enforcement.†

Ehrlich's conclusions on deterrence follow: "The rate of

* The mathematical methods used can be followed in detail only by reading Ehrlich's essay itself ("Participation in Illegitimate Activities.")

† Kobrin, Hansen, Lubeck and Yeaman in an independent study, *The Deterrent Effectiveness of Criminal Justice Sanction Strategies* (Public Systems Research Institute, University of Southern California, 1972), found that about one-third of the variation in crime rates among California counties (more in the more populous counties) could be attributed to variations in the certainty and severity of punishment for crimes. 50 percent of the variation in crime rates was attributed to identifiable "social factors," e.g., age and ethnic composition; 20 percent to unidentified factors.

specific felonies is found to be positively related to estimates of relative gains and negatively to estimates of costs associated with criminal activity." [60] By "relative gains" Ehrlich means gains relative to gains available to the offender from legitimate activities. By "cost" he means the severity and probability of the punishment the criminal can expect. Ehrlich concludes: "The rate of specific crime categories, with virtually no exception, varies inversely with estimates of the probability of apprehension and punishment by imprisonment and with the average length of time served in state prisons." [61] These conclusions are supported by data over three decades. They establish the effectiveness of general deterrence: crime rates can be reduced not only by increasing opportunity for legitimate gainful activity but also by increasing the costs of criminal activity.

Since many doubts about deterrence have emotional rather than factual sources, they are not likely to be resolved by data—even though everyday experience confirms what Ehrlich's work tells us. People are restrained from law violations when unpleasant consequences are threatened. The more likely and unpleasant the consequences are (the higher the costs), the more people are restrained. Ehrlich's work raises as well as answers questions because his conclusions necessarily rest on assumptions as well as data, and in time even the most reasonable assumptions ought to be replaced by hard data. But the quantitative study of deterrence has only begun. Once we accept the fact that general deterrence can be effective, we must seek answers to questions such as the following. In a given situation with respect to specific crimes, what would be the variance likely to be achieved by

1. higher police expenditures (and/or better methods)
2. higher arrest rates
3. higher conviction rates
4. higher actual punishments
5. speedier justice
6. social changes such as better employment opportunities, more expenditures for education, housing, child care, etc?

It is plausible to assume that deterrent effects (output, returns) depend both on what and on how much is done to produce them. Often, the output is not affected until a tipping point is reached—until the input of a productive factor reaches a certain level. Till then, returns may be constant; after the tipping point, they increase; and, probably, if input is increased further, returns from the additions diminish and finally become flat once more. This pattern holds for many activities. If one feeds a cow parsimoniously, she may remain alive but give little milk. If the cow is fed beyond a certain point, the returns of milk increase; the rate of increase diminishes with further feeding, and finally there is no further increase.

Charles R. Tittle and Alan R. Rowe have recently demonstrated that this pattern—or at least the first half of it—applies to criminal arrests.[62] They note that arrest, in the minds of most people, is unpleasant, and that some people find it as unpleasant as conviction and incarceration. Using data for Florida rural counties and metropolitan areas, they found that in areas where more than 30 percent of crime reported to the police resulted in arrests, the correlation between arrest and crime rate was − .58 in counties (with a median crime rate of 11.7) and − .48 in cities (with a median crime rate of 17.8); whereas when the arrest rate was less than 30 percent of crime reported to the police, in counties the correlation between arrest and crime rates was reduced to − .13 (with a median crime rate of 32.5) and in cities to − .19 (with a median crime rate of 33.0). In other words, when more than 30 percent of reported crime was cleared by arrests, the crime rate was significantly reduced. When less than 30 percent of reported crime led to arrests, the crime rate was not significantly affected. In the authors' words: "Certainty of arrest appears to be linked to the amount of crime in a negative direction when the level of certainty reaches 30 percent but not at all when certainty is below 30 percent."

To make sure that their results were not determined by differences other than arrest rates among the areas they investigated, the authors carefully controlled for such variables as age, sex, education, race, income, employment, etc. They found that apart from arrest rates "the lower the socio-economic status [of the area] the higher is the crime rate"—which was to be expected. It was also predictable that the higher the arrest rate the lower, *ceteris paribus*, the crime rate would be. This is not to say that probing, proving, and quantifying what common sense suggests is not a worthwhile enterprise: it was not predictable that increasing returns would set in when the arrest rate reached 30 percent of reported crime or that at this point, and not before, the arrest rate would significantly influence the crime rate.*

The effect of each measure on crime rates is likely to differ according to the crime. Some crimes may respond to harsher penalties, some to higher arrest rates, some to higher conviction rates. In each case, the "tipping points"—of increasing and decreasing returns—may be located in a different area. And the deterrent effect of punishment on property crimes and on crimes of passion differs; in Ehrlich's words, "burglars and thieves are risk avoiders" [63] more often than other offenders. Numerous other factors enter. Deterrence is no panacea. But it can play an important role if we make serious efforts to find out how, where, when, and with whom it works, what it costs, and what alternative measures would cost and would achieve. Amazingly little has been done so far.

---

* Obviously, the next step is to work out quantitative correlations between crime, arrest, conviction, etc., rates at each level and for each type of crime.

XIV

Dimensions of Crime

Statistics Once More

Some overall statistics may help to remind us once more of the dimensions of the problem of crime and punishment—but remember that these dimensions are vague because our statistics are unreliable. Probably less than one-third of all crimes committed are reported to, or by, the police. The ratio of actual to reported crimes varies greatly depending on the victim's location and income, the kind of crime, the reporting police department, etc. Besides, the FBI's *Uniform Crime Reports*, on which one mainly has to rely, usually state crime rates per 100,000 population. If it were reliable, this would still be a very crude measure. The rate of rape is more meaningfully stated as a percentage of the female rather than of the total population. This would give the number of actual rapes as a percentage of possible victims, if not of victimizers. For the same reason, the rate of car theft is most meaningful as a percentage of the automobile rather than (or as well as) of the human population. The FBI also under-reports when multiple crimes are committed on the same occasion, since only the "most serious" crime is reported in such a case. Thus, when an offender assaults the victim, rapes her, burglarizes the house, and steals the car, only the rape appears in the statistics.

There are other difficulties. If stealing more than $500 is grand larceny, and stealing less is petit larceny, then inflation automatically raises the rate of grand larceny. Furthermore, as was indicated before, a more youthful population would make for a higher crime rate, even if the age specific rate remains the same. Or, if homicide rates have not risen as much as aggravated assault rates (they haven't), perhaps it is because medical progress saves more victims of assault, and not because assaults have become less ferocious or homicidal. I draw attention to these difficulties to suggest the need for caution in perusing the statistics.

Because the figures are uncertain, and their interpretation precarious, not all statisticians will ever agree that crime has risen. The sense of public security has diminished, but perhaps because the type of crime has changed rather than the overall frequency or the location or the type of victim. All of these factors could change the sense of public security even if overall crime rates were unchanged. It need hardly be added that a "rise in crime" always denotes comparison with some past period. Usually one can find some periods in the past in which the crime rate is believed to have been still higher than it is at present. However, the farther back one goes, the less one can rely on the data. In any case, though they do not prove it unassailably, the statistics available are quite consistent with a major rise in crime in the last twenty years. The decline in the feeling of public safety seems to reflect not media-instigated hysteria but a correct perception. In the words of the President's Commission on Law Enforcement and the Administration of Justice (1967): "Most forms of crime—especially crimes against property—are increasing faster than population growth."

A rise of (a) crime must not be confused with (b) a rise of the crime rate or (c) of criminality: Crime has risen and the crime rate (crime per 100,000 persons) has risen as well. The crime rate of specific groups of the population, (criminality) e.g., of young males, has risen, too. However, not enough to account for the rise of crime. Much of the rise in overall crime is caused simply by an increased number of young males and would have occurred even if there were no rise whatsoever in their criminality, their proneness to crime. (More than 80 percent of all serious crimes usually are committed by males between the ages of thirteen and twenty-nine.)

All this is of little comfort to the people victimized by the higher general crime rate. The victims do not care whether they are mugged because more young lower class males have become criminals or because there are more young lower class males. However, if there are more young males—and there are—the rate of victimization (the general crime rate as it affects victims) could fail to rise only if a smaller proportion of young males were to commit crimes. Which is indeed what is needed. Meanwhile, most statistics we have refer to the supply and to the suppliers of crime rather than to the victims or consumers. Yet both types of statistics are needed. Together they explain why more people are victimized, and the general crime rate is higher, while the crime rates for specific groups have risen by less: the age composition of the population has been changing.

Even partial statistics, though they cast but a fitful light, can help give a sense of what is happening. Arrests do not prove guilt. But an arrest indicates that a witness, a police officer, or a victim warrants, under oath, that the arrested person committed an offense. In the ten-year period between 1960 and 1970, felony arrests of adults in New York State increased from 40,620 to 114,300. It is unlikely that crime rose less (though convictions did).[64] Or, consider the rise in felony arrests of juveniles under sixteen and between sixteen and eighteen in New York City. (Fifteen- to seventeen-year-olds are arrested more than any other age group, followed closely by eighteen- to twenty-year-olds.)

During the period 1968–73, the juvenile population increased but felony arrests increased more—and not, it seems, because of any greater zeal or effectiveness of the police. The courts have little choice under present law but to release even convicted murderers if they are under sixteen. After a maximum of eighteen months, they are returned to the school system that had proved incapable of controlling or reforming them. Sixteen- to eighteen-year-olds also can count on lenient treatment. Present laws and court practices in effect license them to commit crimes. The law itself probably has become the major "cause" of the rise in juvenile crime.

| | UNDER 16 | | | 16–18 YEARS OF AGE | |
	1968 *	1972 *	1973 †	1970 *	1972 *
murder	27	73	94	97	219
forcible rape	77	152	181	217	353
robbery	2487	4386	4449	6011	8056
burglary	2884	3703		5598	6765
assault				1752	2787

Source: *New York Affairs, Winter 1974; † The Sunday New York Times Magazine, Jan. 19, 1975.

Costs to Society

Consider now the costs, both economic and human. There are about 500,000 police officers in the U.S. They make about 9 million arrests annually (more than 1 million for felonies.) In any year about 500,000 persons are imprisoned. At least 200,000 of these are serving sentences in prison. (The remainder are juveniles or are held for trial or serve short jail sentences.) In addition 700,000 people are out on probation or parole. The number of crime victims is harder to calculate—it must be between 1 and 2 million per year. But that figure is not very meaningful, since it combines burglary with murder victims. Data for separate categories are more meaningful—and horrifying: for instance, there are more than 18,000 murder victims per year in the U.S.—regiments of murdered men and women every year.

The economic costs of crime and crime control are hard to

assess. About $15 billion worth of goods are redistributed through thefts, burglaries, and hijackings in the U.S. every year.* But this is not the most important cost. Actual government outlays for police, courts, and prisons currently (1974) exceed $10 billion per year. Other costs include resources consumed or destroyed by crime or by crime control (hospitalization of the assault victim; earnings lost by criminals and victims; value of the house burned by the arsonist). Finally, and perhaps most important, there are the private costs of crime control: the security guards, watchmen, double locks, electronic gadgets, vaults, insurance expenses, lawyers, private guards and detectives. Altogether it is estimated that "the total cost of all aspects of crime to American society is . . . sixty billion dollars annually." † Certainly a significant cost, however hazardous the estimate.

The punishments meted out to convicts are part of the cost of crime and of controlling it. Can it be reduced? Can penalization itself be made more effective and less costly? A few suggestions have already been made. A brief comparison with other countries may be in order now.

International Comparisons

Even the scanty data and estimates we have make it clear that the U.S. has a comparatively high crime and imprisonment rate. Other nations resort to imprisonment less often, perhaps because they have lower crime rates; or because they use dif-

* *New York Times*, Dec. 29, 1974. This estimate, or informed guess, indicates the cost to the victims, not to society. The social costs of theft are hard to assess, since the goods are usually not destroyed but used—if less than optimally. The social cost of theft control is a separate matter; so is the cost of the indirect effects of theft. Both costs probably exceed the cost of theft itself.

† John C. Ball, Presidential Address to the American Society of Criminology, New York, November 1973, published in *Criminology*, May 1974. The earlier estimate of the President's Commission on Crime is lower, but leaves out many costs and crimes. Moreover, crime has risen since, and inflation has increased the dollar costs.

ferent penalties, such as fines. For instance, Holland has a remarkably low rate of imprisonment, and fines play a major
role. (We do not know enough to tell how effective fines have
proven to be.) In Holland 28 persons per 100,000 were imprisoned in 1972; in the U.S. 118 in 1960 and 96 in 1970, i.e.,
nearly four times as many.* Although one must keep in mind
that the U.S. crime rate exceeds the Dutch rate by at least as
much, it is noteworthy that nearly two-thirds of all Dutch convicts pay fines and that only 30 percent go to prison. The
length of the prison sentences handed out in Holland declined markedly, from 1963 to 1970 while the number of
crimes known to the police increased and the clearance rate
declined. The recidivism rate increased, too, particularly for
multiple offenders. The available data do not permit us to im-
pute these changes to specific variables as yet—i.e., we cannot
say to what degree higher Dutch crime rates occurred despite
of, independently of, or because of, changes in penalties.

So much for the numerical dimensions of the problem. The
statistics give us a framework, but they are, by nature, impersonal. Crimes, however, are human events for the offenders as
well as for the victims. That dimension is best considered by
sketching, at least briefly, offenders as they appear to those directly involved in the criminal justice system.

Crime and Human Misery

Anyone who spends time in an arraignment court † cannot
help being overwhelmed by the amount of sheer human misery he encounters. To be sure, some of the people arrested are

* Holland's imprisonment rate is exceptionally low. Norway's—52
prisoners per 100,000 persons—is more "normal" and still less than 50 percent of the U.S. rate.
† A court that disposes of cases in a preliminary way by setting bail, releasing people on their own recognizance, or dismissing or otherwise deciding
minor cases while holding others over for trial.

hardened criminals, professionals temporarily interrupted in the successful pursuit of their unlawful careers. But the great majority of offenders, many with long records, merely seem to be life's losers: people who assaulted their wives simply because they found no other way of solving (or of expressing) their problems; young people whose life experience made them feel that robbery is an acceptable, even a good, way of getting ahead; rebellious or truculent adolescents who got into fights with shopkeepers or policemen. The courts can try to protect society from the effects of these problems, but I see no way of avoiding or solving them by means available to the criminal justice system—or even to society as a whole. The most one can hope for is to minimize offenses. In this the courts, despite obvious limits, play an indispensable part.

Present law in many states makes public drunkenness punishable. Thus, alcoholics are often arrested.* So, the Bowery bum is dragged into court, where he is promptly released (judges are not interested in crowding the prisons with alcoholics). Surely imprisoning them for a few days solves no problem. But releasing them doesn't either. The most zealous reformers insist that alcoholics be "cured" or at least "treated" rather than imprisoned.† Less optimistic reformers feel that some place should be provided where alcoholics might stay, instead of sleeping in doorways or making nuisances of themselves in the slums of the city. Libertarians opt for simply leaving them alone.

Yet neither the criminal justice system nor the welfare measures proposed as an alternative are likely to solve the problem. Nor does ignoring it. "Public intoxication" is not "vic-

* Since policemen have to testify on their arrests in court, the arrest of alcoholics—no arrest is easier—is often used as a way of earning some easy overtime. Judges and superior police officers are aware of the practice, but nothing is done about it. No one feels it is within his power to act. Strict circumscription of power is quite characteristic of the criminal justice system. It leaves a multitude of matters unresolved when, as is often the case, they do not fall fully into anyone's domain.

† E.g., *Crimes With No Victims*, published by the Alliance for a Safer New York, 1972.

timless." Alcoholics often are a nuisance to others and occasionally a danger. Wherefore they cannot be ignored. Yet alcoholism is not a disease.* Wherefore it cannot be cured. Anyone can be temporarily "detoxified." Some people can be helped to sober up permanently; but others cannot. They re-intoxicate themselves.† To offer the alcoholic a non-penal institution to get him out of the doorway and off the streets helps little. He wants to be in the street. He may have become an alcoholic precisely because he is impelled to become and stay a bum—to be on the street, to sleep in doorways. The very degradation and humiliation, the petty offenses—all the things from which reformers wish to rescue him and from which, if asked, he claims he would like to be saved, are what many an alcoholic is impelled from within to do and suffer. Drinking seems to be as much a part of the drunkard's lifestyle as it is a cause of it. He needs to degrade himself—to live on the social bottom and be shorn of responsibilities and of the anxiety of falling further. The life he craves may include being enough of a nuisance to others to provoke the community to retaliate, even if only by arrest and release.‡

Couldn't we just let the alcoholic go, as libertarians will counsel us to do? Chances are that if he is not arrested for

* The American Medical Association and the U.S. Department of Health, Education and Welfare take a contrary view. However, it cannot be sustained when considered soberly. See Chapter XII.

† The problem persists in different social systems. Thus, a Soviet psychiatrist writes: "After drinking up his last kopeks a drunkard is placed in the comfortable conditions of a psychiatric clinic . . . as soon as he is discharged . . . everything starts all over again." (See *Izvestia*, Oct. 1, 1968, p. 5, quoted in Walter D. Connor, "Alcohol and Soviet Society," *Slavic Review* Vol. 30, No. 3, Sept. 1971, p. 585.) Prof. Connor estimates that the rate of alcoholism—made possible by legal and illegal distilling—is extremely high, generated by boredom and tradition. The government has found no effective remedy. See his *Deviance in Soviet Society* (N.Y.: Columbia University Press, 1972.)

‡ If that is the psychological condition, isn't there a cure for it? Even if "cure" is not a good word, can this lifestyle not be changed by treatment? In some cases, probably, and in others not. There is good reason for research, but no reason to expect anything soon to change significantly the number of alcoholics (about 9 million). I can see no feasible social measure to eliminate the infantile experiences, the anxieties, the guilt feelings, the boredom, the fear of failure, and the myriad other things that may lead to addiction.

lesser nuisances he will be driven to escalate them so that he will be arrested. We should do whatever we can to improve matters. But we should not close our eyes to the obvious. The problem has no neat solution. What we are doing now, though it leaves us dissatisfied, is about the best that can be done to keep the problem manageable. It balances the interests of all concerned, drunk or sober. The idea, now more than ever rampant in so many minds, that a benevolent creator has provided a solution for every problem He created, is not borne out— once we take a hard look at things. We cannot discard the few techniques, however unsatisfactory, we have found to manage the unmanageable, before we have found and tested something better.

Consider another case. The defendant standing before the judge has been found with two stolen sweaters, the sales tags still on them, as he left a department store. No one saw him steal them, though he admitted to the store detective and to the police that he did. His counsel pleads him guilty to possessing stolen property. The record shows numerous arrests and some convictions, all for similar acts committed in an alcoholic haze. He is perhaps sixty, clearly an alcoholic, clearly incapable of mending his ways, clearly more to be pitied than condemned. The judge adjourns the case for six months, at which time it will be dismissed unless he has been brought in again. It seems the most humane thing to do. What is to be gained by putting this man in prison for a few months? And yet if a man who steals in an alcoholic haze is not punished, are we not granting a license to steal? Won't that license encourage what must be discouraged—both drunkenness and stealing?

What about the man who drifts down the street, or into a building, with or without the help of alcohol, and sees what he regards as an opportunity to break into a car, burglarize an apartment, steal from a shop? Quite often the offender seems as much a victim as his victim. A victim, if not of society or of circumstances external to him then of forces within him that

cause him to act as he does. When this offender, this victim of
his own offensiveness, stands before the bench, his suffering
is more impressive, more concrete, and more to be pitied than
that of the victim of his offense, who is represented by a smug
department store detective, an indignant car owner, a well-to-
do apartment tenant, a storekeeper, et al. The temptation is to
say: he suffers enough from his own inability to lead a stable
life. Why heap more suffering on him? Surely it will not reform him. Yet, unless this man is punished, the judge is giving
him—and others—a license to do as he did.

Compassion for the actual offender must not divert us from
the task of discouraging other offenders and would-be offenders. We can do so only by using those convicted as the
means of detering others. We imprison this offender neither to
incapacitate him—we release him after so short a time that it
won't make a dent—nor to rehabilitate him—we know full
well that he will go right on doing what he did before. We
have found no way that promises to change him. We know that
his life circumstances and his customary response to them will
generate his offenses and will continue to do so, regardless of
temporary imprisonment. Thus, this offender is punished for
one of two reasons: (1) as retribution for his offense or (2) to
deter others. Here the retribution itself is justified largely, if
not entirely, by its deterrent effect. We retribute because we
threatened to impose the punishment and must do so to keep
the threat credible. There is little moral reason in cases of the
kind just described to hold the offender fully responsible for
his offense. And often the punishment, though socially necessary, seems disproportionate as retribution. In effect, the offender is used for social purposes—to deter others. (We will
consider whether or not this is justifiable in Chapter XVI.)

XV

What Can Be Done to Curb Crime?

The greatest incitement to crime is the hope of escaping punishment.

Cicero, *Pro Milone*

Rising Crime Rates

In the last thirty years the crime rate, defined as the number of crimes per 100,000 persons, has been rising in most countries for which we have statistics, and for most crimes. By stating the frequency of crime as a rate, allowance is made for changes in the size of the population. But there also have been changes in the relative size of the groups that compose the population. They must be taken into account by stating specific crime rates for each group: young males always have higher crime rates than old males or females of any age. Appropriate analysis shows, however, that the rise in crime rates cannot be attributed only to a greater proportion of young males or other known high crime groups in the population. The rate for each group has risen.

Crime rates for both property crimes and crimes against persons have been rising most steeply in the U.S.* And they have

* The robber and the burglar both want to enrich themselves (motivation), but only the former attacks or threatens a person (intention). The classification

been higher in the U.S. than in most other major nations for a long time.* In the 1970s the rates for murder and rape rose intolerably. (It is likely that there has been some increase also in the reported proportion of forcible rapes, but not of murder.)

Handguns

Many explanations have been offered for the high American crime rates and for their rise in the last decades. Some believe that the easy availability of handguns accounts for the high rate of violent crime. Perhaps. But handguns cannot be blamed for the high rates of rape and larceny which have risen more in the last few years than gun crimes. Nor can handguns be blamed for the great difference between our nonviolent crime rates and those of other nations. At any rate, outlawing handguns is not likely to be more effective than outlawing alcohol: zipguns are even easier to produce at home than bathtub gin.†

Social Reform

Without acknowledging the effect of different social traditions, of different rates of social change, and of different methods of law enforcement, differences in national crime

---

is based on act or intent, not on motive: the robber commits a crime *ad personam*, the burglar *ad rem*, though the motive be the same.

* No statistics are available for the Soviet Union, China, and most of Eastern Europe, and no helpful statistics are available for other vast areas such as Indonesia, India, Pakistan, and most of Africa. Comparisons of crime rates in urban and rural, agricultural and industrial societies, and in different political systems and cultures anyway cast but a fretful light.

† For a comprehensive review of the evidence on gun control and crime, see Mark K. Benenson, "A Controlled Look at Gun Controls," *New York Law Forum*, Winter 1968, pp. 718–748.

rates * cannot be explained. Even so, no fully satisfactory explanation for the worldwide rise in crime rates is available. However, we do know one thing: there has been a worldwide decline in punishment and therewith of respect for law. There also has been a worldwide rise of unmet expectations. The global increase in mobility—social and geographical—and urbanization certainly has contributed to the crumbling of Walter Bagehot's "cake of custom," to the disorganization of communities, and, directly and indirectly, to the weakening of informal social controls. The mutual enforcement of social norms that occurs within small, stable communities is hard to replace. Thus, the pace of industrial change may produce crime as well as prosperity. Plausible and suggestive, and probably correct as far as they go, these ideas are not enough to explain why crime rates have risen so much less in Tokyo than in New York, or why they have risen so much in the last twenty years. Even if the explanation were exhaustive, it would tell us little about how to reduce crime rates; nor does the smorgasbord of explanations referring to motivations, temptations, or opportunities to commit crimes, any or all of which are often believed to have increased, despite—or, perhaps, because of?—more equality, more education, more leisure, more prosperity, more employment, more comfort, and more social services. It is as though one were to argue that the higher incidence of rape must be caused either by more female beauty or by more female reluctance.

Thus, the President's Commission on Law Enforcement and Administration of Justice † found.:

* Intercity comparisons must take into account differences in age, sex, and race proportions among city populations as well as such matters as architectural layout. There are more burglaries and fewer muggings in Los Angeles than in New York. In New York more people live in apartment houses that are harder to burglarize; but since fewer people use cars, they are easier to mug as they walk.

† *The Challenge of Crime in a Free Society*, 1967, p. 15. The commission provided useful statistics and some useful specific proposals. But the general approach left out few clichés.

. . first, that America must translate its well-founded alarm about crime into social action that will prevent crime. . . . The most significant action that can be taken against crime is action designed to eliminate slums and ghettos, to improve education, to provide jobs, to make sure that every American is given the opportunities and the freedoms that will enable him to assume his responsibilities. . . .

and

Warring on poverty, inadequate housing and unemployment, is warring on crime. A civil rights law is a law against crime. Money for schools is money against crime. Medical, psychiatric, and family-counseling services are services against crime. More broadly and most importantly, every effort to improve life in America's "inner cities" is an effort against crime.

The "social action that will prevent crime" amounts to solving all the more prominent or fashionable social problems, "slums . . . ghettos . . . education . . . opportunities . . . medical, psychiatric services." Once we live in Utopia, there will be no crime. The fact that crime increased *with* education with "medical and psychiatric services," and *with* "opportunities and freedoms," is ignored.

Such eclectic explanations of crime, even when in conflict with the known facts, are the bases for most reform proposals, ranging from better housing or employment opportunities to more or better education, mental health, or welfare. In most cases, the effect of the proposed reform on crime is questionable. To be sure, there is some evidence that low employment rates are associated with low employment opportunities and with high crime rates. But not always. It may be that crime pays better than legitimate opportunity, or that offenders are unemployable (as is usually the case with drug addicts). Hence, greater employment opportunities may or may not be much help. Whatever the intrinsic merits of the reforms proposed, there is little to suggest that they would reduce crime rates.* For instance, if "more education" and "better mental health" are *defined* as that which reduces crime, they do so by

* These matters have already been dealt with in Chapters VIII and IX.

definition. But when independently defined, neither has done so in the past. London's comparatively low crime rate obviously is not owed to better housing or to more education. In the U.S.A. as education and social work have increased, so has crime. Surely education does not cause crime. But the evidence indicates that education does not curb crime either: whatever the available educational or mental health institutions actually do produce—as distinguished from an ideal product—does not reduce crime. It seems unlikely that in the foreseeable future we will learn how to produce crime-curbing education or mental health.

We do know, however, that the crime rate "with virtually no exception varies inversely with estimates of the probability of apprehension and punishment . . . and with the average length of time in state prisons." [65] Thus, to increase "the probability of apprehension" and "the average length of time served" is one way to decrease the crime rate. How can we do so?

The Ineffectiveness of the Criminal Justice System

More—or, if you please, less—than an increase of penalties is needed. The penal prescription of the laws he violated is only one of many factors that determine whether an offender serves time and how much. Our prescribed penalties are quite high compared to those of many other countries. Tokyo's crime rate is much lower than the New York crime rate, neither because the Japanese have more money nor because they have more education. They do not. They do not have more severe laws either. However, the two cities have very different ways of handling crime. In 1972 the arrest rate for assaultive crimes in Tokyo was in excess of 90 percent. And 99 percent of all defendants were found guilty. In New York only 19 percent of all reported crime led to arrest. So the actual cost of crime to the

criminal is much higher in Japan than in the U.S., even though
the law does not prescribe more severe punishment.

The penalties served by offenders in the U.S. and, above all,
the probability of serving them are extremely low. For more
than two-thirds of all felonies there are no arrests. And according to Maurice A. Nadjari, New York state special prosecutor,
"there are 97,000 felony arrests in New York City in a year
. . . and only 900 defendants are tried to the point of reaching
a verdict." [66] This means that less than 1 percent of the arrested are tried. The rest either plead guilty to a lesser offense
or are released because it is felt that no conviction could be
obtained. The percentage of those punished (as distinguished
from the percentage of those tried) for a crime is suggested by
a study made in Atlanta, which showed that out of 278 adults
arrested for assault, 63 were convicted and 23 served a jail sentence.* Surely part of the explanation for the difference between the U.S. and foreign crime rates lies in these figures:
American crime rates are high because punishment rates are
low. From 1960 to 1970 the crime rate increased 144 percent
(reported crime increased 176 percent; the difference is accounted for by the increase in population). Reported arrests
increased only 31 percent. The number of convicted offenders
decreased from 117 to 95 per 100,000 population. Thus, arrest
rates declined. And so did rates of conviction. In 1960 118 persons per 100,000 were in prison in the U.S.; in 1970 96 persons, a drop of more than 20 percent. This decline occurred
while crime rates rose 144 percent. *Res ipsa loquitur:* The
matter speaks for itself. The difficulty is in the courts.

Calls for higher rates of punishment used to come exclusively from the right side of the political spectrum. But, as
crime has spread to middle class areas and suburbs, second

* Quoted by U.S. Attorney General William B. Saxbe, *loc. cit.* James Q.
Wilson found that of about 10,000 persons arrested in one year in California
for robbery, only 1,300 were incarcerated. The police released 40 percent. Of
the remainder, only 33 percent were charged with a felony; 20 percent had
the charge dismissed at preliminary hearings. See "Crime and Law Enforcement," in Kermit Gordon, ed., *Agenda for a Nation* (Washington, D.C.:
Brookings Institution, 1968.)

thoughts appear to have seized persons who could normally be counted on to be more solicitous of offenders than of their victims. The trend is not universal, but it is unmistakable. The following will illustrate both the growing outcry for more punishment and the determined opposition.

Margot Hentoff, a far from conservative New York writer, wrote the passages quoted here after she went to court with her husband, who had been mugged. She published her essay in the antiestablishmentarian *Village Voice*, a weekly New York City paper characterized by free-floating, non-party leftism.

. . . As I remembered [the night court], the prisoners used to be mostly hookers, gamblers, and old derelicts who had been found drunk and helpless on the street. But this time it was different. A horde of menacing suspects (with a history of arrest upon arrest for crimes against people) were marched before the judge and, in one way or another, most of them were able to walk out of the building that night with either conditional discharges or extremely meetable bail—especially meetable since many of them had just ripped off enough money to meet it.

After a while, considering what lay ahead in those cases which were not disposed of, it became clear that a complainant would have to appear in court as many times as the suspect, that he was not going to get any of his money back, and that the final disposition of the case would probably send the suspect back out into the city to continue his profitable and only minimally perilous career. In fact, it was a toss-up as to who would be most inconvenienced by the crime—the victim, the perpetrator, or the police.

. . . It struck me that it was indeed true that New York was not so much a city full of criminals as it was a city plagued by a hard core of felons who go about their daily business almost outside the reach of the law . . . in a judicial system which neither corrects the behavior of the antisocial nor removes them from the rest of us.

. . . An act of physical assault is a violation of that fundamental social contract which has as its basic compact the agreement that I can walk down the street and if I don't bother you, you won't bother me. If society has brutalized some people, there is no advantage in allowing the rest of us to be brutalized by the brutalized. And this, I think, is what we must come to terms with in our thinking about crime and the rights of criminals as opposed to the rights of orderly citizens.

This issue relates not only to dealing with adult criminal behavior but to crime by juveniles as well. Many of the problems of city schools stem, in some part, from a falsely humanistic approach which leaves violent and assaulting kids in school with those who are not. I do not think that any of us should have to live scared because we live in cities, but it is far worse that the cities' children are threatened and afraid when they go to public school.[67]

Mrs. Hentoff's views were preemptively opposed by a correspondent who, writing to the *New York Times* from Vermont, depicted offenders as victims of society:

. . . placing blame for a rising crime rate on prosecutors and courts and their failure to jail all criminals is not only simplistic but morally reprehensible. . . . [The] ills within our ghettos, the burdens of our socially and economically deprived and our system's inability to deal with the underlying problems . . . cause most criminality.[68]

Perfect justice is not of this world. The writer of the foregoing letter is right in implying that fires are "caused" (are made possible would be better) by the inflammable material around. Yet he seems to forget that fires can be controlled and even extinguished by firefighters. We can never eliminate all inflammable material or all pyromaniacs. Indeed, the attempt to reach perfection backfires when it leads us to treat lawbreakers as victims and punishment as immoral and simplistic. Those who are victimized by the violence of offenders are victims in a more direct, certain, and tangible sense. It is the primary duty of the criminal justice system to protect these victims. There is no objection to any social reform when it can be shown to be intrinsically meritorious and effective. But it cannot be the only or major protection against crime.

Actual Punishment

Given the offense, actual punishment depends on the probability of (1) apprehension, (2) conviction, (3) the plea entered (or the charge sustained) and the sentence imposed, and (4) the sentence actually served. Most convictions are obtained upon guilty pleas to charges involving far lower penalties than the charges originally made: most offenders are punished not for the offense charged or committed but for a lesser one. And a great deal of time elapses between the offense and the punishment.

Offenders are granted parole for one-third of their federal sentences, unless they seriously misbehave while in prison, and they may be paroled earlier, as they are in most states. In fact, a life sentence usually means imprisonment for from seven to fifteen years. In some states parole is available after shorter periods (six months in Florida). Parole boards, however well intentioned, have few rational rules for deciding whether or not to parole. Finally, if the judge puts the convicted defendant on probation, he does not have to serve time in jail at all if he behaves lawfully over a given supervised period. And in most cases supervision is a formality.

Let me illustrate. According to the *New York Times* (Jan. 27, 1975, pp. 1 and 39), "Among the country's 10 largest cities, New York had the eighth lowest murder rate for each 100,000 residents in 1973. . . . [However] the police reported 1,680 murders in the city during 1973—more than triple the number reported in 1963." (In 1974 the murder rate declined by 7 percent compared to 1973; in 1975 it started to rise again. Most other felonies rose 7 percent compared to 1973, except for larceny-theft, which rose by 28 percent.) The *New York Times* also reported (Feb. 8, 1975): "The 'solved' rate of slayings dropped from 89.3 percent in 1963 to 64.8 percent in 1973. (A homicide is solved or 'cleared' if an arrest is made.)" The decrease in the "solved" rate indicates that more murders are committed by persons who do not know their victims (e.g., robbers). Murders among acquaintances are more often solved.*

Furthermore, according to the *New York Times* (Jan. 27,

---

* See Chapter XIX, pp. 222–3.

1975), "Almost eight of every ten defendants accused of homicide in New York plead guilty to a reduced charge and are freed on probation or receive a prison term of less than 10 years. Of those receiving a maximum 10-year term, most will be eligible for parole in three years." (Eighty percent of the defendants charged with homicide in 1973 pleaded guilty; 4.5 percent received life sentences, whereas 28.5 percent received a maximum of five years and 20 percent received a conditional discharge, or probation.)

The *New York Times* also reported (Feb. 8, 1975) that Hosie S. Turner was convicted of murder after a month-long trial in October 1973. His prior record included "sixteen convictions for robbery, burglary, larceny, parole violation, drug possession and sale. . . . He invariably was allowed to plead guilty to a lesser charge." The practice of reducing charges and imposing minor penalties on persons with a long record of violent crimes continues, according to the *New York Times* (Feb. 11, 1975). In 1974 nearly 80 percent of all felony arrests in New York City were disposed of by the city criminal court by reducing the charges to misdemeanors.

This winnowing out, many in the court system agree, tends to give the defendant the upper hand in bargaining about sentences in Criminal Court. The repeaters know this from experience. The novice learns it from friends or his lawyer.

The *Times* offers the following illustrations:

Willie Poinsette was 48 years old and had a record of 21 previous arrests when, on April 8, 1973, he was charged with robbery and possession of a gun, both felonies. If convicted on these charges he would have faced up to 32 years in prison. Two days later in Criminal Court, Mr. Poinsette pleaded guilty to petit larceny, and was sentenced to two months in city jail.

Melvin Lewis was 19 and had a record of 13 previous arrests when, on Aug. 29, 1973, he was charged with possession of a knife and attempted robbery, both felonies. If convicted on these charges, he would have faced up to 14 years in prison. The same day in arraignment court, Mr. Lewis pleaded guilty to attempted grand larceny, a misdemeanor, and was sentenced to 10 months in city jail. He was conditionally released on parole to a rehabilitation center three months later.

Shortly after disappearing from the rehabilitation center on Jan. 21, he was arrested for assaulting two civilians and a police officer. A week later he was charged with wounding a police officer and killing Mr. Walker.

Whatever the faults of the sitting judges, they cannot be saddled with the whole blame. They must labor under laws, procedures, precedents, and appeals court decisions that so favor the defendants as to compel courts to reduce charges of which defendants are, in many cases, clearly guilty. An overhaul of the whole criminal justice system is needed. Crime rates depend not on statutory prescriptions but on what is actually done to make crime costly to the criminal and to make the cost obvious. At present crime is costly mainly to the victim. Surely it is more beneficial—as well as easier—and more effective to modify the criminal justice system than to undertake the far-reaching social reforms so often proposed.

Delays

About 18,000 murders were committed in 1972 in the U.S. The homicide rate per 100,000 persons increased from 4.5 in 1963 to 9.3 in 1973. This figure, remarkably high by any standard, includes only reported murders and excludes negligent manslaughter and about 55,000 vehicular homicides. In 1972 London (about the size of New York) had 113 murders; New York, 1,700. London had 3,000 robberies; New York, 78,000. London had 150 rapes; New York, 3,300.

All parts of the criminal justice system must share the blame for the fact that so small a proportion of all crimes committed— about 1 percent—ever lead to actual imprisonment of the offender in the U.S. The police can never catch all criminals. Could they catch more? Many people claim that police departments in most cities are riddled with inefficiency, politics, and corruption, and that our criminals are more, and our police less, effective than in most of the Western countries.* Others claim that our police are hamstrung by our solicitude for suspects. At any rate, the behavior of our courts is more important, and most scandalous by far. The sheer incompetence and occasional corruption of many politically selected judges cannot be ignored. But the rules under which even the best-run courts have to operate play much the greater role. Some of these rules are enacted by legislatures. Many more have accumulated as a result of past decisions of appellate courts, including the U.S. Supreme Court. In effect, the courts have become nearly hamstrung by the accumulation of their own past attempts at perfection.†

The probability of convicting the guilty is greatly reduced in the U.S. by (a) delay, (b) the exclusionary rule, and (c) literally endless appeals allowed defendants from state to federal courts. Furthermore, many offenders are classified as juvenile delinquents to be "reformed" rather than punished, and others—far too many—are excused as mentally incompetent. "Reform"—custody for juveniles and incompetents—often means inappropriate terms: too indefinite, too long, or too short. Reformative institutions for juveniles have not been shown to be more effective than simple imprisonment. Incompetents referred to psychiatric institutions may be kept for life or for a few months, depending on utterly capricious psychiatric judgments.

As for the conviction of competent adults guilty of crime, there are innumerable time-wasting procedural hindrances. Some illustrations will have to do. Full discussion of all the drawbacks and advantages of present or proposed judicial practices is beyond the scope of a work focusing on punish-

---

* We must forgo suggestions about better police manpower allocation and utilization. There is a voluminous and growing literature on the topic to which the reader can refer.

† An excellent summary of what has happened is found in Macklin Fleming, *The Price of Perfect Justice* (Basic Books, 1974).

ment. Joseph W. Bishop, Jr., professor of law at Yale University, in a review of Macklin Fleming's book, *The Price of Perfect Justice,* affords the layman a glance at what happens.

. . . the incarceration of even the most obviously guilty criminal is a task comparable to landing a barracuda with a trout-rod and a dry-fly. . . . [There are] numerous techniques by which an accused with an astute, well-paid, and/or zealous lawyer can delay or frustrate his prosecution, litigate the same issue (which may have little or nothing to do with his guilt or innocence) in several different courts, state and federal, and should he actually be convicted, attack the constitutionality of that conviction by endless appeals and petitions for *habeas corpus.* He can start before trial by seeking to enjoin the prosecution on the ground that its threat chills an asserted constitutional right. He can attack the indictment by claiming some ethnic or other group to which he claims to belong—people with Spanish surnames, young people, old people, people with low incomes, people with little education, etc., etc., *ad infinitum*—were inadequately represented on the panel from which the grand jury was drawn. This issue can be litigated, appealed, and reviewed by collateral process in both state and federal courts for months and years. Similar attacks can be made on the composition of the trial jury. Likewise, he can seek to disqualify the trial judge for alleged bias and appeal the judges' refusal to disqualify himself. He can assert that appointed defense counsel is incompetent, before, during, and after the trial. He can demand that he be allowed to represent himself. If the request is denied and he loses his case, he can appeal on that ground; if it is granted, he can appeal on that ground also, arguing that the trial judge should have recognized his unfitness to be his own lawyer. He can move to suppress evidence, even when its truth and relevance are unquestioned, on the ground that it was obtained illegally; Justice Fleming itemizes twenty-six separate state and federal proceedings in which a defendant can challenge the lawfulness of a single search or seizure. Moreover, he can petition for *habeas corpus ad libitum,* hoping finally to find a federal judge who agrees with him and disagrees with all the other judges, for the doctrine of *res judicata*—that an issue finally determined by a court cannot be reopened—does not apply to *habeas corpus,* and a single federal district judge can spring a convict whose arguments have been unanimously rejected by a state's supreme court and other federal judges. If all else fails, the petitioner can argue that the inadequacy of the prison's law library denies him due process or the equal protection of the laws. These . . . are only a small sampling of Justice Fleming's catalogue (all documented by actual cases) of the devices which make it a labor of Sisyphus to put a criminal in jail and keep him there. One who loses at every step can almost claim that that very fact shows he has been denied equal protection of the laws.[69]

Some illustrative comparisons may cast light on our time-wasting procedures. Lord Haw-Haw (William Joyce) was tried in England after the Second World War for broadcasting for the Nazis. He was found guilty by a jury after a three-day trial in September 1945. By December he had exhausted his appeals and was hanged January 3, 1946. Tokyo Rose (Iva D'aquino) was tried in the U.S. for broadcasting for the Japanese. When her trial started, after many delay, it lasted two months. She was found guilty and sentenced to ten years. The last of her numerous appeals was rejected four and a half years later. These are not isolated cases; they are typical. The longest criminal trial in England lasted forty-eight days and the longest murder trial twenty-one. The trial of the Manson "family" in California lasted nine months. Selection of the jury for Bobby Seale (acquitted) took five months. In England it usually takes a few minutes. There is no evidence that the quality of English justice, or juries, is inferior to our own. Other practices that contribute to unjustifiable delays and to uncertainty are too numerous to list. The requirement of jury unanimity often means that the government has to retry a defendant several times to reach a verdict, or give up and let him go. A two-thirds majority might do as well—after all, it suffices to amend the Constitution. As it is, our judicial system seems more designed to blunt the deterrent force of punishment in the rare cases in which it is imposed and to protect defendants' rights than to protect society from crime. It certainly works that way.

Many minor cases in the U.S. are never tried even when they reach the courts. Between ten and twenty postponements are not uncommon. When defense lawyers suspect their client can be shown to be guilty, they delay—with the consent of the judge—until witnesses disappear or become unwilling to

waste another day in court. Without witnesses or complain-
ants, the defendant is safely acquitted. Trial judges, although
given rules about expeditious trials, often have no choice. If
they do not grant adjournments, the appellate courts may reverse the decision despite the rules.*

Minor crimes often are not reported to the police in the U.S.
not only because reporting appears (and is) futile but also because it can be dangerous, the more so if the crime was violent. If the neighborhood bully, or a reputed underworld character or drug addict, assaults you he may be arrested if you
complain. He is let out on bail. Your address is in the com-
plaint and available to him. He, or his friends, may endanger
you and your family before or after conviction. You might be
advised by your friends, or by his, to forget about it. For similar reasons few of your potential witnesses will want to jeopar-
dize their safety. You are well advised not to complain about
minor rackets. The protection offered by our judicial system
against persons who have little to lose is so inadequate that
most persons who do have something to lose prefer to suffer
rather than to make legitimate complaints.

Moralists and the media often lament the unwillingness of
the public to come to the aid of victims of a crime being committed, to help pursue the criminal, or to testify to what they
have seen. In a notorious New York City case, Kitty Genovese
was murdered under the eyes of many people who literally
shut their windows as the dying woman was being pursued
and repeatedly attacked by her murderer. Of course, the moralists are right. Yet none bothers to explain what happens all
too often to those who try to help, if only by calling the police.† They get into a lot of trouble and look in vain for protection by the authorities. A man who in self-defense shoots a

---

* Many of the above data are drawn from Macklin Fleming's "The Law's
Delay" (*The Public Interest*, Summer 1973). A somewhat different light is cast
on the matter in Martin A. Levin, "Delay in the Criminal Courts" (*The Journal
of Legal Studies*, Jan. 1975).

† Foundations support many projects but do not help and reward (a) people
injured in *bona fide* attempts to help the police arrest offenders; (b) people injured in *bona fide* attempts to come to the assistance of victims of violent
crime; or (c) *bona fide* victims of violent crime.

burglar or assailant is more likely to be arrested for illegal possession of weapons than to be congratulated. It can be quite
dangerous, and in any case is hardly rewarding, to denounce
the corner heroin dealer to the police, or the numbers runner,
or to testify to a gang murder, or to become unpopular with a
neighborhood gang of juveniles.

Whereas the protection offered victims and witnesses is
minimal, the protection given suspects often is nearly impene-
trable. Known criminals can live undisturbed in the community, having to fear only other criminals. With so small a percentage of all crimes punished, it is a marvel that the
overwhelming majority of people remain law-abiding. They
do. But we seem to live off the capital of the past. Crime is rising rapidly; the cautionary adage "crime does not pay" is becoming an old wives' tale.

The Exclusionary Rule

English justice, renowned for fairness, does without the "exclusionary rule," which in the U.S. excludes from admission
as evidence anything—documents, photographs, tapes,
weapons, information—seized without legal authority. A confession made before the suspect has been offered a lawyer is
inadmissible. (No lawyer has ever been known to encourage
his client to confess to the police.) Evidence found as a result
of an inadmissible confession is ruled inadmissible, too. So is
evidence seized in a search of persons or places not autho-
rized by warrant or wholly justified by circumstances. The
"exclusionary rule" was established in federal courts * and
has been steadily enlarged and applied to state proceedings. †
Only in 1974 ‡ did the courts begin to limit the rule.

* *Weeks* v. *U.S.* 232 U.S. 383, 1914.
† *Mapp* v. *Ohio* 367 U.S. 643 (1961).
‡ So far in grand jury proceedings only: *U.S.* v. *Calandra* (1974). 414 U.S.
338 (1974).

The exclusion of hearsay evidence is perhaps defensible. (Perhaps. Juries can, after all, distinguish with the help of the lawyers for the two sides.) The exclusion of previous conviction records is unwarranted. To be sure, the previous record tells nothing about the offense at issue. But in practice, verdicts are probability decisions. Previous convictions do help form a judgment about probabilities. If a bishop is accused of robbery, one wants to scrutinize the evidence carefully and give him the benefit of the doubt. If a man with previous convictions for robbery is accused once more of the same crime, one must scrutinize the evidence carefully, to be sure, but one is justifiably more inclined to believe the victim or the witnesses.

Unlawful conduct by the police should be punished. But not by letting a murderer benefit from the error, the impropriety, or the offense of an overzealous law-enforcement officer who obtained the evidence—e.g., the weapon used—without a search warrant. If we want to discourage unlawful police actions, must we do it in so roundabout a way at the price of freeing guilty persons? Must society punish itself rather than the guilty law-enforcement officer? No other country in the world does. Nor does our exclusionary rule keep the police more law-abiding than they are elsewhere.

The rule has caused our trials to take place in a legal wonderland. Courts, instead of trying to find out if the defendant is guilty or innocent, spend their time determining whether or not the evidence that might prove his guilt is admissible.* Any newspaper is entitled to publish illegally obtained informa-

---

* The rule is extended to exclude evidence tainted by unlawful acts, arrests, surveillances, searches or confessions; the case against Daniel Ellsberg was thrown out of court after many weeks of trial because of governmental misconduct. There was such misconduct, and it should be punished—but not by dismissing the case against the defendant. The misconduct of the government was wholly irrelevant to the guilt or innocence of the defendant. No evidence whatever was produced by it. The rule shortchanged both defense and prosecution. But if the governmental misconduct had produced evidence, why should it be disregarded? Why should those who misconducted themselves not be punished instead?

tion. No court is entitled to weigh illegally obtained evidence.

The exclusionary rule has not worked as intended. It has not led to more lawful, but only to less effective, law enforcement. It should be abolished. As Mr. Justice Brennan admitted while yet upholding the rule in its entirety: ". . . we must concede that official lawlessness has not abated." * Lawful and effective law enforcement depend on wholly different matters, such as the recruitment, training, and discipline of the police force. As a matter of fact, the exclusionary rule, by permitting policemen to pretend to enforce the law while deliberately making enough errors to have the evidence excluded and the defendants acquitted, has helped in protecting lawless policemen as well as civilian criminals. It has victimized innumerable law-abiding citizens by letting known criminals go scot free.

The following letter is unusual in as much as the writer bothered to complain and to come to court as often as she did, vastly amusing the defendant.

In early October, 1972, I was mugged at the front door of my house in Hollis Hills, Queens. The mugger was caught within three hours of my report to the police. I pressed charges and six hearings over a span of six months ensued. When my father and I walked into the sixth hearing, the defendant, his wife, and his brother-in-law were overly friendly, waving, smiling, and bidding us good luck. All the evidence which helped catch the mugger was offered: (1) description of car—year, type, color; (2) license plate number—one number off, M instead of W; (3) $40 in the mugger's pocket in the exact bills I reported missing; (4) an autoharp pick—he did not even know what an autoharp is; (5) an almost exact approximation of his height and weight; (6) accurate description of his clothing, etc. . . . The mugger was freed after the sixth hearing because of an illegal search of vehicle by the policeman.

Last night on Channel 5 news, there was an item about the $1 rapist, who was finally caught after raping about 25 women in Queens.

* Dissent *U.S.* v. *Calandra* (1974). Justice Brennan thought it immoral for the government to profit from an illegal act. Surely, then, the government should not tax anything immoral or illegal. The government does and profits. The profit Justice Brennan objects to is not money but the security of the community—it is hard to see wherein it is worse than money.

His name, Leroy Hamlin, was the same man who had mugged me
. . . Mr. Hamlin had several previous arrests prior to mugging me.[70]

Plea Bargaining

We have created other difficulties. Appeals are riskless for the
defendant: penalties cannot be increased nor partial acquittals
overturned. The prosecution cannot appeal. This makes it safe
for judges to help produce acquittals if they so want. At any
rate, they become defense-minded: if a judge errs against the
defendant, an appeal is likely and he may be overruled. If he
errs against the prosecution, the judge is safe. No appeal is
possible. Hence, when in doubt, it is in the judge's interest to
rule for the defense.

Since it is difficult, chancy, expensive, and far too time-con-
suming to obtain conviction through trial in our courts, prosecutors must resort to plea bargaining, however guilty the defendant. More than 90 percent of all cases are settled by
striking a bargain: the defendant is allowed to plead guilty to a
lesser charge than the one originally brought so that in exchange for his lower punishment the trial can be avoided.*
The defendant and his lawyer know that the prosecution cannot afford trial despite sufficient evidence. Prosecutors must
bargain. The risk, the cost, the time-wasting procedures, and
the uncertainties of our legal processes cause the interests of
justice to be protected best by avoiding trial if the accused is
willing to plead guilty to a lesser charge. But these risks and
uncertainties have been created largely by the courts
themselves.

---

* To be sure, the suspect may have been "overcharged"—he may be guilty
of only some of the offenses he is charged with, and only of the lesser ones.
But quite often he is allowed to plead to far less than what he is actually guilty
of.

There is nothing intrinsically wrong with plea bargaining. Defense and prosecution, under the supervision of the judge, may anticipate the outcome of a trial and decide through a bargaining process to accept the anticipated outcome without going through the trial. This well may be in the best interests of all concerned. There is a great deal wrong, however, with the conditions largely created by the past decisions of the courts, that compel prosecutors to allow the defendant routinely to get away with a lesser penalty than that prescribed by law for the offenses he actually committed. In effect, the penalties prescribed by law for the actual offenses are not the penalties applied in most cases, and the penalties applied are not the penalties served. The bargaining power of defense and prosecution depends on the anticipated outcome of the trial and the likely sentence. If it has to be anticipated that the defendant cannot be convicted because of inadmissible evidence, or that if convicted the sentence will be light, the prosecution cannot obtain more by bargaining than it could by trial.

The degeneration of the plea bargaining process is illustrated in the following news story (*New York Times,* May 10, 1975).

> Julio Vasquez, a 31-year-old former convict, was sentenced to a minimum of 15 years and a maximum of life imprisonment yesterday for killing an off-duty police officer . . .
> Mr. Vasquez had a criminal record that included 11 arrests in the last 12 years on robbery, assault and other charges, and five convictions that led to prison terms of less than one year each. His earlier sentences had been arrived at through plea bargaining, which means that he was permitted to plead to a lesser charge in exchange for a guilty plea.

The courts are overwhelmed because of the rise of crime, but even more because of their own time-wasting procedures and inefficiencies, which, in part, account for the rise in crime. They must reform themselves or be reformed. Courts also might be helped by dejudicializing and decriminalizing acts that can be dealt with otherwise. "No fault" traffic accident or divorce regulations are a step in the right direction. It also would help if courts were divested of jurisdiction over such offenses as housing violations and other matters that could be dealt with administratively. The judicial apparatus is too cumbersome to be used where it can be replaced without major disadvantages. But, in the main, courts must help themselves by changing their procedures.

Federal and State Courts

Most crimes are violations of state and local rather than of federal laws. They are dealt with by state and local courts. Yet, it is always possible for defendants after they have exhausted the state courts to allege violation of their constitutional rights and thus to have the case reconsidered in the federal courts. The opportunities for delay are tremendous when cases are referred back and forth. It should not be beyond the wit of man to limit them in the interests of justice.* So far they are being steadily expanded: what used to be an exceptional matter has become routine. After all, the defendant has nothing to lose in wasting the time of the courts and often has something to gain. And courts seem willing, almost eager, to waste their time. Trials are becoming steadily longer, and appeals more frequent.

Juveniles

Children surely should not be held responsible for their conduct to the extent adults are. But should we regard sixteen-year-olds or even fourteen-year-olds as children? They do

* The application of a limited *res judicata* doctrine to *habeas corpus* proceedings might help.

engage in all the activities—except, possibly, work—adults engage in, including crime. Indeed, we make it increasingly hard for juveniles to work and increasingly easy for them to do almost anything else. There is little reason left for not holding juveniles responsible under the same laws that apply to adults. The victim of a fifteen-year-old muggers is as much mugged as the victim of a twenty-year-old mugger, the victim of a fourteen-year-old murderer or rapist is as dead or as raped as the victim of an older one. The need for social defense or protection is the same. Juveniles may be held in custody separately from adults and perhaps subjected to a special custodial authority. But the process of adjudication and the law should be the same. A letter in the *New York Times Sunday Magazine* (Feb. 16, 1975) lends support to this view from an unexpected quarter.

The [juvenile] court purports to address the psychological and social deprivations of all children—that is, to "treat" and "rehabilitate" children whose lives are less than optimal. This "treatment" ratio-nale means that the children who have never committed any crime, but who have "problems" (running away from uncaring homes, refus-ing to attend worse schools) are confined together in the same deten-tion facilities with adolescents who torture, sodomize, rape and mur-der. The young murderer usually stays no more than nine months in training school. The so-called PINS children (Person in Need of Su-pervision—runaways, truants, etc.) will stay 18 months or longer be-cause their parents, who brought them to court in the first place, do not want them.

The length of time that a young criminal is confined ought to be de-termined primarily by the nature of the offense he has committed, with due consideration for the reduced capacity of children to formu-late criminal intent, past records, and the fact that the mere passage of time is more likely to alter the behavior of a 15-year-old than of a 30-year-old.* Neither the juvenile court nor any agency should have the power to confine any child (with the possible exception of a suicidal child) who has not violated the criminal law, no matter what his problems.

Elimination of PINS children from court jurisdiction altogether, and a sentencing system for child criminals which primarily reflects

* Consult Chapter XXI on this point.

the seriousness of the crimes, are reforms that are long, long overdue. They are vociferously resisted, however, by those misguided humanitarians who insist that the coercive power of a court should be a conduit for social services and that "treatment" is holy.

Rena K. Uviller, Director
Juvenile Rights Project
American Civil Liberties Union
New York City

A further illustration (*New York Times*, December 6, 1974, p. 43):

"This is his fourth arrest," Detective Walker said, referring to the 14-year-old boy whose name was withheld in keeping with Family Court laws intended to protect the youth. "All four cases were for assault and robbery only in two cases the result was death."

"He didn't seem shook up," the detective said. "He knows he can only get 18 months. We can't cope with this court system. They're not giving them enough time. There's no punishment."

Anyone under fifteen years old, regardless of how heinous the crime, receives a maximum of eighteen months detention. All too often young boys are simply released back into the community and the school system.

Needed Reform Costless

The catalogue of legal evils can be extended indefinitely. Only the direction in which remedies must be sought for the evils caused or intensified by the criminal justice system can be indicated here: law reform and reform of judicial procedures probably is the most effective way to reduce the crime rate. Per dollar invested it would be far more effective than the prescription of harsher penalties, or better housing, or welfare, or education. Whatever their independent merits, as anti-crime measures these should have a low priority. What is needed is, by and large, judicial reform.

The simplest, least costly, and most effective way to reduce the crime rate is to assure a speedy and reasonable trial for suspects. A trial to determine not the provenience of the evidence or the admissibility of testimony but the defendant's guilt or innocence. Such a reform would not necessarily cost money. On the contrary, it would save some. Reform does not mean more judges or personnel; it means less judicial time-wasting and less judicial indulgence for time-wasting by attorneys.* We are so accustomed to "solve" problems by spending more money and creating more jobs, that chances for needed reforms are dimmed when they require not more money but simply more rational procedures. Since they do not call for expenditures from which some group would directly benefit, no interest group pushes for reforms. Therefore, the reforms advocated, despite their obvious general benefits, are slow to come. Still, we must try.

One final note. Defendants (except when the death penalty is likely) currently must be released on bail, even if they are dangerous to the community in view of their record. The law prescribes that the amount of bail should not exceed what is needed to assure that the defendant will not leave the jurisdiction of the court pending trial. (No amount of money could ensure that if the death penalty were likely. But otherwise bail is hard to deny.) When danger to the community is accepted as a reason for not granting bail, the burden of proving the danger at present lies on the prosecution, and the evidence required rarely can be provided. This should be changed. As long as suspects are brought to trial within three months, it would seem reasonable to enable judges to deny bail to those with previous convictions for serious crimes. Perhaps also to those who present a clear danger to the community.† At least this

* Almost any system of nominating to judicial office is superior to the one based on political connections, whether or not confirmed by elections, that now prevails in most states and even in the federal courts.

† The argument that this amounts to punishment without conviction does not seem persuasive here. It is implied in the previous conviction of the suspect that the community is entitled to treat him as more dangerous than others. Just as he may not serve as a policeman, or be licensed as a funeral director, so he may not be released on bail if dangerous. As for people without

would eliminate many of the crimes now committed by people out on bail. Furthermore, penalties for persons who commit crimes while out on bail should be automatically 50 percent higher than penalties prescribed for the crime otherwise.

Our law-enforcement system makes punishment uncertain and late. Only a few of the factors causing uncertainty and delay have been identified here. But it seems obvious that reforms are overdue and that the major reforms must occur in the area of criminal procedure. Arrests are of no use unless the guilty are punished.

How To Go About It

How can the necessary reforms be enacted? They require legislation. Legislative committees must be charged with drafting proposals to (1) identify the factors that produce (a) our low clearance rate for crime, (b) our low conviction rate, (c) our trifling penalties for many of those convicted, and (d) the fact that so much crime is committed by offenders out on probation, parole, or bail; (2) change laws and procedures in such ways as are likely to increase clearance rates by 30 percent; (3) increase conviction rates by 30 percent. Further, to propose laws that (4) prohibit probation or suspended sentences if a defendant is convicted for the second time or had more than three arrests not leading to conviction; and (5) minimize parole for a man convicted for a second time. It is this type of change and this type of mandate to bring it about that is needed in both state and federal jurisdictions—but above all, in state jurisdictions.

---

previous convictions, they should be deemed dangerous only on the basis of specific evidence that entitles society to protect itself as it does against (equally unconvicted) madmen.

PART THREE

KINDS OF PUNISHMENT

XVI

Philosophical Quandaries

"Legal punishment . . . never can be inflicted on a criminal *just* as an instrument to achieve some other good for the criminal himself or for civil society . . . for a man may never be used just as a means to the ends of another. . . ." [71] In Kantian terms it is legitimate to use a person as a means if he freely consents, either because he shares in the ends for which he is used, or because his own ends require that he allow himself to be used by others. For either reason we often volunteer to be used as means to other people's ends. The doctor volunteers to be used as a means to your health, the taxi driver as a means of transportation, the cook as a means to feed you. Kant, aware of this, only opposed the use of a person "just" as a means, i.e., against his will, or when it does not suit his, the person's, ends. No society fully lives up to this Kantian ideal. A society that did would be unlikely to survive. Thus, we draft people, some against their will, to go to war; and we may confine a person who suffers from a contagious disease against his will.

A Means To Deter?

Still, if Kant's injunction is to be taken seriously, we must ask if and to what extent we are morally entitled to punish offenders in oder to deter others from committing crimes. Kant insists only that "a man may never be used *just* as a means." If we punish an offender primarily because he commits an offense, and only secondarily to deter others, he is not "used *just* as a means." Thus, the question is: To what extent can we use an offender, punished for the sake of justice, to deter others when he has not consented to be so used? Or has he?

I should argue that criminals have consented to be used as a means to deter others, that they are no more used against their will than policemen are. I realize this sounds strange. Who ever heard of criminals volunteering for punishment? They don't. But neither do policemen volunteer to be shot at and, perhaps, killed. Yet they do volunteer to become policemen, knowing that they risk being shot at. Policemen accept this risk voluntarily, though, no doubt, they will attempt to minimize it. Thus, whether for their own private ends (e.g., income) or for the sake of the public ends they have made their own (e.g., social protection), policemen volunteer to take the risk of being shot at. It is in this sense that offenders volunteer. Although they will try to minimize the risk of punishment, they voluntarily assume it by breaking the law. They voluntarily forfeit the right not to be punished—and therewith the right not to be used as a means to deter others—by committing offenses. Society can use offenders to deter others, and thereby to protect itself, as it uses policemen. By volunteering for their respective activities—crime or crime control—both offenders and policemen knowingly assumed the risk of being used for social protection in ways they would prefer to avoid. This risk is inherent in what they volunteer for. Thus, neither the criminal nor the policeman is used "just" as a means any more than the doctor or taxi driver is.

Policemen, to be sure, usually share in the social purpose for which they are used whereas offenders do not. Yet, as long as offenders voluntarily risk punishment for the sake of their own ends, as long as they volunteer to risk to be so used, they consent—just as a gambler consents to risk losing his money, though he hopes to win. Furthermore, offenders usually are interested in sustaining the social order as much as other citizens. Murderers do not care to be murdered, thieves to be stolen from or to be murdered. Offenders need the social order which they violate so that they may take advantage of it, just as parasites need the body of their unwilling host. They do share, or benefit from, the general purpose for which they are used when punished.

Retributive punishment must be proportionate to the gravity of the crime, as the legislators measure it. Even if nobody needs to be deterred, because nobody is tempted, punishment must be inflicted for the sake of justice because it is deserved.* It is this idea that led Kant to insist (in a rather infelicitous illustration) that "even if civil society decided . . . to dissolve . . . the last murderer in prison must first be brought to justice" else "society would become . . . a party to a public violation of justice." Deterrent effects are hoped for. But they are neither necessary nor sufficient for punishment. Only a crime is. Yet, once a person is guilty of a crime, society is entitled to make his punishment deterrent because, by committing the crime, the offender voluntarily risked no less.

Thus, the legislator's view of the gravity of the crime to which the punishment must be proportionate may include—though it cannot be reduced to—what is needed to deter others from it. If the crime is grave, so is the need to deter others from it. Although the severity of punishment can be no less than required by the gravity of the crime, it can be as much more as is required to deter: the criminal has voluntarily taken the risk of being used to deter others.†

* See Chapters II and III.

† A more purist retributionist view might regard the deterrence of others as a less than legitimate element in deciding the severity of punishment. In practice this would not make much difference. The "gravity" of the crime and the punishment "proportionate" to it might be so defined—and would be—as to serve the deterrent purpose, even though this may not be openly avowed. It is hard to see how any society could act otherwise if it is to minimize the acts it prohibits, as it must. It is advantageous, nonetheless, to state the deterrent separately from the retributive purpose, for one can analyze and ultimately legislate more rationally if the requirements of each are considered separately, even though they can be conflated analytically and ultimately must be combined in practice.

A Means To Rehabilitate?

Since offenders voluntarily take the risk of punishment, and since punishment may include treatment thought suitable for correction, the Kantian injunction not to use anyone just as a means, even for his own benefit, need not prohibit the rehabilitative treatment of offenders as long as it remains incidental to but does not replace retributive justice. Yet attempts to rehabilitate often do, and even were meant to, replace retribution.* In the nature of the matter, "correction" requires individualized, i.e., different, treatment for each criminal, treatment linked to him rather than to his crime, whereas retribution and deterrence are linked to the act not the actor, and unlike rehabilitation require the same punishment for the same offense. Thus, rehabilitative treatment unless incidental to retribution—unless it neither decreases nor increases the punishment imposed for the offense—tends to be inconsistent with justice, whereas deterrence is not.

The utilitarian theories, which stress the correction of offenders, have found wide acceptance in modern times. Thus, the late Mr. Justice Black wrote: "Retribution is no longer the dominant objective of criminal law. Reformation and rehabilitation of offenders have become important goals of criminal jurisprudence."† The idea that "punishment" is primarily for rehabilitation is:

. . . subscribed to by many if not most psychiatrists, by most practioners of the behavioral sciences who think about problems of the criminal law, by the overwhelming majority of "professionalized" workers in the correctional field—probation officers, case workers, and the like—and by an increasing number of those popular writers who perform the extremely important function of translating the

---

* The only criminal code that acknowledges rehabilitation of the offender—individualized treatment—substantially unaffected by the gravity of the crime as its major goal is that of Greenland. However, Greenland is an exception also owing to historical traditions and the nature of its society.

† Dissenting in *Carlson* v. *Landon,* 342 U.S. 254, 547 (1952).

ideas of the intellectually advanced into current popular terms. Its catchwords—"treat the criminal, not the crime," "punishment is obsolete," "criminals are sick," and the like—are standard fare in large circulation magazines, and show that the popular culture has absorbed, even if it has not yielded to, the behavioral approach to crime.[72]

Concerned with the future personality and conduct of the offender, the "behavioral approach" replaces the justice model of punishment with a therapeutic one. Hence Barbara Wootton [73] urges that "the formal distinction between prison and hospital [be] . . . eventually obliterated altogether." * A similar view is expressed in a letter to the *New York Times* (Dec. 27, 1973): "We on the left should be careful not to violate the principles we preach, among which are the following: Acting in revenge is wrong . . . prisons, if they do not reform, should be closed." The writer rejects punishment (which he confuses with revenge) and believes that if society cannot rehabilitate convicts, it must release them. He does not believe incapacitation or deterrence useful. He is joined by renowned philosophers such as Richard H. Brandt, who proposes:

. . . if an accused were adjudged guilty, decisions about his treatment would then be in the hands of the experts, who would determine what treatment was called for and when the individual was ready for return to normal social living . . . it would be criminal-centered treatment, not crime-centered treatment. [For] it is doubtful whether threats of punishment have as much deterrent value as is often supposed.[74]

Because they intend to meet the individual's needs, and concentrate on helping rather than punishing him, the future-oriented treatment theories often are regarded as more rational, charitable, and humanitarian than retributive theories, which punish past acts according to legal definitions and prescriptions and ignore individual rehabilitative "needs." What

---

* Samuel Butler (in *Erewhon*) anticipated (or produced) Lady Wootton by suggesting that criminals be hospitalized. However, his hospitals prescribed flogging.

could be more humane than to deal with everyone according to his individual "needs"? To forget about guilt and the past, and to try to cure or correct for a better future? To help the criminal rather than to punish the crime? What could be more rational? *

One can argue that the justice model is more just than the therapeutic model, but the argument may amount to a disguised definition. It is more interesting to ask which model is ultimately more helpful to the offender and to society. With regard to the offender, the charity of the therapeutic model is suspect because it is compulsory. Convicts do not volunteer to be corrected. Most do not feel sick at all and do not want to be cured. They are held in a correctional institution to be treated against their will.

In the justice model the convict, punished according to desert, leaves when he has served his time, as legally prescribed for the crime for which he was convicted. He does not depend on the approval or disapproval of his jailers. The correctional or therapeutic model implies that he will leave when his needs have been met. The needs, however, are not those he feels but those he is felt to have. Experts and prison authorities decide on them, and on the length of his stay. The "needs" they attribute to the convict derive from their own notions about proper behavior and lifestyle. At best, experts define the convict's needs according to their reading of the significance of his prison behavior (or, sometimes, of his way of life) in predicting his conduct when released. If he is held because bad behavior is predicted, he is, as it were, made to suffer in advance for his expected future acts. Perhaps these social precautions can be justified as such, but not as punishment nor as a treatment. For treatment in the medical sense

* Strictly speaking, the humanitarian motive must be distinguished from the corrective-therapeutic one. The latter is instrumental and in principle could lead to painful or cruel, as well as humane, measures, depending on what is effective, whereas humane treatment is a moral precept, justified not by effects but by its intrinsic moral rightness. In practice, however, "humane" treatment is usually justified by the expected therapeutic effects.

surely is in the convict patient's interest as he defines it, and punishment refers to past offenses only.

Justice, at any rate, becomes irrelevant. There can be no "just correction," no "just therapy." Correction or treatment can be effective or ineffective, needed or not, but neither can be just or unjust any more than an appendectomy can be, or Vitamin C. The link between guilt and the punishment deserved by it—justice—is severed and replaced by a link between therapy and expected future conduct. Dr. Karl Menninger [75] acknowledges the therapeutic view when he writes: "The very word 'justice' irritates scientists." *

To be an involuntary patient and to depend on the uncertain judgment even of competent and well-intentioned authorities is also demeaning. The correctional model might well mean that offenders are released when they are sufficiently submissive—when they get along with prison authorities, including psychiatrists and social workers. David Greenberg's "The desire to help when coupled with a desire to control is totalitarian," [76] exaggerates only a little. Furthermore, psychiatry is not an exact science. Hence, capricious detention for involun-

---

* Those who originally sponsored rehabilitation as the main goal of legal sanctions against law violators are beginning to recoil having seen the consequences. Thus, *Struggle for Justice, A Report Prepared for the American Friend's Service Committee* (Hill and Wang, 1971), although still encumbered with many clichés, suggests that at least some among the Quakers to whom we owe the rehabilitative emphasis have seen the light. *Partial Justice* (Alfred A. Knopf, 1974) by Willard Gaylin, a psychoanalyst, reports on interviews with some forty federal judges which led Gaylin to conclude that sentencing becomes capricious when discretionary, more influenced by the divergent life experience of each judge than by the crime or the criminal. Gaylin might have spared himself the interviews by looking at any of the classical texts on criminal law. One reason Bentham advocated uniform sentencing standards determined by the crime and independent of the individual criminal was that sentences tailored to the criminal would necessarily be unequal and never above the suspicion of bias. Furthermore, he knew that the sentence would depend not on the criminal but on the judge who evaluates him. It would be unavoidably capricious. Yet physicians, psychiatrists, and psychoanalysts have long advocated discretionary procedures for the sake of rehabilitation. It is good that some of them finally have come to regret their advocacy. Gaylin concluded: "We must mechanize justice because we are not yet up to the love and understanding that is essential if discretion is to serve justice." "Not yet"? There is no reason to believe that we will ever be.

tary treatment is hard to distinguish from detention based on a *bona fide* diagnosis. Once the therapeutic model replaces a definite punishment with indefinite, involuntary "correction," it may turn out to be less humane, as well as less just than the retributive model.

Is It Effective?

Rehabilitative treatment has not been shown to be effective in reducing recidivism: the recidivism rates of those treated in different programs by different methods do not differ from the rates of those not treated at all, whether in the U.S. or elsewhere. Attempts to rehabilitate need not be given up, although the result so far is discouraging. A way may yet be found. And even if it does not portend rehabilitation, humane treatment is always justified for its own sake, as is justice. However, given the evidence we now have we should no longer regard rehabilitation as a major purpose to which punishment is suited. Retribution, deterrence, and incapacitation should have priority. Let me quote from an extensive report to substantiate the above.

With few and isolated exceptions, the rehabilitative efforts that have been reported so far have had no appreciable effect on recidivism.

The survey was limited to the rehabilitation methods generally in use during the period from 1945 through 1967, including small caseloads on probation or parole, intensive supervision in specialized caseloads, early releases from confinement, variation in sentence length and degree of custody, casework and individual counseling, psychotherapy, group therapies of various kinds, so-called "milieu therapy," halfway houses, pre-release guidance centers, tranquilizing drugs, plastic surgery, and other factors. Methods not evaluated included work release, methadone maintenance, recent forms of so-called "behavior modification," and what have come to be called diversion methods.

The weight of the evidence is that the addition of treatment elements ("programs" of the kind evaluated) to the system has no appreciable effect in changing offenders into non-offenders.

Those placed on probation do no worse than those imprisoned and may do slightly better. Small caseloads on probation do no better than standard caseloads. Probation supervision (as currently practiced) is not an effective "treatment," i.e., does not substantially improve the behavior of those supervised over what would be expected. A large number of treatment programs took place outside prison. The burden of evidence is not encouraging.[77]

Prof. Ulla Bondeson found in Sweden "that different methods of confinement do not create any different effects." Bondeson "compared four different types of correctional institutions; Christiansen, Moe & Sehnholt (1972) compared two different types of imprisonment; and Uusitalo (1972) compared open labor camps with closed prisons. The effects did not differ." Bondeson concludes: "Despite shorter terms of confinement, more open institutions, and more treatment resources given both during and after institutionalization, the Swedish correctional institution seems to produce recidivism rates as high as the American. . . ."[78] (If drunken driving is excluded, the recidivism rates still remain as high as in the U.S.)

These results are not unknown, but unceasing efforts are being made to ignore or deny them. Thus, Dr. Seymour L. Halleck still insists that "rehabilitation is a more important goal than punishment."[79] And the following revealing note appeared in *New York* magazine:

Theoretically, "work release" contributes to the rehabilitation of prison inmates by freeing them for outside jobs under certain conditions. The *New York Post,* for example . . . editorializes that "the repeater rate has been significantly cut; therefore so has crime." Nothing about the program could be further from the truth.

. . . More than one out of four in the program escape; a substantial number cause so much trouble that they're returned to prison; the recidivism rate for the program's "graduates" is so high that when it is combined with the other statistics, the probability is that "work release" participants are more likely to commit future crimes than the average prisoner released directly to the streets.[80]

A large bureaucracy of professionals and quasi-professionals has gained a vested interest in "rehabilitative" activities on which its power, prestige, and income depend. Hence, the pressures for ever more "rehabilitation."

Why Rehabilitation Does Not Work

There are three major reasons for the failure of rehabilitation, even under favorable circumstances. In unfavorable circumstances prison may lead to criminalization more readily than to rehabilitation.

1. Only diseases can be cured by treatment. Few offenders are sick. There is no convincing independent evidence that convicts are more sick than non-convicts.* Those who feel that all offenders suffer from some disorder to be corrected by treatment confuse their moral disapproval with a clinical diagnosis. Theoretically, it seems likely that many offenses are rational acts on the part of the offender; to minimize offenses one must change not the offender but the cost-benefit ratios that cause offenses to be rational.

2. Even the offenders who are clinically sick—some certainly are—are not likely to be rehabilitated coercively. As Norval Morris puts it, "facilitated change" must replace "coerced cure" [81]—i.e., the comforts of the prisoner and the duration of his incarceration must be entirely independent of his acceptance of a treatment program, which should be addressed only to those who want it. However, Prof. Morris has given no evidence of an available program that, if uncoerced, would be successful. It is one thing to point out that coerced rehabilitation does not work; it is quite another to show that if uncoerced it does work.

3. Rehabilitative treatment is necessarily ineffective, unless it follows or is part of independent retributive punish-

* See Chapter XI.

ment for another reason as well. When a person decides *sua sponte* to undergo psychotherapy (or for that matter medical treatment), he does so because he is dissatisfied either with his state of mind—e.g., he may suffer from anxiety—or because he is dissatisfied with his own behavior. However dimly, he realizes that he does not achieve what he intends to or succeed in the relationships or careers he wants because he defeats himself, perhaps because of an unconscious conflict. He seeks treatment to help him decide what he wants and to help him achieve it.

In contrast, the offender's intention is defeated by his own behavior only inasmuch as it is punished. Otherwise he need have no reason for dissatisfaction. It is the punishment that makes his behavior unrewarding and thus, perhaps, causes him to wish to change it. Unless his offense is punished, his behavior need not be self-defeating or irrational; therefore he has no reason to desire the change that the psychiatrist might have helped him make had he desired it. To be a successful thief may be immoral, but it is not self-defeating or irrational. To be an unsuccessful one may be. A criminal becomes unsuccessful inasmuch as he is punished. Rehabilitative efforts make sense only if offenses are made unrewarding, self-defeating, irrational, and ultimately painful. Only punishment can achieve this.* Hence rehabilitation can follow, but it cannot take the place of punishment.

Can the Punishment Fit the Crime?

Granted that the guilty deserve retribution as threatened by the law they violated, how much retribution do they deserve? What should the law threaten for each crime? What is de-

* To be sure, there are offenders who offend because they unconsciously seek punishment. There is evidence for the existence of such offenders, but none to indicate that their number is significant or that the unconscious need for punishment is decisive in producing their offenses.

served by its gravity? How is that "gravity" determined? 'Gravity" includes harm but cannot be reduced to it. Intention is important.* Rehabilitative or deterrent measures are justifiable as means to the degree they are effective.

Anticipated effects determine their size and shape. There can be no such test for retribution which is as independent of affects as promise keeping is.† Relative to others the size of each punishment is justifiable. But the size of any retributive punishment standing by itself is arbitrary—unless tradition and feeling (itself largely produced by tradition) are taken to be justifications. We may comfort ourselves with the thought that most things can be justified only in relation to others, within an order, and not by themselves.

Marvin E. Wolfgang asked police officers, judges, and university students to assign numerical weights to 141 offenses (he does not explain why he asked so unrepresentative a group) and developed "a set of scale scores denoting the relative mathematical weights of different crimes." [82] Thus, homicide scored 26, forcible rape 10, etc. Wolfgang's scores reflect the seriousness of crimes. Given the number of crimes, the scores help to measure trends of crime more fully by assigning a weight to each type of crime. Thus, Wolfgang's scores make the F.B.I.'s Uniform Crime Reports more meaningful.‡ Wolfgang also proposed that his scores be used—in a way "akin to the motor vehicle point system used in some states"— to assign "cumulative offense scores" to each offender, and to administer punishments "not in relation to a specific offense at a given moment but in relation to the accumulated social harm over a period of time."

Wolfgang believes that his scores contain an "element of justice" because they are consistent and additive. He realizes that such a point-scoring system measures not an objectively

---

* See Chapter III, p. 27.
† See Chapter II.
‡ Alfred Blumstein ("Seriousness Weights in an Index of Crime," *American Sociological Review*, Dec. 1974, pp. 854–864) has thrown some doubt on the usefulness of Wolfgang's work for this purpose.

extant "gravity" of crimes but merely a shared subjective evaluation— indeed, "gravity" is a metaphor—and an equally subjective evaluation of the appropriateness of sanctions. Now, the attempt to quantify such evaluations may help clarify them. But when driven too far, it gives an illusion of precision where precision is impossible. And scores reached by various mathematical averaging processes give an illusion of consistency and representativeness, of shared reaction, that can be quite misleading—as misleading, say, as Jeremy Bentham's "felific calculus" was. Even a correct average of evaluations may not correspond to any single evaluation and thus be quite unrepresentative. Furthermore, I have some misgivings about adding, say, 3 points to a man's score for one episode of picking pockets and 26 points for homicide. The motor vehicle point system deals with one coherent activity for which a license is granted. Violations cause the same kind of harm. But different crimes are not homogeneous enough to be meaningfully added to one another. Social harm, caused by unlawful actions, is no more a homogeneous quantity than "happiness" is. Still, Wolfgang's procedure sheds some light on how people view the relative harm done by crimes.

The *lex talionis*—an eye for an eye—is a simpler way of determining sanctions.* It appeals aesthetically—to our sense of symmetry if not of justice—to make "the punishment fit the crime." But it is not feasible, if it were desirable, to do so literally. Punishments do not and cannot match in kind the crimes for which they are inflicted. Punitive fines for some property crimes, or execution for murder, are among the few exceptions.

Thomas Jefferson tried, rather too valiantly, to make the punishment fit the crime by proposing in his 1779 "Bill for Proportioning Crime and Punishments": [83]

Whosoever shall be guilty of rape, polygamy, sodomy with man or woman, shall be punished, if a man, by castration, if a woman by cut-

---

* Historically, the rule was used to limit rather than to demand retribution. It also served as a basis for negotiating monetary compensation.

ting through the cartilage of her nose a hole of one half inch in diameter at the least. [And] whosoever shall maim another, or shall disfigure him . . . shall be maimed, or disfigured in the like sort: or if that cannot be, for want of some part, than as nearly as may be, in some other part of at least equal value. . . .*

Jefferson was always an egalitarian—an eye for an eye, each eye being of equal value, regardless of the status, age, sex, etc., of the possessor or of the offender. There are valid objections to such literalness which need not be detailed. These objections, however, are irrelevant to attempts to proportion the severity rather than the kind of retribution to the gravity of the crime. Our laws try to do so because it is "a precept of justice that punishment for crime should be graduated and proportioned to the offense."† The precept is universal. "There is no society where the rule does not exist that the punishment must be proportioned to the offense," according to Émile Durkheim.[84]

It is impossible, however, to measure the absolute gravity of different crimes or the specific (cardinal) difference in their gravity. Therefore, we cannot justify the absolute (cardinal) amount of retribution—in whatever form—for different crimes. We can, at best, justify why one is punished less or more than the other. G. W. F. Hegel was right in stating that "reason cannot determine . . . any principle whose application could decide whether justice requires for an offense (1) . . . forty lashes or thirty-nine, or (2) a fine of five thalers or four. . . ."[85]

Homogeneous penalties such as detention can be cardinally measured by taking their length as the relevant quantity; so can the differences among them. But the gravity of even reasonably homogeneous crimes cannot be measured in cardinal terms. Burglary, with breaking and entering, is more grave an offense than theft. But how much more grave? Assault is less

---

* Jefferson felt that "victimless" acts, such as consensual "sodomy," should be harshly punished. His libertarianism did not extend to what he felt was contrary to moral rules, which he attributed to nature but was quite willing to have the government enforce.

† *Weem* v. *United States*, 217 U.S. 349 (1910).

grave than assault with intent to kill. But how much less? And how much more (or less) serious is assault than burglary? Even when they are measurable, the absolute sizes of, and the cardinal differences among, penalties are not justifiable. But ordinal differences usually are. We cannot measure intervals between degrees of gravity, but we can order crimes according to whether they are more or less grave, and penalties according to their severity; the order of severity of punishments can and should match the order of gravity of crimes. Only when crimes are very different in kind, or when penalties are, does the order of sizes become questionable too.

Still, even the order of relative severity of punishments that responds to the relative gravity crimes are felt to have, is largely subjective. It is shaped by cultural and historical factors, and differs from place to place and over time. A minor theft a few hundred years ago could bring the death penalty in England, whereas now even a murder does not. But though it be different from what it once was, there is a felt gravity of crimes and a corresponding order of severity of punishments at any given time. If legal punishments are less or more severe than justice is felt to require, the law loses its effectiveness. If legal punishment is felt to be insufficient, there will be private vengeance. If the legal punishment is felt to be excessive, juries may refuse to find guilty defendants they know to be guilty so as to avoid what they feel is excessive punishment. Juries do not have the authority, but they have the power to thwart the law in such cases.* Either way justice is defeated. Finally, the law must take account of the deterrent effect of the size of punishments. If the crime is to be minimized, the threatened punishment must be sizable enough to achieve deterrence. Although we know that a more certain and severe threat produces more deterrence, we do not know how much more deterrence added threats produce for different crimes under various circumstances. Much research remains to be done.

* This happened with the death penalty when it was felt to be too severe for the offenses for which it was mandated.

XVII

The Decline of Corporal Punishment

The Shrinking Range

In times past the variety of punishments inflicted on criminals would have satisfied the most exigent sadist. In modern times the wide range has been narrowed, the variety diminished. We no longer impose most of the harshest punishments. The ingeniousness that went into torture instruments now displayed in European museums and still in use two hundred years ago amazes us, and the cruelty seems stunning. Any pain that human beings can wreak on one another was used for punishment. Courts did not hesitate to prescribe horrifying physical tortures or gruesome bodily mutilations. The Middle Ages were as inventive as antiquity, the West as zealous as the East. Death, meted out for trifling offenses, was thought too mild a punishment for serious crimes or, perhaps, too dull. So dying was artfully drawn out into agony beyond belief by a succession of progressively more painful mutilations inflicted in multifarious ways.

Courts also used to impose some mild punishments which have fallen into disuse. Thus, democratic countries no longer banish people or exile them to faraway places, although offenders—political or otherwise—may prefer to seek asylum abroad rather than face the courts at home. But self-exile is not deportation. In some nondemocratic countries, banishment or exile of citizens is still quite popular. But only aliens can be deported from the U.S., and there is neither banishment nor exile within the country.* Forfeiture of all goods is rare. Offenders still are deprived punitively of civil rights, licenses, and the right to enter certain occupations, usually in connection with other punishments. But in the main our courts impose three basic penalties: death, imprisonment, and fines. Each raises questions that warrant separate consideration. But some preliminary reflections on the shrinking range of penalties and, particularly, on the decline of corporal punishment may be in order.

Torture

In the past torture was used legally to obtain evidence, confessions, recantations, penitence, or to punish crimes. It is no longer used legally at all. Nonetheless, in some democratic countries torture is inflicted, clandestinely and sporadically, to obtain confessions; and in nondemocratic states torture is used widely, often with the tacit encouragement of the authorities. However, torture has been legally abolished everywhere as a means of judicial inquiry, and nowhere is it used routinely in nonpolitical cases now.

The humanitarian reasons for this welcome change are obvious. But some pragmatic reasons for discarding torture bear rehearsing. As a means of judicial inquiry, torture is irrational, unlikely to separate the guilty from the innocent or truthful from false testimony, while yet indiscriminately inflicting

* The advantages and drawbacks of banishment or exile as an alternative to prison are discussed in Chapter XXII.

pain on innocent and guilty alike. The testimony extracted by torture tells more about the ability of the tortured to withstand pain than about guilt or innocence: to stop torture people will confess to what they have not done or seen.

But whether justified or not, *non*judicial torture is still likely to be used to extract information deemed essential for preventive purposes.* If the prisoner is the only one who knows the location of the bomb, which will go off in four hours and kill ten persons, and if he refuses to tell where it is, the choice may be between his suffering torture and the certain death of ten innocents. Sparing the prisoner and allowing the victims of the bomb to die instead may be regarded as humanitarian and principled by some, and attacked as sentimental weakness by others.[86] Such dilemmas, fortunately, are not frequent; and they are seldom as clearcut as in the illustration. The prisoner may be suspected of having the information needed, but he may not have it. Similarly, those who feel justified in using torture may not actually have the immediate and humanitarian purpose that might justify it, but a punitive, sadistic or ideological one.†

Punitive Pain

Torture was inflicted in the past for punitive as well as interrogative purposes. Mutilation also was used punitively. Unlike punitive torture, mutilation—relabeled, of course—has

* This end may or may not justify this means, depending on the need for the kind of information sought. Ends justify means when (a) suitable (effective and efficient) (b) the means do not defeat other primary ends, and, finally (c) the means are proportionate to the ends. Ends never can justify all means but always do justify some.

† Whether torture is more securely confined by clear distinctions, or by rejecting it in all cases and thus giving it uncontrolled *sub rosa* existence, is a matter of tactics that cannot be analyzed here but that merits serious thought—not the well-intentioned non-thought, which is customary on the subject.

survived in two forms: castration for sexual offenders and cutting out parts of the brain for some others.* The professed purpose is medical—to help rather than to punish the convict—and the mutilation is carried out by a physician. But the "informed consent" of people in custody is usually open to doubt. And unless it is entirely voluntary, the amputation cannot be distinguished from a punishment, such as cutting off the arm of a thief as was done in the past. This is still, or again, done in some Islamic and African countries. (After the third conviction in Saudi Arabia and earlier in Yemen, Lybia, and Uganda.)

To the modern Western mind, mutilation seems an excessive punishment. In the past even great humanitarians thought otherwise. Times were more brutal and people lived on more familiar terms with death, pain, and injury. What to us is nearly incomprehensible was quite acceptable to them. Perhaps cutting off the hand of the burglar would prevent recidivism and serve as an effective deterrent to others. Most of us would rather tolerate more burglaries than curb them by this means. The stolen goods can be replaced, and stealing is an act. But the severed limb cannot be. Mutilation becomes a permanent condition.

Desirable still to Jefferson,† retaliatory mutilation would horrify us today. Times have changed. Punitive mutilation has become unacceptable even as retaliation for irreversible bodily injury. Indeed, we have become repelled altogether by any form of corporal punishment. Nobody seriously proposed to punish the Nazi concentration camp guards, or their commanders, with the kind of torture they inflicted on the inmates. Though surely deserved, no pain was deliberately inflicted on them. They served prison terms as though guilty of

---

* Involuntary sterilization, as carried out, e.g., in Denmark, prevents reproduction but does not interfere with sex, and can be justified when there are hereditary diseases or defects: it does not punish anyone, and may reduce future suffering. Castration, which Denmark also inflicts with the consent of the convict, in preference to keeping sexual offenders in jail, is more questionable.

† See Chapter XVI.

offenses just a trifle worse than embezzlement. A few were executed, like ordinary murderers. Except for death, bodily pain is no longer inflicted judicially. And the death penalty surely is not imposed for the sake of the pain incidental to it, but, if anything, despite it: one of the virtues originally ascribed to the electric chair was painlessness; one of the objections raised to it now is that it has been found painful.

Mutilation and fatal torture now seem, in the words of the eighth amendment to our Constitution, "cruel and unusual punishment." Still, our practice of avoiding all punitive physical pain could reflect emotional bias. Is every corporal punishment more cruel than imprisonment? Is a thief better off incarcerated for two years than receiving sixty lashes? Is incarceration more humane, even if the thief would prefer flogging? Is prison better for him? or for us? Rational notions of avoiding excesses, ineffectiveness, or cruelty cannot explain the abolition of every kind of corporal punishment. There appears to be a change primarily of feeling, although it has been disguised as much as it has been justified by argument. We reject corporal punishment out of hand as somehow illegitimate. We are revolted by it. Our notion of human dignity now includes the inviolability of the physical person: we feel that corporal punishment would dehumanize offenders as well as those who inflict it. We have become queasy about touching bodies for any reason other than medical, sexual, or perhaps in sport. This widely shared feeling about the inviolability of the physical person does not rest on the arguments used to rationalize it. Some conjectures may help explain it.

Changes in the Conception of the Person

In the past we did not own our bodies and souls inalienably. Ownership of one person by another was accepted. It was an effect of birth into slavery, or of defeat in war, or of sale by parents who were thought to own their children. It is only recently that the soul and, with the abolition of slavery, the body too became the inalienable property of the individual. The unwillingness of society to infringe on anyone's body without his consent may be the culmination of this development. To imprison is an arm's length interference, a deprivation rather than a direct physical intrusion. To flog is to transgress on what is now accepted as inviolably private. The distinction does not have much logical support. But we are dealing with a psychological matter, and the distinction is undeniably felt. We now are reluctant to inflict corporal punishment, even on children. England, long a holdout, is about to abolish flogging in schools (for practical purposes, it largely has been abolished). In the American middle class, children are rarely beaten. In the past cruelty to children (and, of course, by children to each other) was the norm.[87] Now it is the exception, and in some cases a crime. Adults who were beaten frequently as children tend to accept corporal punishment of adults more easily. Our treatment of children, then, may be both an effect and a cause of the change. Only animals are still punished bodily. In our minds physical punishment would reduce people to animals. Human dignity requires *noli me tangere*.

Our reluctance to lift the physical immunity we have created, even for criminals, may be an expression of our alienation from our bodies and from each other as well as of greater humaneness. We live in a far more abstract world than our ancestors did. Few of us till the soil or herd cattle. Most of us work with lifeless matters or with abstract symbols, and are rewarded by money, by abstract "purchasing power." Far more than in the past, we deal with each other at arm's length, by telephone or in writing. People or events often are seen as images on screens or heard as disembodied voices. Bodies have become private, intimate things, not to be invaded without consent for any public purpose.

When they were the norm, corporal punishments also served as public entertainment. People took their families to

attend hangings, beheadings, drawings and quarterings, dis-
embowelings, burnings, or torture on the rack. Far from feeling guilty or squeamish about torture, or deriving but a furtive
pleasure from it, people publicly rejoiced and enjoyed a spectacle as cruel as anything the Romans ever were blamed for.
They did not doubt that the forces of good were carrying out
God's will. Having relegated them beyond the pale, law-abiding citizens enjoyed the suffering of criminals as a spectacle.*
Justice was as haphazard as it was cruel. Still, there was remarkable little empathy; people did not identify with victims.
Wrongdoers deserved what they got, and God was in his
heaven. We must remind ourselves also that society was far
more cruel and indifferent to all victims—to the insane, the
sick, the crippled, the hungry—than it is today. (Religion was
concerned with these victims, but the concern was as often
spiritual and abstract as it was material and concrete.) Criminals were no exception. The powerless were treated cruelly,
and cruelty was physical.

Pain also was far more familiar than it is today. Extreme
physical suffering was routine. Anesthetics were unknown,
and surgical patients, the victims of accidents, the wounded,
and the sick suffered horrendously, as did women in
childbirth.

Modern medicine has made pain unfamiliar to most of us
and almost inhuman. (At least so we hope.) And we no longer
feel as sure as we did in the past about what is good and evil,
about our ability to know, and about the responsibility of those
whom we condemn. Thus, we no longer want to punish. "Correct," rehabilitate, yes, or if worst comes to worst, get rid of the
incorrigible or the intolerable as painlessly and as privately as
possible. Keep them behind walls. But punish—we hesitate
and prefer not to. The indirect and abstract suffering in prison
may be seen as rehabilitative, as is the suffering that takes

---

* After all, St. Thomas Aquinas held that those in heaven "will see the
punishments inflicted on the damned, so that their ecstacy will be greatly
heightened."

place in a hospital. Originally, it was meant to be. Prisons still are called "correctional institutions" though no longer "penitentiaries"—we no longer expect penitence. But the punitive nature of corporal punishment is too obvious: flogging as a form of treatment is hard to credit. It is obviously punitive. Imprisonment, on the other hand, we can justify to ourselves—it allows for rehabilitation.

To us pain is the greatest of evils, and its deliberate infliction is never justified—certainly not in the name of justice. When we depict torture in comic books or movies, the good guys never torture the bad guys. Those who deliberately inflict pain are *ipso facto* bad. The good guys manage to sneak pain in—but only when incidental to self-defense, never as punishment. Eichmann was executed—as painlessly as possible—not *coram publico* and with rejoicing but in the presence only of official witnesses. We will try to protect ourselves; we will try to rehabilitate the criminal or remove him from our midst. But whatever the criminal did, the responsibility for deliberately inflicting bodily pain is more than we can bear. To deprive him of liberty, or (rarely) of life, may be necessary. But bodily pain or harm as punishment—never.

A Psychological Presumption

The conjectures so far listed rest on social developments in the past two centuries. However, these developments could not wholly explain the modern recoil from corporal punishment without a psychological surmise to be hazarded now.

In the Western world corporal punishment became sexualized in the eighteenth century; it was abolished in the nineteenth. Once sexualized, the rational, instrumental functions of inflicting physical pain were overwhelmed and ultimately had to be given up. Ego (rational, instrumental) activities often become inhibited altogether when sexualized—i.e.,

once they are used as, or felt to be, vehicles for the direct gratification of libidinal (or aggressive) drives. They become fused
with the drives they express and are blocked when these are.
The ego activities, then, cannot be used any longer as means
for realistic (ego) purposes, regardless of how useful they are.
Psychoanalysts are familiar with the inhibition in individuals
of activities such as reading, walking, writing, or mentation as
a result of such a fusion, such an invasion by the libido which
overwhelms rational functions. Something analogous has happened to society with respect to the punitive conditioning of
individuals by means of deliberately inflicting pain. Infected
with, or tainted by, sexual gratification, corporal punishment
became inadmissible, just as tainted evidence is inadmissible
in our courts. Business and pleasure do not mix. Corporal punishment now is perceived as debasing sexual exploitation,
even as homosexual rape. (By the eighteenth century, pain
was inflicted mainly by men on men.)

Although named much later by Krafft-Ebing [88] and explained later still by Freud, the sexualization of deliberately
inflicted pain began to be publicly recognized during the
Enlightenment, most obviously with Rousseau (1712–1778).
It was apotheosized by the Marquis de Sade (1740–1814).
Rousseau wrote that when Mlle. de Lambercier spanked
him for some childish transgression, he "discovered in the
shame and pain of the punishment an admixture of sensu-
ality" that left him eager for repetition. He presents his own
"common and unfortunate case" in his *Confessions* to warn
against corporal punishment, for "received at the age of eight
at the hands of a woman of thirty [it] would determine my
tastes and desires, my passions, my very self for the rest of
my life. . . ." Indeed, Rousseau did become what later
would be called a masochist.*

Rousseau's sensual enjoyment of "shame and pain" in hav-

---

* Rousseau suffered from sexual and other psychic disturbances, to which
the early experiences he describes must have contributed. However, in his
case, and in most others, the term "masochism" (after the Austrian writer
Sacher-Masoch, 1835–95, who described this peculiarity in his novels) ob-
scures as much as it enlightens.

ing corporal punishment inflicted on him had to wait more than a century to receive a name and to be widely acknowledged as a sexual possibility that can become a perversion. Meanwhile, the sexual pleasure drawn from inflicting pain on others was starkly revealed, painstakingly elaborated, and relentlessly glorified by Rousseau's contemporary, the Marquis de Sade, after whom it was named. Sadism could be more readily acknowledged than masochism—one surmises because it fitted the historical ideals of masculinity, which it obsessively exaggerated.

Both sadism and masochism involve a merging of aggressive and libidinal drives. A psychic identification of the sadist with his victim, of the masochist with his punisher, also is involved. The sadist violently denies the humanity of the victim identified with his passive drives and derives pleasure from the de-identification. But the pleasure lies in the process of de-identification, endlessly repeated, not in the result. An object one has never identified with is incapable of yielding sadistic gratification, which rests on the initial empathy with the victim on whom the sadist projects what must be punished. In turn, the masochist introjects (identifies with) the aggressor who punishes him.

The feeling popularized by Karl Menninger [89] that we punish ourselves in criminals and actually need them for this purpose, and that we fear ourselves in them, is clearly related to the sexualization of corporal punishment, which would be impossible without such identifications. In Menninger's attenuated, desexualized sense, what has been said about corporal punishment may well apply to all punishments. Yet his argument for abolition, expresses, as much as it analyzes, the motives he has detected and his reaction. For from the investigation of psychological motives or functions of punishment, nothing follows about moral justification and, above all, social usefulness. To think otherwise is to commit the genetic fallacy to which psychoanalysts are all too prone. The sexualization of corporal punishment helps explain its abandonment but does not tell us whether that abandonment is right just as the sexualization of his writing tells us why the author who suffers from a "writing block" abandoned it but does not tell us whether he should stop writing.

Rousseau is a political philosopher of the first rank, whereas de Sade had no originality of style or substance in his nonsexual theories. However, the political ideas of the Enlightenment which they shared are not incidental here. Unlike the *ancien régime*, the Enlightenment and finally the French Revolution assumed the psychic identity and equality of all mankind.* Tocqueville [90] quotes Mme. de Sévigné to testify how alien feelings of universal solidarity were to prerevolutionary France. A kind and considerate lady, she wrote her daughter describing with amused indifference the hanging and quartering of rebellious peasants all around her. They were beyond the pale to a lady of her status, and she could not feel their suffering any more than the peasants would have felt hers.†

Liberté, Égalité, Fraternité recognized, or created, universal human empathy and identification, regardless of social status. Ralph Waldo Emerson may have been anachronistic when he maintained that all "governments have their origin in the moral identity of men." But postrevolutionary governments grew from it. This identification was essential to the recognition of a universal pleasure yielding process of de-identification by means of the infliction of carnal pain. With the infliction of pain thus sexualized, it became inhibited and could no longer be used for punishment. Punishment had to be disembodied, restricted to depriving criminals of liberty or life, while touching them as little as possible and avoiding their sight.‡

---

* The idea of organic relationship ascribed to Menenius Agrippa (in, e.g., Shakespeare's *Coriolanus*) is ancient but quite distinct from the revolutionary idea of identity.

† Robert Nisbet was kind enough to draw my attention to this passage.

‡ Such a development might also be explained as a final prevalence of the Christian feelings of charitable empathy. But it is hard to see why these feelings should not have prevailed in the Christian Middle Ages and should have come into their own after the de-christianizing Enlightenment.

XVIII

The Death Penalty: Arguments For

The Problem

Rehabilitation, concerned with the convict's conduct after his release, is irrelevant to the death penalty since the convict is not released. And although helpful, death ordinarily is not indispensable for incapacitation. That leaves but one moral and one utilitarian justification for the death penalty. Moral: death may be required, or at least permitted, by considerations of justice; utilitarian: capital punishment * may be a more effective deterrent than the alternatives.

Too Severe?

Most people believe that death is a more severe punishment than the usual alternative, life imprisonment. A minority, including Prof. Jacques Barzun (and, therefore, a weighty mi-

* From the latin *caput* (head), capital punishment originally may have referred to beheading.

nority), do not share that belief; [91] some claim that they would rather die than live in prison. However, those actually confronted with the choice have usually preferred life in prison—unwisely, perhaps, but it is hard to argue with them. Fortunately, the question need not be answered. One may advocate death because it is kinder than life in prison, or because it is not. One may also oppose it for either reason.* (Prof. Barzun advocates it because he regards death as more humane than prison.)

Most abolitionists regard the death penalty as too severe, and I shall focus on their arguments. Humanitarians object on grounds of justice, or "humanity": to put a man to death deliberately is sometimes unjust but always morally wrong and "inhumane" they feel.† Utilitarians (who may be humanitarians as well) claim that imprisonment, lifelong if necessary, would be at least as effective a deterrent as death, which, since it is not required for any useful purpose, is cruel.‡

The Only Threat Available

It is always difficult to know how many crimes are not committed because of a threat. But it can be shown logically that the death penalty is the only threat that could (could, not necessarily will) deter members of three groups.

* The convict sentenced to life in prison might be offered a choice. It seems wrong not to grant people capable of rational choice the right to choose death. But the issue here is not optional suicide but obligatory execution.

† Michael Meltsner's *Cruel and Unusual* (New York: Random House, 1973) indicates the scope of organized efforts to abolish the death penalty by all legal means, such as "Last Aid Kits" distributed to lawyers to help gum up the wheels of justice and make it practically impossible to execute convicts. These efforts have very nearly succeeded now, although, as Joseph W. Bishop, Jr. points out (*Commentary*, February 1974), they attempt to foreclose judicially what is clearly a legislative decision: abolitionists attempt to get the courts to do what legislatures have not done because it is opposed by the majority of voters.

‡ Religious sentiment also is appealed to. But holy writ and religious tradition could support either side of the controversy. So could appeals to personal taste. The answer to the question, Would you be an executioner? may be negative but irrelevant. You might not want to be a butcher or a chicken farmer,

1. Convicts already serving a life term are incapacitated insofar as the world beyond prison walls is concerned, but are left quite capable of committing crimes within. Such crimes are frequent. Without the death penalty, these convicts are immune to threats of further punishment. It seems unwise to grant convicted criminals this heady immunity not available to non-convicts, who are less dangerous. The federal prison system currently has custody of an offender who, since being confined for murder, has committed three additional murders on three separate occasions while in prison. The following item appeared in *Newsweek* (June 11, 1973).

Two hard-case inmates apparently wangled their way into the warden's offices and stabbed the warden and his deputy to death with sharpened mess-hall knives.

. . . investigators said that the death mission had been specifically ordered the night before at a meeting of Muslim inmates because Fromhold had resisted their demands "once too often." Fromhold was stabbed thirteen times in the back and chest; Warden Patrick Curran, 47, who dashed into his deputy's first-floor office, was stabbed three times in the back.

Neither inmate had much to lose. Burton was doing life in the cold-blooded execution of a Philadelphia police sergeant, and Bowen was awaiting trial in another cop-killing and the shooting of an elderly couple.

Ways could be found to deprive these inmates of nearly all capacity to harm each other, or the prison personnel. But to achieve this, prisons would have to become truly inhumane. Convicts would have to be permanently chained or isolated. If rehabilitation, or merely decent treatment, is to be attempted, if prisons are to do anything other than to incapacitate inmates totally, the threats of the law are needed to control those who still might commit crimes, including murder. The death penalty is the only threat that could restrain those already serving life terms from further homicides.

---

either, yet approve of eating meat or eggs. Nor is compassion decisive. Felt with the man to be executed, it may also be felt with his victim: if the execution spares future victims of murder, supporters of the death penalty may claim compassion as their argument.

2. Without the death penalty, those already threatened with a life term for kidnapping, skyjacking, or murder, but not yet apprehended, have no reason to refrain from additional crimes. They may murder third persons or the kidnap victim. Above all, they will be able to kill the arresting officer with impunity. This won't make the policeman's job easier. The effective impunity granted for additional crimes to suspects already threatened with a life term invites them to murder the officers trying to apprehend them.

Logically, as long as there are fewer degrees of punishment than of crime, even the threat of the death penalty would not have a restraining effect on *all* further crimes. Once the first kidnap victim had been killed, murdering the second could bring no additional penalty—one can die but once. But, because of the threat of execution, the first victim might never be killed. And if there is some discretion in sentencing: criminals threatened by the death penalty feel that further murders worsen their situation and that the killing of police officers ensures their own death.

3. Prospective spies in wartime, or violent revolutionaries in acute situations when there is a present danger of the government being overthrown, can be restrained, if at all, only by the death penalty.* They believe that they will be released from prison when their side wins. They may even expect a reward. In an acute situation only the threat of an irrevocable penalty could effectively deter them. Unlike imprisonment, death cannot be revoked; it may cause the expected victory to come too late.

The Deterrent Effect of Irrevocability

Turn now from logic to emotion, to the expectations people are likely to have. Irrevocability probably makes the death penalty more deterrent than life imprisonment. For, however

---

* In democratic regimes revolutionaries may include totalitarian rightists or leftists; in dictatorial ones, democrats or rival dictators.

unfounded or irrational, the hope of revocation inheres in all revocable penalties because the possibility does. Even if revocation is *de jure* excluded and the chance remote, a revocable penalty is always less deterrent than an irrevocable one because of the *de facto* "animal faith" * that leaves us only with death: "where there is life there is hope." Anyone, if at all deterrable, is more deterred by the threat of death than by the threat of life imprisonment, which can be revoked and usually is. Only death is irrevocable.†

Additional Sources of Fear

Unlike prison, death is not known: we have reports on dying but not on being dead. Most people are unable to imagine their own end and fear it more than anything. The intensive fear of the death penalty—suggested *inter alia* by the agitation for abolishing it—in part is fear of the unknown. It also springs from confusion: death is attributed to the penalty as though it caused an otherwise avoidable event. Yet, unlike a prison sentence, the death penalty does not take from us what we otherwise would keep: people not legally deprived of freedom are free, but people not legally deprived of life still die. A death sentence but hastens and sets a date certain for what must happen to all of us.‡ Yet the fear that has death as its original object is displaced to become fear of the penalty that quickens it, as though certain death itself could have been eluded had there been no death sentence.

Since we often hurry death, or risk doing so, by hazardous actions—or by ordinary habits such as smoking—the fear of

---

* An expression coined by George Santayana.

† Most punishments are irreversible but revocable. Fines are reversible as well. Prof. Charles L. Black, Jr., in his *Capital Punishment* (New York: Norton, 1974), p. 31, evokes this linguistic (though not the factual) distinction on the dubious authority of George Bernard Shaw.

‡ John Stuart Mill, et al., pointed out as much in urging Parliament to retain the death penalty. See Hansard, Parliamentary Debates, April 21, 1868.

the death penalty strictly speaking cannot be fear that death will come sooner. That fear does not restrain people from smoking. Nor can the fear be produced by expectations of pain: execution is no more painful than natural death and in most cases probably less so; at least the pain does not last as long as natural pain often does.* Much of the fear of the death penalty and of its deterrent effect probably spring from heightened awareness, from the confrontation with an implacable certainty.

Another source of fear may be more important. To be put to death because one's fellow humans find one unworthy to live is a very different thing from reaching the end of one's journey naturally, as all men must. To be condemned, expelled from life by one's fellows, makes death not a natural event or a misfortune but a stigma of final rejection. The knowledge that one has been found too odious to live is bound to produce immense anxiety. Threatened by disease or danger, we usually feel that death is in an indecent hurry to overtake us. We appeal to friends and physicians to save us, to help delay it, and we expect a comforting response. Death is the common enemy, and it calls forth human solidarity. Not for the condemned man. He is pushed across by the rest of us. To die by the inscrutable decree of higher powers—somehow necessary and, perhaps, benevolent, but at any rate addressed to all of us—is one thing. To be singled out as too loathsome, as unfit to live, by the solemn judgment of one's fellow men is the most desolating of rejections.

The Symbolic Meaning of Abolition

The degree to which penalties stigmatize crime and criminals as hateful depends not only on the social climate in which punishment takes place but also on the penalties themselves:

---

* We could find better methods of execution. Those now used certainly seem more painful than necessary.

as these become milder, crimes appear less odious and criminals are less ostracized. Traditionally, death has been the expected penalty for murder. The *lex talionis* has psychological plausibility: we expect outraged nature to strike back, to be done to us as we have done to others. That expectation—and its deterrent effect—ultimately ceases when it is no longer met. Social traditions, beliefs, customs, expectations and fears may linger on long after the circumstances that gave rise to them have changed, long after they are rationally justified. But not forever.

No matter what can be said for abolition of the death penalty, it will be perceived symbolically as a loss of nerve: social authority no longer is willing to pass an irrevocable judgment on anyone. Murder is no longer thought grave enough to take the murderer's life, no longer horrendous enough to deserve so fearfully irrevocable a punishment. When murder no longer forfeits the murderer's life (though it will interfere with his freedom), respect for life itself is diminished, as the price for taking it is. Life becomes cheaper as we become kinder to those who wantonly take it. The responsibility we avoid is indeed hard to bear. Can we sit in judgment and find that anyone is so irredeemably wicked that he does not deserve to live? Many of us no longer believe in evil, only in error or accident. How can one execute a murderer if one believes that he became one only by error or accident and is not to blame? Yet if life is to be valued and secured, it must be known that anyone who takes the life of another forfeits his own.

The Burden of Proof

Does the death penalty actually deter more persons, or deter them more effectively, than other punishments? If so, does the added deterrence warrant the added severity?

The general idea of the penal system is that, all other things being equal, the more severe the penalties the more deterrent they are. Higher penalties for drunken driving, rape, or theft deter more than lower ones. This much is borne out by every-day experience and by statistical demonstrations.* Death is perceived as the most severe penalty. The claim that it does not add to deterrence runs counter, then, to the known general relationship between severity and deterrence. This does not disprove the claim; the death penalty could be an exception. But those who feel that it is must bear the burden of proof by showing that diminishing returns (of deterrence) set in as severity is added and that marginal returns are reduced to zero as the death penalty is reached.

So far we do not know if and where diminishing returns set in and reach zero as severity is added.† No way has been found as yet to determine the exact amount of the marginal (added) deterrence produced for each crime by a specific amount of added severity. The elasticity of the supply of crime—its response to different negative prices (cost)—may vary: each crime may have a specific elasticity of supply. The response of prospective drug addicts to an increase of the average penalty may differ from that of prospective burglars to the same increase. The supply of some kinds of murder, such as murder by professionals and murder in the course of robberies, may be highly elastic; such murders may be much more deterred by the death penalty (by a very high cost) than murder in the course of intrafamilial disputes. (There are good grounds for suggesting as much but little evidence to prove or disprove it.)

Our ignorance of elasticities and of the points where diminishing or zero returns set in extends to all penalties. There is no evidence to show that ten years of prison deter 100 percent more people, or deter them 100 percent more effectively, than

* See Chapter XIII.

† It seems likely that this happens with, but not before, death. Since people find nothing more fear-inspiring than death, painfulness when added to the death penalty—as used to be done—is probably ineffective as a deterrent.

five years. Possibly, if we prolong the penalty to fifteen years, the last five years add zero deterrence. Possibly not. No study has established the degree of marginal deterrence by comparing states that impose five years with states that impose ten years of prison for the same crime, or states before and after abolition of the ten-year penalty, or states before and after reinstatement.* Proof of added deterrence is not demanded for any other penalty. It is demanded for the death penalty, and the (alleged) lack of proof of marginal deterrence is the most common argument for abolition.†

Inconclusive Statistics

Until recently, statistics did not show the presence or absence of a deterrent effect of the death penalty. Prof. Thorsten Sellin testified on this point in Great Britain.

8916. We cannot conclude from your statistics . . . that capital punishment has no deterrent effect?—No, there is no such conclusion.

8917. But can we not conclude that if it has a deterrent effect it must be rather small?—I can make no such conclusion because I can find no answer one way or another in these data." ‡

If indeed it were shown that after abolition the capital crimes rate had consistently decreased, or that upon rein-

---

* Ehrlich (see Chapter XIII) found that more punishment deters more. But he did not investigate the addition to deterrence produced by each addition to punishment.

† Selective insistence on such proof is not justified. Still, scientific investigation of the deterrent effect of penalties should be high on the agenda of the social sciences.

‡ Royal Commission on Capital Punishment, 1949–1953 Report. Prof. Sellin has opposed the death penalty in many writings and feels that the burden of proving it deterrent lies on those who wish to retain it. He feels that the statistics available to him cannot be used to show that the death penalty has or has not additional deterrent effect over alternatives. Others have been less cautious. Not being able to show that the death penalty has (additional) deterrent effects is not to be confused with showing it does not. Not showing presence is not the same as showing absence.

troduction it had consistently increased, neither showing by itself would prove or disprove the claim that the death penalty deters over and above alternative penalties. (Actually, the capital crimes rate does not change consistently upon legal abolition or reintroduction.) Had the death penalty been retained, the capital crimes rate might have declined more; and in the second case, had the death penalty not been reintroduced, the capital crimes rate might have risen more. In the absence of conclusive statistical proof of its effectiveness or ineffectiveness, the case for or against the death penalty as a deterrent rests on one's preference for one of two risks.

1.   If the death penalty does not add deterrence and we carry out death sentences, we lose the life of the executed convict without adding deterrence.
2.   If the death penalty does add deterrence, and we fail to pronounce and carry out death sentences for murder, we fail to deter murderers who could have been deterred had the death sentence been pronounced and carried out. We lose the lives of the victims who would have been spared had we been willing to deter their murderers by executing other murderers.*

Factors That Influence the Capital Crimes Rate

It would be a mistake to relate the frequency of marriages exclusively to legal costs and economic benefits. So with crimes. There are historical, moral, psychological, and cultural variables that affect marriage and crime, and they cannot be reduced to costs and benefits. Crime rates, therefore, can change independently of changes in penalties: the threat of legal punishment is only one current in a stream of motivations and nonpenal factors such as opportunities, customs, or stimuli,

* If the death penalty adds deterrence, the question whether or not it adds enough can be answered if we know (a) how much deterrence it adds and (b) how much is enough. (See p. 217)

which contribute to crime rates, as they do, *mutatis mutandis*, to other social actions. The rates at which fiction, sociology textbooks, Vitamin C, or pantyhose are produced all depend not only on cost-benefit ratios but also on motivation, opportunity, fashion, etc. There is no doubt, however, that higher costs, e.g., via taxation, do reduce the rate at which anything is produced. The degree of reduction depends on the elasticity of the supply. Changes in costs (penalties) are as likely to influence the supply of crime—including murder—as they are to influence the supply of anything else.

New Evidence

Since the statistical evidence for the marginal effect of the death penalty was found inconclusive, a new analysis has been published by Prof. Isaac Ehrlich.[92] Ehrlich points out that Sellin's findings are produced by "simple correlation techniques and rough measures of the conditional risk of execution [which] failed to identify a systematic association between murder and the risk of execution. . . . The actual enforcement of the death penalty . . . may be a far more important factor affecting offenders' behavior than the legal status of the penalty; [so may] the probabilities of apprehension and conviction." Prof. Ehrlich's "simultaneous equation regression model" suggests that over the period 1933–1969 "an additional execution per year . . . may have resulted on the average in 7 or 8 fewer murders." The importance of this conclusion is obvious. It remains to be seen if further research will support or refute it.

XIX

The Death Penalty:
Arguments Against

"Answer not a fool according to his folly,
  lest thou also be like unto him.
Answer a fool according to his folly,
  lest he be wise in his own conceit."

Proverbs 26:4,5

According to Boswell, Dr. Johnson noted pickpockets plying their trade in a crowd assembled to see one of their number executed. The episode demonstrates that not all offenders are deterred by the death penalty. The conclusion usually drawn—that deterrence does not work—would follow only if no fewer pocket-picking episodes had occurred than would have in a crowd that size in the absence of the execution.

Injustice

Because of the frailty of human judgment, innocents may be convicted of capital crimes as of other crimes. Since executions cannot be revoked, demonstrations of innocence would come too late.* This is factually correct and relevant to retributionist arguments for the death penalty, but not to most utilitarian or humanitarian arguments against it.

Innocence is irrelevant if the death penalty is rejected on grounds of insufficient deterrence (utilitarians) or of "inhumanity." Either argument asserts that convicts should be spared execution, whether guilty or not. Hence, it does not matter which they are. If guilt is irrelevant to the penalty, so is the lack of it. Arguments from likely irrevocable injustice are relevant only if justice (desert) is relevant to punishment, if guilt is a necessary and sufficient reason for imposing it. Strict utilitarians and humanitarians, then, cannot use miscarriages of justice to argue for abolition of the death penalty. What about retributionists, for whom justice is the paramount criterion of penalization, or at least an essential one?

Errors would not justify the abolition of the death penalty for retributionists. Many social policies have unintended effects that are statistically certain, irrevocable, unjust, and deadly. Automobile traffic unintentionally kills innocent victims; so does surgery (and most medicines); so does the death penalty. These activities are justified, nevertheless, because benefits (including justice) are felt to outweigh the statistical certainty of unintentionally killing innocents. The certain death of innocents argues for abolishing the death penalty no more than for abolishing surgery or automobiles. Injustice justifies abolition only if the losses to justice outweigh the gains—if more innocents are lost than saved by imposing the penalty compared to whatever net result alternatives (such as no punishment or life imprisonment) would produce. If in-

* This is the burden of *Capital Punishment* by Charles L. Black, Jr. (New York: Norton, 1974). Black stresses that criteria for the death penalty should be more stringent than for any other, and also that, as a matter of fact, some degree of "capriciousness" (discretion) is impossible to avoid. He is right on both counts. However, to insist that only the total elimination of "capriciousness"—which he knows to be impossible in the prosecution of any crime and generally in human affairs—would make the death penalty legally or morally justifiable is a counsel of perfection meant to exclude a disliked policy, and not a serious argument.

nocent victims of future murderers are saved by virtue of the
death penalty imposed on convicted murderers, it must be retained, just as surgery is, even though some innocents will be
lost through miscarriages of justice—as long as more innocent
lives are saved than lost. More justice is done with than without the death penalty. It is always a logical error to reject a rule
because of individual cases. Rules and the results they produce must be compared with alternative rules and with the
results they produce, not with individual cases.*

Discriminatory Application

Abolition often is advocated for the sake of equality, or non-
discrimination, because of statistics which suggest that the
death penalty has been applied more often against the poor
and the black than against others. Since a higher proportion of
the poor or black are guilty of capital crimes,† the fact that
more of them are sentenced to die than of the rich or white
does not by itself imply discrimination. However, if a higher
proportion of the guilty poor and of the guilty black were executed than of whites or non-poor who are as guilty, it would
suggest unwarranted discrimination. In the past, if not in the
present, this appears to have been the case.‡

Now, since abolitionists remain opposed to capital punishment even where it is distributed without discrimination, e.g.,
where populations are nearly racially homogeneous, as in
England or Sweden, it appears that the discrimination argu-

---

* In *The Death Penalty in America* (New York: Doubleday, 1967), Hugo
Adam Bedau—a fervent abolitionist—found that altogether eight (out of 7,000)
men executed in the U.S. in the 20th century were innocent. He adds (*Federal
Probation*, 35, June 1971) "that it is foolish sentimentality to argue the death
penalty should be abolished because . . . an innocent person may be executed when the record fails to disclose that such cases occur."

† See Chapter IX.

‡ In *Furman* v. *Georgia*, the Supreme Court decided against the death
penalty mainly on this ground.

ment is used to screen objections to the death penalty that do not depend on that argument. At any rate, objections to unwarranted discrimination are relevant to the discriminatory distribution of penalties, not to the penalties distributed. Penalties themselves are not inherently discriminatory; distribution, the process which selects the persons who suffer the penalty, can be. Unjust distribution—either through unjust convictions or through unjust (unequal and biased) penalization of equally guilty convicts—can occur with respect to any penalty. The vice must be corrected by correcting the distributive process that produces it. There is no reason to limit such a correction to any specific penalty. Nor can much be accomplished by abolishing any penalty, since all penalties can be meted out discriminatorily. The defect to be corrected is in the courts.

Crimes of Passion

It is claimed frequently that the death penalty is unlikely to add deterrence because most capital offenses are crimes of passion not easily deterred by any legal threat. Crimes of passion can be roughly defined as assaultive crimes among persons acquainted with each other (although such crimes are not always caused by "passion": one may dispassionately and with premeditation kill one's wife for the sake of her money.) Although many are "crimes of passion," other types of capital crimes are associated with robberies or power struggles among gangsters, or caused by politics, resistance to arrest, drugs, arson, kidnappings, etc. Abolitionists who rest their case on "crimes of passion" would be more logical if they urged that the death penalty be abolished only for these crimes. They would run into an open door since death hardly ever is demanded for crimes of passion in the U.S.

The contention that crimes of passion are not deterred by

threats is plausible. But there are many difficulties with it. Are all crimes of passion not deterrable? If they were merely less easily deterred, more severe threats of punishment might deter where milder ones have not. This would actually argue in favor of the death penalty. If, however, they are altogether nondeterrable, should crimes of passion not be punished at all? Would that not so outrage the sense of justice as to lead to crimes of revenge by the injured—which also would be crimes of passion? Would non-punishment (or mild punishment) not then encourage endless "crimes of passion"? At any rate, it seems too sweeping to say that all, rather than some, "crimes of passion" are nondeterrable. "Passion" is not a distinct homogeneous quality characterized by nondeterrability. There are degrees and the borderlines are blurred. "Passion" and "non-passion" are continuous, not wholly separate, qualities. Crimes of passion rise as punishment declines and decline when punishment rises.* At least some are deterrable.

Finally, if it were granted that they are not deterrable as a rule, the fact that among capital crimes the proportion of "crimes of passion" is high would not indicate that the threat of death is futile. On the contrary, it would indicate that the threat has deterred the crimes that can be deterred, leaving only the "crimes of passion," which cannot be. Success in deterring all but the least deterrable murders does not argue for abolition of the death penalty.

The murder rate in the U.S.—always a multiple of that in Western Europe and Japan—has risen terrifyingly in the last decades. Most ominous, a greater proportion of murders now involve political motives, robberies, and assaults in which the victim and the murderer do not know each other. One explanation is that in the past, the death penalty restrained all but the most impassioned. Its practical disappearance reduced that restraint. Thus, in the 1960s the victim and the murderer

---

* That severity and certainty of punishment influences the homicide rate, as it does, (see the study by Gray and Martin, Chap. XIII) is inconsistent with the theory that "passion" is not deterrable at all and/or that murder is mainly a crime of passion.

were acquainted with each other in about 80 percent of all cases in New York. By 1974 the "stranger murder rate" had increased to 34 percent of all cases.[93]

Beccaria on Brutalization and Comparative Deterrence

Cesare di Beccaria was perhaps the first to contend that the death penalty brutalizes the community: "The death penalty cannot be useful because of the example of barbarity it gives to men . . . it seems to me absurd that the laws . . . which . . . punish homicide should themselves commit it." [94] Beccaria presented no evidence for the exemplary nature of the barbarity of execution. Moralists of a different persuasion might claim that failure to punish murder by execution is barbarous and brutalizes the community. The Romans thought that *homo homini res sacra* ("man should be a sacred thing to man")—but for this very reason they unflinchingly executed murderers.

Beccaria's view that by imposing the death penalty the law commits "homicide" or, as others have it, "legalized murder" rests on a confusion (unless it is simply a more emphatic way of expressing disapproval). When an offender is legally arrested and imprisoned, we do not speak of "legalized kidnapping." Arrest and kidnapping may be physically undistinguishable. But legal punishment need not differ physically from crime. Punishment differs because it has social sanction and a legitimate purpose. In capital crimes the law may inflict as punishment on the criminal the same physical act that constituted his crime: we deprive him of his life as he did his victim. In other cases we deprive him of freedom, or money, as he might have his victim. If it were "absurd," as Beccaria thought, to punish homicide with execution—to do as a punishment to the criminal what he did to his victim—it would be

equally absurd to fine an embezzler or to deprive of freedom a
man who deprived others of freedom. Not the physical act but
the social meaning of it distinguishes robbery from taxation,
murder from execution, a gift from a theft.

Beccaria also rejected the death penalty because he thought
it less deterrent than life imprisonment.

It is not the intenseness of the pain that has the greatest effect on the
mind, but its continuance. . . . The death of a criminal is a terrible
but momentary spectacle and therefore a less efficacious method of
deterring others. Perpetual slavery . . . has in it all that is necessary
to deter the most hardened and determined, as much as the punishment of death. I say it has more. There are many who can look upon
death with intrepidity and firmness; some through fanaticism, and
others through vanity . . . others from a desperate resolution to get
rid of their misery, or to cease to live; but fanaticism and vanity fore-
sake the criminal in slavery, in chains and fetters, in an iron cage; and
despair seems rather the beginning than the end of their misery.[95]

Beccaria's contention here disregards the brutalization that
surely inheres as much in "perpetual slavery" as in death.*
Whether or not imprisonment is actually more deterrent than
death can be decided ultimately only by the kind of factual
knowledge that has been presented already. Yet, although
Beccaria's argument does not lack persuasiveness, intuitively
one feels that the fear of irrevocability (see Chap. XVIII) will
have a greater deterrent effect than the fear of "perpetual slavery." At any rate, Beccaria's alternative to the death penalty is
not really available now. It is most unlikely that we would
keep "the criminal . . . in chains and fetters, in an iron cage
. . . in perpetual slavery." As a sentence, "life" today means
not life but some years of it. And during his imprisonment the
convict, far from being kept in fetters, is entertained by TV
and social workers and may have sufficient freedom to commit
additional crimes. We feel that once we keep a person alive,
we owe him humane treatment. Compared to the actual alternative, Beccaria might now regard the death penalty as more
deterrent.

* See also Barzun *op. cit.*, pp. 207–208.

The "Sanctity of Life"

Some opponents of capital punishment claim that it is inconsistent with "the sanctity of life." It is not easy to see what "sanctity" could mean outside of its religious context other than the assertion, disguised as proof, that it is wrong to put criminals to death.* To punish is to deprive people of a good, to inflict an evil in proportion to the crime. If life is the highest of goods, death must be the greatest of punishments and, therefore, appropriate for the taking of life. Liberty is second only to life and, indeed, sacred to many people. We do deprive offenders of it as a punishment. To be wrong, the death penalty would have to exceed some natural proportion, or limit, beyond which we cannot, or should not, go. Unless one resorts to a religiously or, in some other way, revealed source, one cannot show that society, unlike the murderer, must hold life unconditionally inviolate; and the fact that the nonreligious urge it so religiously cannot commend this precept to believers. The death penalty has been part of all major religious traditions: Graeco-Roman, Judaic, Islamic, and Christian.†

Cruel and Unusual?

Cruel

When the Eighth Amendment to the Constitution prohibited "cruel and unusual punishment," the death penalty was not unusual or regarded as cruel in any prohibited sense. Has it become so since? The Supreme Court (in *Furman* v. *Georgia*, 1973) left this matter open.

---

* Oddly enough, persons who feel that the life of murderers is sacred sometimes do not object to euthanasia for others.

† Sometimes the high cost of imposing the death penalty—the many courts involved—is used as an argument against it. Yet life imprisonment usually costs more: the "lifer" can keep even more courts busy considering ever new arguments for release than the prisoner on death row.

"Cruel" may have several meanings. It may be a moral evaluation by the court. In *Furman* the Supreme Court neither
claims to have made a moral discovery—that the death penalty
is cruel—nor suggests a basis for such a discovery, which
would supersede previously held moral ideas. At times, some
of the justices seem to imply something of the sort; but none
asserts it explicitly.

"Cruel" may refer also to the acceptance by the community
of a new moral norm violated by the death penalty. If that
were the reason for abolishing the death penalty, it should be
abolished by the political process rather than by a judicial one.
The Supreme Court is not elected or meant to legislate
changes it detects in public opinion. Legislatures may do so.
This version of "cruel" does not seem to be the basis for the
court's decision, although there are some *obiter scripta* in that
direction. As ascertained by polls, and in some states by refer-
endum, majority opinion does not regard the death penalty as
"cruel" and favors its retention. Educated opinion is more
often abolitionist. This may reflect greater wisdom, or perhaps
the fact that the higher socioeconomic groups suffer violence
less frequently, or, finally, that these groups have suffered in-
doctrination in college courses more frequently.*

"Cruel" may also mean onerous punishment. But punishment is defined as legal infliction of suffering. "Cruel" punishment, then, must be understood to be irrational punishment inasmuch as the evil inflicted does not, or cannot,
achieve its rational objective, or exceeds what is needed to
achieve it. This idea played a role in some of the opinions in
Furman. The justices who held this view regard general deterrence as the rational purpose not achieved by the death
penalty to such an extent as to justify it. However, the statistics
presented in some of the opinions to show as much have been
refuted by recent work.† Anyway, the reasoning proves too

---

* The Marvin Field poll found that 49 percent of all Californians favored
the death penalty in 1956, and 74 percent in 1975 (*New York Times*, March 26,
1975).
  † See Chapters XIII and XVIII.

much. It would authorize abolition of any penalty that does not demonstrably deter. On the other hand, any penalty that does might be constitutional. Chances are that "cruel" is best interpreted to mean excessive and morally wrong. If this is the interpretation, no reason is given why we should hold the death penalty to be cruel, or that the Framers did or might do so today.

Unusual

"Unusual" may mean infrequent or unfamiliar.* But in the Eighth Amendment "unusual" seems to mean "capricious," i.e., not guided by known rational rules which permit prediction. In *Furman* the court found that the death penalty is imposed capriciously in Georgia, perhaps discriminatorily and inequitably, and therefore unconstitutionally. Since many state laws leave as wide discretion to judges or juries on whether or not to impose the death penalty as the law does in Georgia, the decision invalidated these laws. By 1975, nearly thirty-two states had fashioned new statutes making the death penalty mandatory for some crimes.† They expect these laws to be found constitutionally valid. Unfortunately, at least some are drawn so inexpertly as to raise doubts.‡

The court's reasoning raises an interesting question: when is judicial discretion not capricious? Modern practice often gives wide discretion to judges to impose short, lengthy, or indefinite prison terms; standards for the use of this discretion hardly exist. Usually, this discretion is justified by rehabilitative aims which require that punishment be adapted to the individuality of the offender and to his progress rather than meted out according to a tariff for crimes. (Judges, in turn, often give wide discretion to parole boards.)

* The death penalty has become unusual in this sense by the recent action of the courts. They cannot use their own action as its justification.

† I think it beyond the scope of this work to specifically suggest what crimes should be punished by death. It need be said, however, that death being the ultimate penalty, it should be inflicted only for the gravest crimes, in their most aggravated form, e.g., not for rape, but for rape-murder.

‡ See Charles L. Black, Jr., *Capital Punishment* for an analysis of the new Georgia and Texas laws.

If imposing the death penalty according to the judge's or jury's view of the prospects for rehabilitation gives too much discretion and too little guidance, can the same not be said about prison sentences when their length is determined not by law but by the sentencing judge or by parole authorities? Conceivably, such sentences also may be held to violate the "cruel and unusual" clause of the Constitution, unless replaced by mandatory sentences within a narrow range. Everything that can be said about possible capriciousness in applying the death penalty can be said about imprisonment as well; and it would be as true. Thus, the *Furman* decision consistently applied may mean a return to punishments fixed by law with very little discretion given to judges. The crime rather than the criminal's "needs" would determine the punishment. Perhaps, then, the *Furman* decision will reestablish punishment according to law.

XX

Fines

In the U.S. fines are usually regarded as unjust and ineffective. They are widely used, but mainly as penalties for what are thought trifling or at least not odious offenses: parking violations, noise, littering, traffic violations, etc. Or fines are imposed for financial offenses—a remote echo of the *lex talionis*. For more serious offenses, fines are imposed at most as adjuncts to imprisonment. A mere fine for a vicious crime, a *malum in se*, is felt to be incompatible with the dignity of the law; the punishment might taint justice with "materialism." It also would appear to punish heinous crimes with a trifling sanction, as fines are thought to be.

In contrast, some European countries, particularly Holland and some Scandinavian countries, recently have begun to impose fines for a wide range of serious offenses. They do not regard fines as less effective or less just than prison terms. Effects of this innovation are as yet not clear enough to reach definitive conclusions.* But a theoretical analysis of fines as an instrument of penal justice seems in order, and may be helpful if we are looking for alternatives to imprisonment. For prison sentences are increasingly unpopular with the judi-

* In a sense, this innovation goes back to quite early ages when even murderers paid restitution money and what we would call punitive fines to the family of the victim if that family consented not to retaliate.

ciary and are generally regarded as unhelpful, as more evil than necessary.

Objections

In the U.S. most fines are set by statute (or precedent) as an outright sum of money or one to be determined by the judge within narrowly fixed limits. This is the source of the major objections to the effectiveness and to the equity of fines.

A fine sufficient to enforce the law at one time can become insufficient later. It is practically impossible for legislation to keep up with rises in the price level; therefore, as the value of money declines through inflation, most fines become ineffective. Thus, fines levied against landlords, or prostitutes, or parking offenders, often become a negligible part of the cost of doing business. Because their ineffectiveness is known, police are not eager—or successful—in enforcing fines or initiating proceedings that lead to them.

As now imposed, fines are strikingly inequitable. The same fine (the same of money) is imposed for the same offense. Rich offenders are punished by paying what to them is a trifle; poor offenders pay the same fine but bear a much heavier burden. When the alternative is to go to jail or to pay a fine, the poor often have to go to jail, whereas the rich pay easily. Wherefore, fines are regarded as outrageously unjust.*

Since the rich find it easy to pay them, fines that may deter the poor will not restrain the rich from wrongdoing. The rich thus have a privilege.

License Fees?

What seems unjust when fines are regarded as penal sanctions may be justified when they are regarded as license fees—i.e., if the acts for which fines are currently imposed are not de-

* These objections were already noted by Jeremy Bentham, (*Theory of Legislation*, Chapter IX).

fined as crimes. As a penal sanction, a parking fine of $25 imposed equally on a person in a high and another in a low income bracket is unjust. But as a rental or license fee for an hour's parking, $25 may be all right. There is no objection to giving parking priority to those willing or able to pay the price. The point of having money (and the incentive for making it) is to be able to do, or get, what money can buy. Wealthy persons can rent apartments or parking spaces less wealthy persons cannot afford. But, although the fine for a parking violation might be regarded as a rental fee, society certainly does not intend to license murder, or even theft. Hence punishments for these offenses, which must always be defined as crimes, never can be regarded as licenses. These punishments must be severe enough to deter, yet equitable enough to be accepted as just. As presently imposed, fines do not meet these tests.*

Bail

Lest the argument based on inequity be misapplied, it should be noted that it cannot be extended to bail. For, in the first place, judges can, if they wish, omit bail or adapt it to the wealth or income of the defendant as well as to the gravity of the crime. Presently they can do this with fines only within much narrower limits. Bail, to be sure, is inequitable. A poor and friendless defendant may be detained until his case is decided, whereas a rich one can bail himself out. Even if later

---

* Gary Becker (in *Essays On the Economics of Crime and Punishment,* ([New York: Nat'l Bureau of Economic Research, 1974], p. 29) ably argues for a fine equal to the harm done by the offense. In his view, the fine should always be the price of the offense and should not depend on the offender's income. Rich and poor would pay the same price, as they do now for a car. This view disregards the retributive function of punishment and, though ingenious, seems unpersuasive: societies, since Aristotle, have distinguished penal from cummutative (exchange) justice. Fines must be prohibitive for all rational people when the crime is at all serious; they must therefore be proportioned to the offender's income, as well as to the harm done.

found innocent, the poor suspect may have to spend months or even years in jail while the rich man does not. Yet this inequity can be avoided only by a greater injustice. There may be no other way than detention to guarantee the appearance in court of a poor defendant unable to furnish bail.* Now, wealthy defendants able to post bail also could be detained for trial, as is done in most of continental Europe. Equality could be achieved this way, but not justice. We would throw out an advantage simply because it cannot benefit everybody equally. Yet the only real alternative to bail for those who might not otherwise appear in court is pre-trial detention for all. It seems better, then, to free at least those whose appearance in court can be secured by bail than to detain all suspects.†

Fines of Income Days

Whereas bail necessarily produces unequal burdens, fines need not. They can be imposed so as to be as nearly equal, equitable, and just as punitive imprisonment is.

Objections to fines cannot be eliminated altogether. But

* The Vera Institute of Justice and the Bail Revaluation Program of the Department of Corrections have demonstrated in New York that bail is not needed for many poor defendants who are unlikely to flee because they are well-rooted in the community. Some New York judges have gone overboard with the notion. Unwittingly, they have demonstrated that bail is needed when the defendant's penal record, or insufficient community roots, or chances of being severely punished, make voluntary appearance much less than certain.

† The disadvantage of permitting those set free to commit crimes while out can be remedied by appropriate selectivity rather than by either detaining or freeing everyone who has been indicted. (The law would have to be changed to permit selectivity based on dangerousness.) William M. Landes, in "The Bail System: An Economic Approach" (see *Essays on the Economy of Crime and Punishment* [New York: National Bureau of Economic Research, 1974]), has worked out an alternative bail system in which detained suspects would be paid for the time spent in detention if found innocent, and credited with it if found guilty. It is an intriguing idea.

they would lose their sting if all fines were imposed not as sums of money but as days of income (from all sources). A fine of five days' income may amount to $15,000 for one person and $100 for another. But the fine would be equal: five income days in both cases. The burden for the two offenders would be equal.* (Poor persons also might be allowed to pay fines in installments.) Were they fined the same sum of money—say, $500—the burden would be much less equal. Imposition of the same number of "income days" for the same offense would make fines as equitable as prison sentences. Rich and poor alike would be deprived of the same number of days of freedom, or of income, for the same offense. Since they would be no less equitable, fines could replace prison sentences—if they are as effective. Unless the convict must be incapacitated to protect the community, a fine could replace any term of imprisonment. The retributive, deterrent, and rehabilitative aims of punishment might be attained as well, or better, by fines. How, then, can fines be utilized?

Stigmatization

Tradition makes fines less stigmatizing than imprisonment. Since stigmatization is an emotional as much as a rational matter, that tradition might not change readily. Anyone who has been burglarized, raped, or assaulted, or whose brother has been murdered, will be infuriated to find the guilty party set free upon conviction. He will not feel that a fine is a sufficiently serious penalty. And if it is believed to be trivial, a fine becomes psychologically trivial, a less stigmatizing penalty than imprisonment. The branding effect of any punishment depends, after all, on the significance people give to it. If it is desired, then, to help stigmatize a crime as odious through

* Not altogether of course: the same deprivation never burdens two persons equally.

its punishment, it still might be necessary to imprison offenders even when they need not be incapacitated. However, after one to two years in prison, the convict could be allowed to serve his punishment outside, by surrendering to the authorities most of his income above the minimum he needs to live. It is unlikely that additional prison years would add much to the stigma of the punishment. Thus, even a life sentence might be served by depriving the convict of most of his income after he has served, say, two years of prison.*

Advantages

Imprisonment is still necessary when a need for incapacitation is felt. But in many cases incapacitation is not needed. And reform normally fails in prison. Criminalization is as likely as reform, for the prisoner becomes part of a community that approves antisocial behavior—directed against society at large—and forms his loyalty to illegitimate ways of life. Outside prison, reform is more likely, criminalization less. A person allowed to live a normal life, even if deprived of most of his income, is more easily rehabilitated than one kept with other convicts in a situation in which antisocial resentment is communally cultivated and no models for fruitful and legitimate activities are available. Unlike prison sentences, fines do not disrupt the occupational career of the convict nor his ties to his family and other affectional ties. Unlike prison sentences, fines do not leave him to draw all his emotional support from fellow convicts. On the contrary, fines require the convict to pursue an occupational career and can be used to give him an incentive to do so.† His ties to legitimate ways of life are

---

* Incidentally, offenders would not profit financially—by publishing their memoirs or lecturing—from the notoriety their offenses brought them if their punishment were a fine proportioned to their income.

† Evidence to support, or refute, the reformative effect of fines over imprisonment is presently lacking. The advantages of fines over imprisonment do not depend on it.

strenghtened. Furthermore, the enormous monetary expense of keeping a person in prison is avoided. Instead, the fines exacted should more than pay for all the expenses connected with extracting them.

There is no reason, then, why even major crimes, such as assault, robbery, or some kinds of homicide, should not be punished by fines—provided that fines are fashioned into serious punishments and dissociated from the trifling amounts imposed for trifling crimes. A man who previously would have received a life sentence and might have been paroled after about seven years is not necessarily less punished if he spends, say, fourteen months in prison and is otherwise punished by a fine of, say, seven years' earnings. The convict might pay over a longer period by paying a high percentage of his income as long as needed to cover seven years' earnings. His "earnings" may be calculated by considering his actual earnings in peak years. Or, if the convict has not earned a regular legitimate income before his conviction, his earning capacity may be calculated by considering the earnings achieved by others with his skills, and so forth. Either way, a monetary punishment can be made just as punitive as a prison sentence.

Confiscation

A penalty related but not identical to fines that has fallen into disuse is confiscation. Confiscation deprives the convict of all or a portion of his wealth, and may be imposed in conjunction with fines. It seems odd that at the present time we are willing to deprive a criminal of his freedom—even of his life—but not of his wealth. Confiscation, although it may be imposed on rich and poor alike, would be effective only with wealthy persons. Dependents may suffer. But they would suffer also from a breadwinner's business loss. There is no reason why they should suffer less from his crime. Partial confiscation may also

be needed to punish a wealthy convict who has a low legitimate income and as a matter of equity between two convicts
who pay the same fine, based on the same crime and on the
same income when one is wealthy and the other is not.

A fine may be paid either out of wealth or out of income. A
wealthy person may pay a fine of, say, six months' income out
of his wealth, whereas a poor one may have to hand over the
fruits of his work. He would bear a burden the wealthy convict
would have been spared. To avoid this inequity, a fine stated
as a percentage of property owned might be added to the fine
stated in income days. It would be effective with wealthy convicts and nugatory with poor ones.

Restitution

Another advantage of fines is that they do not preclude payment of restitution as prison sentences do in practice. Restitution is owed whenever a loss was suffered. The relatives of a
victim of murder are entitled to it no less than the victims of a
burglary. The amount of restitution can be determined by procedures now used to determine what is owed the victim of accidents by the party responsible for damages or injuries. The
amount should be independent of the offender's ability to pay
and dependent on the financial loss suffered. However, ability
to pay should determine the rate of payment. Restitution has
been neglected in modern times mainly because imprisonment prevented it. This obstacle would be removed when
fines take the place of prison.

Proof of Loss

Whenever the amount of restitution is to exceed the maximum
fixed for petit larceny, the burden of proving the loss, damage,
or injury should fall on those who claim to have suffered it.

Restitution should equal the demonstrated loss. However, a victim of crime should not be asked to prove the loss suffered if the amount claimed is below the amount fixed for petit larceny. Restitution should be automatic if the loss claimed seems probable to the court.*

Costs

Anyone convicted of a crime should bear the costs of his defense. If he is unable to do so while on trial, the cost should be added to what he owes as restitution. Anyone not convicted should be entitled to reimbursement of the costs of his legal defense. For this purpose the costs of legal defense should be determined by a fee schedule.

Punitive Fines

The issue of restitution should not obscure the punitive uses of fines. Fines are quite separate from restitution and are to be levied independently. Restitution compensates victims. Fines are the punishment imposed by society to vindicate its laws. Restitution depends on the loss suffered. In contrast, the fine depends on the gravity of the crime which determines the punishment: the income days, or years, or the proportion of his wealth the convict is to be deprived of. The fine having been determined, the rate at which income (or wealth) is to be taken from the convict depends on the following considerations.

1. No convict should be deprived of all the income he earns or is capable of earning above the minimum he needs to live. When his income increases, he should retain a greater sum

---

* The amount of restitution should be fixed during penal proceedings, as is done in France (Articles 2–10 of the French Code of Criminal Procedure).

than when it does not. The added amount he retains should suffice to give him a strong incentive to earn more to maximize his earnings, even though a major part, at least temporarily, does not go to him. This will facilitate enforcement.

2. When the fine is stated in days or years of earnings, or as a percentage of what is, or could be, earned, the convict might keep his earnings temporarily low, or postpone them until the fine is paid. There is probably no way to prevent this altogether. But any minimization of the fine the convict attempts by minimizing, postponing, or hiding his earnings can in turn by minimized. The court may state the fine as a percentage of earnings beyond a minimum over a period of time, or as a number of days' total actual earnings (paid in installments). But courts also may calculate the convict's potential income on the basis of either his past earnings or of average earnings of persons in his occupation. The daily amount of the fine might be no less than the appropriate earnings based on theoretical earning capacity, whether or not the convict chooses to use it or alleges he has not or cannot. This kind of calculation also will be essential with convicts who before conviction had no record of earnings from legitimate sources. Attempts to hide property may be counteracted in similar ways.

3. Since the offender needs a minimum income to maintain himself, all calculations of rates of payment must be applied to his net income, after deduction of maintenance, after taxes, and after deduction of restitution payments. Despite its disadvantages, imprisonment must be retained as a means of enforcing fines on those who display unwillingness to earn or pay. A man sentenced to seven years income may chose to earn less than he could or to hide his earnings. He will be dissuaded from attempting this if he realizes that the alternative to earning and paying in good faith is to spend the time in question imprisoned.*

* Fines should be reduced if payments occur in advance of schedule to give an incentive to make them. (They can ultimately be forgiven if the convict's payments and behavior make this advisable.) There is no reason not to apply parole or probation to fines as is done to imprisonment.

4. The convict should remain under court supervision as long as he has not paid his fine in full. Attempts to hide earnings or property unlawfully should be an offense punished by prison sentences.

5. There remains the formidable problem of convicts unable to earn enough to provide their own minimum living expenses, let alone pay a fine. Many of these are presently on welfare. If, because of their miserable condition, they were let off without punishment when convicted of an offense, they would be, licensed, in effect, to commit crimes with impunity. Since they are unable to earn enough to pay a fine, they will be unable to benefit from this option. Thus, if convicted of a crime, they will have to be imprisoned. However, it may be that while in prison their earning capacity increases, whether because of the acquisition of new skills or because of changes in motivation. (It also may be that the threat of imprisonment will increase earning capacity.) Therefore prison sentences should be transformable into fines, each prison day becoming equivalent to a day's earnings, calculated by the criteria suggested before; the rate of payment should be set according to ability to pay.

6. People able and willing to earn enough money to pay their fines but unable to find a job that would permit them to do so should be hired by public institutions as employers of last resort. The alternative would be prison, certainly more costly and less helpful.

7. When a fine is imposed, the offender must agree in writing to the terms of the sentence and be made aware that imprisonment is the alternative to meeting them.

It would not be fruitful to anticipate all the problems that will arise. A system of fines is likely to generate problems that can be solved more or less well but are not easily foreseen, just as a system of taxation does. Some inequity, some excessive harshness, and some excessive mildness will occur. Yet, whenever incapacitation is not imperative, a system of fines seems immensely preferable to imprisonment.

Incapacitation

Fines and the stigmatizing prison term (if needed) should be determined by statute, as prison terms are now although in more determinate ways. But the law cannot and should not always decide whether a particular offender must be imprisoned or fined. However, judicial discretion in making this decision should be limited so that days or years of imprisonment should be neither fewer nor more than the income days of which the fine would have consisted had it been imposed. The need for punitive and non-punitive incapacitation should be determined in ways to be discussed in the following chapter.

XXI

Who Should Be Imprisoned?

Obviously, only the guilty can be sent to prison, but who among them? There are three groups:

1. Those whose crime must be branded as odious in the public eye beyond what anything short of imprisonment could accomplish. But unless they are dangerous, these convicts should be kept in prison only as long as is needed to stigmatize their offenses. After, say, two years they might be released and subjected to fines. In such cases, the sentence may stipulate both the term of imprisonment and the fine.
2. Convicts originally sentenced to fines who willfully fail to meet the obligations imposed on them.
3. Offenders who must be incapacitated because they are dangerous to the community. These, in turn, fall into three groups:
   a. Those whose punitive prison terms, deserved by their offenses, coincide with the period over which they are deemed dangerous (e.g., dangerous offenders sentenced to life or near life terms). This is no problem—the sentence automatically sets both the prison and the (coterminous) incapacitation period.*
   b. Those who because of developments such as age or irreversible disease cease to be dangerous while still in prison. The remainder of their prison term might be indefinitely sus-

---

* However, I doubt that lifelong incapacitation is ever needed. Offenders grow less dangerous as they grow older. Few are dangerous after age forty, hardly any after age sixty.

pended or converted into a fine, each prison day being equivalent to an income day. Release would be decided on during the prison term by an appropriate authority.

c. Those who continue to be too dangerous to the community to be released after serving the punishment deserved by their offense. They constitute the real problem to which we must turn now. The original sentence could do no more than transfer the decision on post-punishment incapacitation to an appropriate authority.* At present, this decision is made by parole boards within limits set by the sentencing judge. This has proved unsatisfactory both in protecting the community and in protecting offenders from capricious judgments.

In the past, when deciding on a prison term, one of the purposes judges or parole boards had in mind was to incapacitate the convict until he would be likely to be law-abiding. This seems common sense. Why release someone who is still dangerous to the community? The danger is real enough, according to the *Wall Street Journal* (Jan. 16, 1975):

Los Angeles police officials say that slightly more than half of all those convicted of robbery and burglary in the first six months of 1973 had been free on parole or probation for earlier crimes. Philadelphia police recently asserted that almost half of all crimes reported in that city are being committed by persons who are on bail, probation, or parole for previous arrests. Two-thirds of all crime nationwide is estimated to be committed by repeaters. Yet . . . despite a crime rate that more than doubled between 1960 and 1972, there were fewer prison inmates at the end of that 12-year span than at the beginning." †

Incapacitation and Punishment

Although persuasive, the argument for keeping an offender in prison because he is still dangerous leaves one uneasy. Can we keep a man in prison solely because we think he will com-

* Those who commit new crimes while paying a fine for previous ones, and are thereupon held to be in need of incapacitation, constitute an analogous problem, which does not require separate treatment here.

† The *Journal* adds: ". . . Criminals are being released because of the assumption that crime is largely a reflection of underlying social and economic problems . . . it is a rare criminal who is imprisoned for any length of time."

mit crimes again if released? If punishment is to be given only for what is deserved by what the convict has done in the past, how can he be punished for what is feared of him, for what he may do in the future? We cannot punish offenders just to protect society from anticipated danger. "Punishment" refers only to what is deserved for a crime already committed. Nobody can be punished for being dangerous or inclined to violence. Character—a set of dispositions to act—cannot be punished; only acts can be.

Must we then let offenders go after they have served their time, even when we foresee danger? If justice were our only aim, we could do nothing else: *fiat justitia pereat mundus.** But the preservation of society and the security and welfare of its members are legitimate political ends beyond justice.† It is for the sake of the security or welfare of society, not of justice, that we quarantine persons with contagious diseases, or carriers thereof, and confine psychotics deemed dangerous to others, when they have not, or not as yet, harmed anyone. We do not punish, but nonetheless deprive, these persons of freedom, because they constitute an excessive hazard. And in war we imprison enemy aliens, though they have broken no law, simply because they imperil our country. Surely, then, once having punished offenders for their offenses, we may incapacitate them when we have reason to believe that they will unlawfully harm others if released and that the harm and the likelihood of it are great enough to outweigh the harm the preventive restriction on their freedom does to them.

But the precautions we must take to preclude recidivism must not be punitive. The dangerous offender whose future offenses are to be prevented by incapacitation cannot be punished for something he has not (yet) done. The West German penal code quite properly makes this distinction: offenders are punished according to desert; thereafter, if adjudged still dangerous, they are kept confined until no longer so.‡ The

* See Chapter IV.
† See Chapters IV and XVI.
‡ See also the Italian Penal Code on p. 38. My view here partially overlaps with that of jurists who advocate "social defense" as the guiding principle of

trouble with this "dual track" system is that the offender may find it hard to distinguish one track from the other, the punitive incarceration from the non-punitive incapacitation. To be sure, arrangements could be made to make the post-punishment incapacitation "measure" as non-punitive as possible. Thus, within the limites required to isolate him from society, the detained person may share his confinement with his family, or with anyone who volunteers. And there is no reason to deprive him of any reasonable amenities. Yet, though it can be minimized, the punitive effect of incapacitation cannot be removed altogether.

The incapacitated offender is *ipso facto* deprived of freedom—what could be more painful? Meeting this problem will be difficult at best. Let me deal with some prior ones: (1) What kind of danger should lead to incapacitation? (2) What authority is to make the decision on whether or not that danger is present? (3) On what basis is that authority to decide who among offenders is dangerous and for how long?

1. If one grants that we can discover it, the danger against which post-punitive confinement should protect society is above all violence. Offenders highly likely to engage in violent crimes upon release must be confined for the duration of that likelihood. (The likelihood often diminishes with age and other circumstances.) Anyone with a second conviction for an assaultive felony—such as robbery, rape, or assault—should be eligible for post-punishment confinement, particularly when there have been additional arrests. Even when non-assaultive offenses are involved, a case for preventive incapacitation can be made, although more stringent criteria of selection, such as additional convictions or arrests, should be used. Yet, when it is almost certain that they would continue their unlawful careers upon release, there is every reason to

---

criminal justice. However, unlike these jurists, I do not believe that the latter can be reduced to the former. For a contrary view, see Henry W. Seney, *Wayne Law Review* 17 (1971), 18 (1972), and 19 (1973).

prevent the habitual drug dealer, fence, car thief, et al., from resuming their careers after having served their punishment.

2. The judge who passes the original sentence also must decide if the punishment is to include prison. When, on the basis of the record, the judge passes a prison sentence for reasons including the possible danger to the community, the sentence should be brought to the attention of a different authority, which must decide on possible post-punishment confinement. Such confinement might be mandatory when there is no less than a 60 percent chance of recidivism by persons previously convicted of assaultive crimes; the probability might have to rise to 75 percent for non-assaultive felonies. But how do we know what the probability is?

Predicting Dangerousness

3. Predictions of dangerousness are hazardous. In 1966 the Supreme Court released 967 offenders held in New York psychiatric institutions beyond the term of their sentences because they were considered dangerous. (They had been confined without proper procedures.) * Researchers who followed the subsequent careers of these persons for four years found that only 2 percent were returned to institutions for the criminally insane; more than half were not readmitted to any institution.[96] However, the criteria by which these persons had been declared dangerous in the first place are questionable, and they had been held an average of thirteen years beyond their sentences. By then, probably many were too old

---

* *Baxstrom v. Herold* 383, U.S. 107 (1966). The case has no legal bearing on the post-punishment incapacitation discussed in the text, for we do not assume that the persons to be confined are sick; they are to be classified as dangerous on the basis of purely legal categories (e.g., previous convictions). No hearing on their individual personality characteristics is required, although a judicial decision on the legal factors bearing on incapacitation is needed in each case.

for violent crime, which is usually a young man's activity. Thus, the oft-quoted Baxstrom "test" of predicting dangerousness may be less than fair to our ability to predict.

Kozol et al. applied a procedure for predicting dangerousness to 435 high-risk incarcerated offenders; they compared the post-release careers of those they had judged dangerous with the careers of those they had judged harmless. Four times as many of the offenders termed dangerous committed violent crimes.[97] Obviously, if properly applied, predictive techniques can produce results significantly higher than chance. (Similar techniques can predict non-assaultive recidivism.) Yet not all of those classified as violent turned out to be, nor did all those predicted harmless turn out to be. It seems doubtful that human action will ever be *fully* predictable in practice.

The Categorical Method: Wolfgang's Study

How great a probability of dangerousness warrants incapacitation? The answer depends on balancing the impingement on the offender's post-punishment freedom against the danger to the community. I have suggested a provisional answer: we should keep an offender incapacitated when the probability of assaultive recidivism exceeds 60 percent, or when the probability of non-assaultive felonious recidivism exceeds 75 percent. But how do we predict or measure these probabilities? Two kinds of measurement are possible: categorical—dependent on the general categories into which the offender falls, such as the number of previous convictions and arrests, the type of crime, his age, sex, etc.—or individual—dependent on the individual's history, which produces something like a psychiatric profile. In principle, the two kinds of measurements do not differ; after all, a case history, explicitly or implicitly, has to be interpreted through theoretical categories that indicate the prognostic significance of the individual's behavior. And the behavior included in the case report is selected with a view to these theoretical categories. However, the categories used in case histories are often based on psychological theories, whereas those used for categorical prediction are based on statistical experience. Furthermore, the compilers of case histories may stress rehabilitation as much as the security of the community.

Above all, the two methods of prediction—case and categorical—differ greatly in practice. The case method maximizes individual judgment in two senses: The prognosis depends on the peculiarities of the individual and on interpretation by the individuals who study his case—i.e., on the idiosyncrasies of their (intuitive?) judgment criteria. The categorical method minimizes the influence of the peculiarities of the individual case and of the individuals who pass on it. The decision depends on our actual experience with the prognostic significance of such objective matters as age, previous convictions, etc. For this reason, the categorical method of prediction is much to be preferred. The results of categorical prediction should be modified by the peculiarities of the individual cases only when exceptionally weighty, and only to a limited degree.

Is the categorical method reliable enough to bear the burden of prediction? Paul Meehl finds "it difficult to come up with so much as one single well-designed research study in which the clinician's predictions are better than the statistical table or formula; in most studies, the clinician is significantly worse." [98] Consider another study. Marvin E. Wolfgang traced the involvement with the criminal justice system of "9,945 boys, all born . . . in 1945 who lived in Philadelphia at least from ages ten to eighteen. . . ." [99] More than one-third were picked up by the police for something other than traffic offenses, but half of those had no further contacts with the police. Specifically, Wolfgang found that "the probability of committing a first offense of any type is 0.3511. The likelihood of a second offense is 0.5358, the probability of a third is 0.6509. Beyond the third offense the likelihood of further offenses ranges from 0.70 to 0.80." In other words, the probability of committing further offenses increases with the offenses already committed, and becomes very high, almost a certainty, after the third offense. And the few boys—7 percent—who had committed five offenses before their eighteenth birthday, accounted for more than 50 percent of all offenses of the cohort and for two-thirds of all violent offenses committed by it. Often arrested, they were rarely deprived of freedom for any length of time. Not unexpectedly, Wolfgang found

The chances of becoming an adult offender are much higher for persons who had a delinquency record than for those who did not. The probability of being arrested between eighteen and twenty-six years of age, having had at least one arrest under age eighteen, is three-and-one-half times higher than the probability of being arrested as an adult, having had no record as a juvenile . . . the chances of recidivating from a juvenile to an adult status are higher than commencing an adult arrest record—at least up to age twenty-six.[100]

Wolfgang also observed that "the cumulative probabilities of ever being arrested rise much more rapidly and dramatically up to age seventeen than they do after that age." His data indicate that between ages twelve and seventeen the probability of at least one arrest increases by more than seven times. "However, this probability . . . climbs much more slowly after age seventeen and [is] by age twenty-six only one-and-one-half times as great" so that "the probability of ever being arrested, as well as of committing offenses generally, declines with age, beginning with the eighteenth year." [101]

Wolfgang's data indirectly question legislation that, in most states, provides for young offenders to be treated with leniency and for no public record-keeping of their arrests or convictions.* The legislation is based on the belief that young of-

* The *New York Times* (editorial, March 4, 1975) states: "It is dangerously unrealistic . . . to forbid the criminal justice system to keep records on juvenile offenders. The purpose of such records is not to stigmatize the youngsters but to prevent them from using their ages as a sanctuary from the law. It makes

fenders can be reformed more easily than older ones. Wolfgang's data indicate that such optimism is not supported by facts and becomes positively wrong after the third arrest of a juvenile. Legislation should be changed accordingly. After the age of thirteen, juveniles should be treated as adults for indictment, trial and sentencing purposes. Once they are in penal institutions or in confinement, they may be held separately and treated differently. But not to hold them responsible for their offenses or not to punish them is to license and encourage juveniles to commit offenses. To be sure, most juvenile offenders come from particularly trying backgrounds and home situations. However, there is no evidence that such home situations have become worse compared with what they were twenty years ago. Yet there are more offenders among juveniles. They are the product of the leniency of the law—of the privilege granted them—as much as of anything else.*

The available data tend to support what Wolfgang's study shows for the birth cohort he followed. Still, one must be wary of relying altogether on just one study, albeit a very solid one. It is possible that what is true for Philadelphia may not be quite as true for Los Angeles, or that what is true for the 1945 cohort may not be quite as true for a 1960 cohort, or that Wolfgang's result was affected by variables, some known— e.g., ethnic and economic composition of the cohort—and others not. With all these qualifications, the following conclusions seem reasonable enough to permit categorical predictions:

1. The more offenses a young person commits, the greater the risk of further offenses while still a juvenile. After the third offense he is almost certain to commit other offenses.

---

no sense to deprive the courts of the option to separate from society truly dangerous juvenile criminals until such time as they can safely be released. There need be no contradiction between the protection of public safety and compassion for troubled youths."

* The increase in the proportion of one-parent families—fostered largely by the welfare system—probably contributes something to juvenile delinquency.

2. The chances of becoming an adult offender are much greater—three-and-one-half times greater—for a person who was a juvenile offender than for a person who was not.
3. The chances of committing offenses climb fastest before age seventeen and much more slowly thereafter; the frequency of committing offenses reaches a plateau by age twenty-six.

Although uneasy about the justice of post-punishment confinement, I believe the protection of society must have priority over the freedom and the comfort of offenders. It is better to confine an offender, even after he has served his punishment, than to let more harm come to innocent victims, as long as there is good reason to believe that he still is dangerous. An offender found to be still dangerous who actually is not is in the same unfortunate situation as a suspect found guilty who actually is not. We must do our utmost to minimize these cases, short of failing to punish the guilty and not confining the dangerous.

Post-Punishment Incapacitation and the Crime Rate

Would post-punishment confinement really reduce the crime rate? In Chapter V it was pointed out that if a crime is attractive to offenders for rational reasons, if it is profitable, the incapacitated offender is likely to be replaced by others. Incapacitation *per se*, then, would not reduce the crime rate, even though it reduces the number of crimes that the incapacitated offender can commit. Why then confine dangerous offenders after punishment?

In some respects criminal conduct may be likened to gambling.* If the odds were better, more people would gamble; if the odds were worse, fewer people would. The best way to reduce the rate of gambling is to worsen the odds, to increase

---

* The reverse comparison does not follow, although it helps explain why some people abhor gambling as though a crime.

the cost of gambling, and to reduce the net benefit. People who gamble casually, or rationally for the sake of actual net benefits, will stop once they get burned and can see that the odds are loaded against them. That takes care of most people. But some persons will continue to gamble however unfavorable the odds are. They have become addicted enough to continue gambling, however irrational it has become. Now, if the odds are already sufficiently unfavorable so that most people, most of the time, avoid gambling, the total rate of gambling would be reduced greatly if these addicts were incapacitated. (On the other hand, as long as the odds remain favorable, it helps little to incapacitate the addicted gamblers.)

Mugging, robbing, raping, assaulting, burglary, and car theft have their addicts who will continue however much the deck is stacked against them. It is most important to rig the odds so that most would-be offenders are deterred. (As much as possible, it also is important to make legitimate opportunities available.) Yet even if relatively few (perhaps irrational) persons are addicted to these offenses so that they will continue to commit them despite harsh and certain punishment, these few can and do account for a disproportionate number of the offenses committed. Given unfavorable cost-benefit ratios, incapacitating these few, then, would greatly reduce the number of offenses. Hence, post-punishment confinement of very likely recidivists is a necessary measure of social defense. More than half of all serious crimes now are committed by a relatively small group of recidivists. They can be identified and their activities predicted with a high degree of probability. A good case for post-punishment incapacitation can be made then. I have deliberately not tried to specify all the criteria for post-punishment confinement, beyond suggesting who should be incapacitated on what basis, for I wish to suggest a legislative principle rather than actual legislation, which would require much more elaboration than is suitable here.

XXII

A Note on Confinement and the Operation of Prisons

The substitution of fines for prison terms has already been suggested, as have other reforms. Now I shall sketch—in no more detail than is needed to betoken feasibility—recommendations for new—or reestablished—measures such as banishment or exile, and for the operation and supervision of all court-ordered forms of confinement. My proposals imply a far less radical departure from existing institutions than prisons themselves were when, in 1790, a "penitentiary" was first established in Philadelphia; and they rest on far more realistic beliefs than the widespread use of probation and parole to which we have become inured in the last thirty years; finally, they are less utopian by a long stretch than Federal District Judge James E. Doyle's oft-quoted *obiter scriptum:* ". . . the institution of prison probably must end . . . it is as intolerable . . . as was the institution of slavery." *
Prisons cannot "end" because nothing else is in sight to pro-

* *Morales* v. *Schmidt,* 1972 (W.D. Wisconsin). His decision was reversed on appeal by the 7th District, 1973.

tect the community from offenders who are too dangerous to be let loose. Yet many offenders can be punished, or incapacitated, by as effective and less gruesome means; and prisons can become somewhat more humane and functional.

Types of Confinement

Offenders ought to be incarcerated only when their offenses have to be stigmatized as shameful, or when they are so dangerous that they have to be fully incapacitated while being punished, or, as a last resort, when they fail to obey prior court orders. Otherwise, fines, or other non-confining sanctions, are always preferable.

In some cases, incapacitation may be necessary not only during but even after punishment. If offenders are still too dangerous to be let back into the community after serving their punitive prison terms, they should be confined in non-penal institutions (to be discussed anon). But for some offenders, whose continued criminal careers depend on the resources of cities, banishment from metropolitan areas might do and should be preferred. In other cases, exile to a specific place may be necessary. Such post-punishment measures should be imposed for determinate periods of time, based on categorical criteria of prediction. People do not remain equally dangerous as they grow older.

Banishment and exile sound startling to contemporary American ears, too reminiscent of emperors and czars, of olden times and retrograde social orders. But if we clear our minds of historical associations and prejudices, I believe it will become evident that banishment and exile are often better than confinement to institutions.

Supervision

All institutions that hold people against their wishes need outside supervision, for, by definition, they lack the internal
checks and balances that make such supervision unnecessary
elsewhere. One can check out of a hotel if abused, but not out
of a prison. Prison staffs—which, unlike hotel staffs, can also
totally circumscribe the activities of inmates—have extensive
coercive power that must be checked by an outside authority
if it is not to be abused.* While sharing the purposes of the
penal system, the outside authority should be altogether independent of the management of the institutions it is to super-
vise and of its personnel. (The general supervisory power of
the judiciary is too cumbersome and has not proven sufficient
anywhere.) Such outside authorities exist abroad.† In Great
Britain a "Board of Visitors" deals with violations of prison
rules and with complaints by prisoners. In France a *juge de
l'application des peines* is presumed to do so, and in Italy a
guidice di sorveglianza.

The needed "supervisory court" should be concerned with
anything that affects prison life and the carrying out of confining sentences, including crimes committed by and against
confined persons. The court should have full judicial status,
hold hearings, try cases, pronounce sentences, and issue
directives in the usual fashion. An appeals division might
have a nearly final say, with grounds for further appeal being
kept few and narrow. The supervisory court also should hold
primary hearings on all *habeas corpus* applications and on any
other application for rehearing by anyone confined against his

* Because of the endogenous helplessness of many patients, this principle
also applies to nursing homes and psychiatric hospitals. (Prisons differ by
producing helplessness exogenously.)

† In many states in the U.S. there exist outside supervisory boards. But they
have not proven effective anywhere. They tend to be political in origin and to
lack judicial status, appropriate powers and full time personnel.

will. (The courts that hitherto had jurisdiction might retain the ultimate ability to overrule.) * Supervisory courts also could try all complaints of offenders about their treatment while confined.

The first and the main task of the supervisory courts is to determine the length of the convict's post-punishment confinement, if any. An adversary hearing should be mandatory on the application of the prosecution. Such an application should be permissible whenever the offender had been sentenced to prison. The criteria for decision are to be categorical (as described in the previous chapter). The supervisory court also would decide on the form of post-punishment confinement: banishment, exile, or the non-penal institution to which the offender might be sent after serving his punishment.† In these decisions the court should be assisted by a statistical research section, which is to help set and revise categorical criteria.

If the jurisdiction of the supervisory courts were to include the matters listed, parole boards would become unnecessary; so would classification centers which now group prisoners and send them to different penal institutions. The sentences of the original trial judges would determine the punishment—fine, and where necessary, imprisonment. All other matters would be decided by the supervisory court.‡ Consider, now, the forms of partial incapacitation that the supervisory court might decide on after the original sentence has been served.

* Those who doubt the need for this reform may want to read "What Hath Habeas Corpus Wrought?" by Julian Hawley (*N.Y. State Bar Journal*, October 1974). He describes how a prisoner, complaining, by means of *habeas corpus*, about an orange not served him at breakfast, managed to keep dozens of state and federal courts busy. *Habeas corpus* was extended by courts and can be restricted by them, with some legislative help.

† The usual trial courts, which retain the (prior) punitive sentencing power, also might follow categorical criteria in deciding on incapacitating or non-incapacitating punishments.

‡ Prison administrators should retain the right to take off a month per year (prorated) of the original punitive sentence for good behavior. This facilitates prison discipline, and should remain an independent prerogative of administrators.

Banishment

Banishment is helpful when the offender's illegal activities depend on his presence in any of a few areas from which he can be banned. Banishment is cheaper than incarceration, for, by banishing a person from a given area, the government does not take any more responsibility for his support than it does for that of other citizens. And the offender banished from certain areas would be better off than confined to any institution. He might be obligated to report his whereabouts; and additional means of supervision can easily be imagined. There would be problems, but they would not be insurmountable. It would scarcely be in the offender's interest to show up in the places from which he was banished; imprisonment would be the alternative.

Exile

Exile to a specific place is useful when it seems likely to preclude the offender's unlawful activities. Banishment even from many areas may not be enough in some cases. But there are places too small and distant for a wholesaler in stolen goods, a hijacker, a mugger, or a drug dealer to ply his trade. The problem with exiling an offender to a small and distant place is that he may be unable to make a living there. The government (state or federal) responsible for the exile may have to reimburse the local welfare department for his support. The locality in question also should be reimbursed for whatever other expenses accrue in connection with the exile. Still, the cost would remain below that of imprisonment. Other advantages are obvious, not least the avoidance of prison life. The major problem probably would involve intergovernmental relations; not many communities would volunteer to accept exiles. But this problem can be solved and is worth solving in view of the advantages of exile over prison.

Non-Penal Confinement

As was mentioned above, some offenders may have to be confined after their prison terms for the sake of the security of the community. Banishment or exile may not be enough. Their confinement must be secure, but it should be as non-punitive as security permits. The confined offenders may live in apartments shared with family or friends. They may get an allowance as well as income from work made available within the compound. They may cook for themselves and lead the life they would lead outside as much as possible, except that they would not be allowed outside. They should be able to receive visitors. (Needless to say, if a confined person uses these amenities disruptively, he would have to be transferred to a more restrictive institution.) Other than security and cost, there are no reasons for depriving offenders confined after their punishment of any amenities. Educational or rehabilitation programs also may be offered to those who want them. However, the period of incapacitation, determined categorically, should in no way depend on these programs. Behavior within institutions rarely indicates much about behavior outside; and treatment programs are useless unless actually desired by those who participate.

Penal Institutions

Prisons, much as one might hope for improvement, will remain a necessary evil at best. However, they need not be quite as evil as they are now. In penological circles it is often said that offenders are "sent to prison as punishment, not for punishment,": prison personnel should not arbitrarily impose or permit punishments beyond the incarceration ordered by the court. But a more questionable interpretation seems to have taken hold lately in the public mind: prisons should be made into altogether non-punitive institutions—as though offenders were sent to penal institutions for non-penal purposes. Perhaps the notion, already discussed, that the overriding purpose of prisons is to rehabilitate and that rehabilitation calls for the exclusion of all punitive elements is responsible for this misinterpretation. At any rate, the idea of non-punitive prisons not only has proven unhelpful but also has made prisons far more painful and harmful than they need be. "Never is evil done so thoroughly or so well as when it is done in a good cause," Blaise Pascal tells us. Our prisons certainly bear him out.

In most cases, the prisoner's lot is worse than deliberate punitiveness would have made it. Once incarceration is no longer intentionally, officially, and directly meant to be punitive or penitential, the staff seems to have no more idea of the purpose of prisons than the inmates. And neither has confidence in the proclaimed corrective purpose—if they heard of it. Prisoners, then, are left at the mercy of an odd mixture of creaky bureaucratic regulations, individual abuses (sometimes well-meaning), and, above all, *laissez-faire*. *Laissez-faire* has come to mean that prisons are effectively run by the prisoners.* "Correctional officers" are content to enforce self-protective regulations without effectively protecting prisoners from one another. Hence prisoners who have achieved dominance—by virtue of strength, aggressiveness, organization, etc.—abuse other prisoners. Homosexual rape is commonplace. To avoid violence, injury, or death, most prisoners are compelled to submit to threats by bullying inmates. The

---

* There is a parallel here to what has happened in many educational institutions where coercion has been replaced not by leadership and discipline but by peer-group dominance.

effect is brutalizing and criminalizing—the very opposite of what benevolent reformers meant it to be. Attempts to structure the activities of prisoners meaningfully and to prepare them for law-abiding conduct upon release cannot be taken seriously under these circumstances.

It is not what is done but what is not done that makes our prisons inhumane and produces recidivism. The staff tolerates, even fosters, a social order run by and for the dominant prisoners. The prison subculture, which grows on the soil untended by the staff, allows the hierarchy of prisoners to form and foster attitudes that necessarily counter any salutory effects imprisonment could have. Although in other countries prison systems cannot be said to do better in reducing recidivism, the treatment of prisoners, though less luxurious and costly, is often more humane in England, France, Germany, and Italy simply because the biggest bullies among them are not allowed to dominate the prisoners.

What leads to our *laissez-faire* "system"? The prison staff is not entirely to blame for adopting a hands-off policy. There are many constraints beyond its control. And the staff itself too often is untrained, badly paid, and overworked. Furthermore, many prisons are far too big to be manageable. Still, the staff doesn't like to make waves: it is easier to ignore what goes on among prisoners than to take responsibility for controlling it. The difficulties are ideological as well: Americans have been so imbued with the doctrine that everyone should be free to pursue happiness his own way that they automatically apply it even to children (who need instruction) and to prisoners. We forget that the doctrine was never meant for prisoners; it is inconsistent with reform as well as with punishment, i.e., with the very purpose of penal institutions. After all, his way of pursuing happiness was what landed the prisoner in what he calls "the slammer." He is there so that he may not continue to pursue happiness in his own way, so that others may be deterred from following his way, and so that he may learn legitimate ways of pursuing happiness. *Laissez-faire* is what did him in.

It is to be suspended while he is not free—while he is in prison.

The controversy over "behavior modification" in prisons illustrates our confused overextension of the doctrine of freedom to penal institutions. "Behavior modification" attempts to devise techniques to systematically change undesired behavior traits. In the case of private patients, the desire for change comes from them, and the only question is one of efficacy. With prisoners the desire does not come from them. Thus there are good reasons for avoiding drugs, surgery, or any painful ways of modifying behavior even if effective. These would amount to unwarranted punishment. The consent of a prisoner can hardly be regarded as freely given if his release depends on it.* He must be protected rigidly against overzealous experimenters who, under the guise of helping prisoners, may inflict unauthorized punishments on them. So far so good. But pain or drugs are not always required. "Behavior modification" only requires a reward structure (and, to the extent to which deprivation is failure to reward, a deprivation structure) meant to make the desired behavior more profitable to the subject and the undesired behavior less. And that is what prisons are meant to do anyway. Prisons exist to modify behavior.

Prisons certainly can elaborate systematically attempts to modify the behavior of prisoners in as much detail as is effective, provided that no additional punishment is visited on them. Prisoners are entitled to a nutritive diet fit for human consumption. They are not entitled to special palatability. However, they may be rewarded for behavior modification with particularly attractive food. The same goes for numerous other privileges that may be extended or restricted for the sake of rewarding or sanctioning behavior: mail or visitors beyond the legal minimum, access to radio, TV, magazines, recreational activities, etc. Any privilege may be used for behavior

* One might argue—inconclusively—about psychiatric patients.

modification as long as no right is interfered with. I have some doubt on the efficacy, but none on the legitimacy, of behavior modification, as long as no unwarranted punishments are imposed. The purposeful withholding of privileges is not an unwarranted punishment, nor can unequal treatment be claimed to be, when behavior changes are systematically and equally rewarded for all those who make them. All human interaction relies on continuous behavior modification—there is no reason why prison should be an exception.

A word finally about work. We have swung away from the original workhouses—but too indiscriminately. In most institutions there is too little work for prisoners. They have far more leisure than they can put to any productive use. After all, neither family life nor the social activities or entertainments that fill (or kill) leisure time outside are available. With proper incentives most prisoners prefer to work and to use or acquire skills to a far greater extent than is now possible. They should be helped. At the present time prisoners are not able to substantially increase their net income by means of harder or better work. They should be. More work, and work more appropriate to their actual or potential skills, with more financial incentives would help solve many prison problems.* Present efforts to allow prisoners to work according to the skills they have or may be able to acquire are wholly insufficient. And prisoners are paid only token wages instead of the current market wages their work deserves.† This is surely counterproductive: legitimate work is held out as a part of their punishment. This will not help prisoners to see legitimate work as a rewarding experience.

---

* Prisons could produce nearly the whole gamut of goods and services now produced outside. To avoid competition with outside industry, the prison output might be sold exclusively to government agencies. (There is hardly anything the government does not buy at present.)

† From the wages paid prisoners, reasonable amounts for room and board and, where indicated, for restitution for harm done might be deducted.

XXIII

Epilogue

From an analysis of punishment and justice as idea and institution (Part One), we have proceded to the social control of crime (Part Two) and finally to the kinds of punishment available (Part Three). To end with the nuts and bolts of the last chapter seems anticlimactic. A summary would be redundant, but a brief look at an underlying issue might not be.

"He that spareth his rod, hateth his son: but he that loveth him chasteneth him betimes," the Bible tells us (Proverbs 13:24). Punishment—if not the only, or the first, or even the best means of making people obey laws—is ultimately indispensable. In our time many fathers seem to hate their sons. Or have they forgotten? The sons have not. They respond in kind, to the fathers and to the *parens patriae,* to the society that must chastise them when their fathers did not. Punishment is visited on the adult who had been spared as a child, whose parents abdicated their responsibility for full, firm, and loving guidance, thereby compelling society to meet its responsibility for punishment.

Punishment is painful. And pain, if not the supreme evil, certainly is evil. One wishes, therefore, that it need not be inflicted. The wish has never been far from our minds. Often it has been confused with its fulfillment; yet James Madison reminds us that we could dispense with laws and punishments only "if men were angels." The constitution he helped draw up rests on the conviction that men are not. It is the greatest document of institutionalized mutual distrust ever produced (wherefore it proved durable). The framers knew that non-angelic societies need laws, have law-breakers, and must punish them to enforce the laws. They worked out principles of checking both law-breaking and law-making.

Idealists always have found it hard to believe that we need courts and punishments to moderate what Christians used to call corruption and Freudians inborn unconscious impulses. The very restraints the law demands of us, the very punishments it threatens and inflicts, are blamed for what they restrain. J. J. Rousseau's delusion that "nature has made man happy and good, society corrupts him and causes his misery" all too often is taken to mean that a better society could do without laws and punishments. Despite the preaching of the ancient Christian fathers, and the information gathered by anthropology and psychoanalysis, we find it hard to believe that paradise has been lost and harder still that it cannot be regained in this world. The less we are sustained by faith in a world beyond, the more reluctant we are to give up the hope of paradise this side of eternity. Innumerable reformers and revolutionaries have conjured up countless utopian visions, religious and secular, of a prelapsarian paradise to be regained here and now. No conflict there, no evil, no need for law and punishment. Ovid, in his *Metamorphoses,* already described such a society: *sine lege . . . sine iudice erant tuti* ("without law and judges all were secure"). What Ovid found in the Golden Age, and Genesis in the state of innocence from which we have fallen, we still long for. Christian heretics never ceased in one form or another to proclaim, as Pelagius did originally: *homo sine peccato esse potest si velit* * ("man, if he so wills, can be without sin"). From Rousseau to Marx to Mao,

---

* The spirit is Pelagian, but the words are by Coelestius or Marius Mercator (all about fifth century).

they always concluded that if man nonetheless seems sinful, it is because of the corrupting institutions of society.

Somehow bad social institutions always seem to corrupt naturally good men. The possibility that naturally bad men corrupt good institutions is rarely considered. None ever satisfactorily explained why naturally good men create bad institutions, and by what means revolutionaries manage to remain uncorrupted so as to lead us into the millennium. Divine grace may work for religious saviors, but how do the others do it? Wealth used to corrupt, but now poverty does as well. And power tends to corrupt according to Lord Acton; but now so does powerlessness, according to those who have discovered that the powerless are as corrupt as others. The powerful are able to do what they wish, and the powerless are not—the ability is depicted as corrupting; so is the inability. Could natural wishes be corrupting to begin with rather than the ability or inability to carry them out—wealth and power, or poverty?

What, then, produces the corrupt intent, the *mens rea?* It would be silly to deny that social opportunities, pressures, temptations, and encouragements add to nature's inheritance. Society surely helps form and direct the use we make of the possibilities that nature grants us. "How but in custom and in ceremony/Are innocence and beauty born?" W. B. Yeats asked. Social institutions curb as well as produce innocence and beauty, guilt and ugliness. The threat of punishment issuing from society only reins in what society unavoidably played some role in creating. Yet there could be no society without the opportunities, pressures, temptations, and encouragements, the institutions—the social order—that make crime possible and likely and laws and punishments necessary. And no society could do less than hold individuals responsible for what they do with the opportunities available to them.

The outlook of this book has not been chiliastic, enthusiastic, or antinomian. Not relying on divine revelations (*entheos,* from which we derive enthusiasm), I cannot see the millennium (*chilios*) coming nor feel that in view of its proximity we can do without law (*nomos*). Legitimate opportunities for all should be fostered; they can reduce the lure of crime. But they can only reduce, not eliminate, crime. Laws, and punishments to enforce them, are needed in any foreseeable social order. The task, then, as I saw it, was not to dream up an order that can do without punishment but rather to consider how punishment can be just and effective—neither less nor more harsh and certain than required to secure life, liberty, and the pursuit of happiness.

Notes

I / *To Secure These Rights*

1. Franklin E. Zimring and Gordon J. Hawkins, *Deterrence* (Chicago: University of Chicago Press, 1973), p. 336.
2. Ramsey Clark, *Crime in Urban Society* (New York: Dunellen, 1970), p. XII.
3. Jerome Hall, "Justice in the 20th Century," *59 Cal. L. R.* 3 (1971), p. 753.
4. *The Crime of Punishment* is the title of a book by Karl Menninger, M.D. New York: Viking, 1968).
5. Abraham Lincoln, *On the Perpetuation of our Political Institutions*, 1838.

II / *Retribution, Vengeance and the Future*

6. Quoted in Sanford H. Kadish and Monrad G. Paulsen, *Criminal Law and Its Processes* (Boston: Little Brown, 1969), p. 64. See also Justice Marshall's concurring view in *Furman* v. *Georgia* (1973).
7. Hall, "Justice in the 20th Century," n. 3.
8. James Fitzjames Stephen, *A History of the Criminal Law in England* (Macmillan: London, 1863), II, p. 80.
9. Edwin H. Sutherland, *White Collar Crime* (New York: Dryden Press, 1949).
10. David Hume, *A Treatise on Human Nature*.

III / *Justice and Utility*

11. H. L. A. Hart, *Punishment and Responsibility* (New York: Oxford University Press, 1968).
12. Aleksander I. Solzhenitsyn, *The Gulag Archipelago* (New York: Harper & Row, 1974).

IV / *Justice, Order, Charity*

13. *The Theory of Moral Sentiments* in *Adam Smith's Moral and Political Philosophy*, Herbert W. Schneider, ed. (New York: Harper Torchbook, 1970), pp. 129–130.

14. Ibid.

15. Isaiah Berlin, *Four Essays on Liberty* (New York: Oxford University Press, 1969).

V / *Utilitarian Functions of Punishment*

16. Carl B. Klockars, *The Professional Fence* (New York: Free Press, 1975).

VI / *Some Indirect Effects of Punishment*

17. Herbert L. Packer, *The Limits of the Criminal Sanction* (Stanford: Stanford University Press, 1968), p. 45.

18. Robert Nisbet, *Twighlight of Authority* (New York: Oxford University Press, 1975).

19. Packer, *Limits of Criminal Sanction*, p. 149.

20. Ibid.

21. J. F. Stephen, *A History of the Criminal Law in England* (London, 1883).

22. Johannes Andenaes, *Punishment and Deterrence* (Ann Arbor: University of Michigan Press, 1974).

22a. Ibid.

22b. *City in Terror*, N.Y., 1974.

VII / *What Causes Crime?*

23. Edwin Sutherland, *White Collar Crime* (New York: Holt, Rinehart & Winston, 1949), p. 234.

24. See Robert Merton's "Social Structure and Anomy" in his *Social Theory and Social Structure* (Glencoe, Ill.: Free Press, 1957).

25. Travis Hirschi, *Causes of Delinquency* (Berkeley: University of California Press, 1972).

26. For a careful discussion see R. Mansfield, L. C. Gould, and J. Z. Namenwirth, "A Socioeconomic Model for the Prediction of Societal Rates of Property Theft," 52 *Societal Forces* 4 (June 1974).

27. "Crime and Punishment, an Economic Approach," in *Essays in the Economics of Crime and Punishment*, ed. Gary S. Becker and William M. Landes (New York: National Bureau of Economic Research, 1974).

VIII / *Poverty*

28. Enrico Ferri, *Criminal Sociology* (abr. English ed., London, 1895), p. 76ff.

IX / *Black and White*

29. "Finality in Criminal Law and Federal *Habeas Corpus* for State Prisoners," 76 *Harv. L. Rev.* (1963).

30. F. B. Graham, "Black Crime: The Lawless Image," *Harper's Magazine,* September 1970.

31. M. A. Forslund, "A Comparison of Negro and White Crime Rates," *Journal of Criminal Law, Criminology and Police Science* 61 (June 1970); E. R. Moses, "Negro and White Crime Rates" in *The Sociology of Crime and Delinquency,* ed. Wolfgang et al. (New York: John Wiley, 1970); R. M. Stephenson and F. R. Scarpitti, "Negro-White Differentials in Delinquency," *Journal of Research in Crime and Delinquency* (July 5, 1968).

32. D. J. Black and A. J. Reiss, Jr., "Police Control of Juveniles," *American Sociological Review* 35, (January 1970); E. Green, "Race, Social Status and Criminal Arrest," *American Sociological Review* 35 (June 1970).

33. Enrico Ferri, *The Positive School of Criminology* (1906; reprint ed., Chicago: Charles H. Kerr, 1913), p. 60.

34. Enrico Ferri, *Criminal Sociology,* (Boston: Little Brown, 1917), p. 242.

X / *Free Will, Responsibility, Rationality, Deterrability*

35. John Stuart Mill, *System of Logic,* Book VI, Chapter II, Section 3.

36. *Nichomachean Ethics* 74–74, J. Thomson, trans., 1114, W. D. Ross, trans.

37. Barnes and Teeters, *New Horizons in Criminology.* (Englewood Cliffs, N.J.: Prentice-Hall, 1959.) pp. 817–818.

38. Barnes and Teeters, *New Horizons in Criminology,* fn. 37 (pp. 337–338).

39. "The Purposes of Criminal Punishment," 21 *Modern L. Rev.* 117, 1958, pp. 122–125.

40. Paul B. Horton and Gerald R. Leslie, *The Sociology of Social Problems,* 4th Ed., New York: Appleton-Century-Crofts, 1970, p. 167.

41. George Antunes and A. L. Hunt, "The Impact of Certainty and Severity of Punishment on Levels of Crime in American States: An Extended Analysis," (Evanston, Illinois: Center for Urban Affairs, Northwestern University, 1972.)

42. Barry F. Singer, "Psychological Studies of Punishment," 58 *California Law Review,* 405, 1970.

XI / *Are They Sick?*

43. Gwynn Nettler, "Shifting the Load," *American Behavioral Scientist* January/February 1972.

44. Ramsey Clark, *Crime in America,* (New York: Simon & Shuster, 1970) p. 220.

45. Nigel Walker, *Crime and Punishment in Britain,* (Edinburgh: Edin-

burgh University Press, 1970.) See also his *Crime and Insanity in England,* (Edinburgh: Edinburgh University Press, 1968.)

46. See Guze, Goodwin, and Crane, "Criminal Recidivism and Psychiatric Disorders," *Am. J. Psychiatry* 132, 1970.

47. H. A. Overstreet, *The Great Enterprise* (New York: Norton, 1952) p. 115.

XII / *Addiction*

48. James Q. Wilson, Mark H. Moor, and David Wheat, Jr., "The Problem of Heroin," in *The Public Interest,* Fall 1972.

49. George Bigelow, Ira Liebson, Roland Griffiths et al., "Alcoholic Drinking: Suppression by a Behavioral Time-Out Procedure." (Baltimore, Maryland: Department of Psychiatry, Baltimore City Hospitals, 1973.)

XIII / *Does Punishment Deter? Statistical and Experimental Evidence*

50. Gregory Zilboorg, *The Psychology of the Criminal Act and Punishment,* (New York: Harcourt Brace & Co., 1954) p. 27.

51. "The Myths of Thomas Szasz," *Bulletin of the Menninger Clinic,* Nov. 1974, p. 502.

52. See Charles Tittle and Alan R. Rowe, "Fear and the Student Cheater," *Change,* April 1974. Also by the same authors, "Moral Appeal, Sanction, Threat and Deviance," 20 *Social Problems,* 48 (1973).

53. William Chambliss, "The Deterrent Influence of Punishment," *Crime and Delinquency* 12: 70–75, 1966; and Richard Salem and W. Bowers, "Severity of Formal Sanctions as a Deterrent to Deviant Behavior," *Law and Society Review* 5: 21–40, 1970. An excellent survey and analysis of what has been published by sociologists and criminologists on the subject is found in Charles R. Tittle and Charles H. Logan "Sanctions and Deviance: Evidence and Remaining Questions" *(Law and Society Review,* No. 3, Spring 1973). As good a survey of what economists have written on the subject is found in Gordon Tullock, "Does Punishment Deter Crime?" *(The Public Interest,* Summer 1974).

54. Crime, Punishment and Deterrence," *Social Science Quarterly,* 48: 515–530, 1968.

55. "Punishment and Deterrence: Another Analysis of Gibbs' Data," *Social Science Quarterly* 50: 389–395, 1969.

56. "Criminal Homicide, Punishment and Deterrence: Methodological and Substantive Reconsiderations," *Social Science Quarterly* 52: 277–289, 1971.

57 "The Impact of Certainty and Severity of Punishment on Levels of Crime in American States: An Extended Analysis," (Evanston, Ill: *Center for Urban Affairs,* Northwestern University, 1972).

58. Isaac Ehrlich "Participation in Illegitimate Activities: A Theoretical Investigation" *The Journal of Political Economy,* May/June 1973, pp. 521–565. Ehrlich acknowledges the work of a number of predecessors, mainly economists such as George Stigler and Gary Becker.

59. Ibid.
60. Ibid., p. 560.
61. Ibid., p. 545.
62. Charles R. Tittle and Alan R. Rowe, "Certainty of Arrest and Crime Rates: A Further Test of the Deterrence Hypothesis," 52 *Social Forces* 4, June 1974, pp. 455–462.
63. Ehrlich, "Participation in Illegitimate Activities." (See n. 58).

XIV / *Dimensions of Crime*

64. *New York Times* editorial, Dec. 28, 1974.

XV / *What Can Be Done to Curb Crime?*

65. Ehrlich, "Participation in Illegitimate Activities."
66. The *New York Times*, Sept. 24, 1974.
67. "We can't all be victims of society," *The Village Voice*, October 10, 1974, p. 42.
68. *New York Times*, October 6, 1974.
69. *Commentary*, July 1974. pp. 101–104.
70. *The New York Times*, April 12, 1975.

XVI / *Philosophical Quandaries*

71. Immanuel Kant, *Gesammelte Werke*, (Berlin: Cassirer Edition, 1922) VII, pp. 138–40.
72. Herbert L. Packer, *The Limits of the Criminal Sanction*, (Stanford: Stanford University Press, 1968) pp. 12–13.
73. Barbara Wootton, *Crime and the Criminal Law*, (London: Stevens and Son, Ltd., 1963).
74. Richard H. Brandt, *Ethical Theory*, (Englewood Cliffs, N.J.: Prentice-Hall, 1959) p. 504.
75. Karl Menninger, *The Crime of Punishment*, (New York: Viking, 1968) p. 17.
76. "Rehabilitation Is Still Punishment," *The Humanist*, May-June, 1972.
77. Summarized by Robert Martinson in "What Works?—Questions and Answers About Prison Reform," in *The Public Interest*, Spring 1974. Lipton, Martinson, and Wilkes, *The Effectiveness of Correctional Treatment* (New York: Praeger, 1975).
78. "Evaluation of Correctional Treatment: A Survey and Critical Interpretation of Correctional Treatment Studies in Scandanavia, 1945–1974," a report prepared for the Crime Deterrence & Offender Career project, 1974.
79. Seymour L. Halleck, *Psychiatry and the Dilemmas of Crime*, (Berkeley: University of California Press, 1971) p. xiii.
80. Michael Kramer, "The City Politic," April 1, 1974.
81. Norval Morris, *The Future of Imprisonment*, (Chicago: University of Chicago Press, 1974).

82. "Seriousness of Crime and a Policy of Juvenile Justice," in *Crime, Justice and Society,* James F. Short, ed. (Chicago: University of Chicago Press, 1975).

83. Quoted by Walter Kaufman in *Without Guilt and Justice* (New York: Peter H. Wyden, 1973).

84. Émile Durkheim, *The Rules of Sociological Method,* English transl. (Glencoe, Ill.: The Free Press, 1952).

85. G. W. F. Hegel, *Philosophy of Right,* English tranl. (New York: Oxford University Press, 1971).

XVII / *The Decline of Corporal Punishment*

86. See also Charles L. Black, Jr., *The Occasions of Justice* (New York: Macmillan, 1963) p. 99.

87. See Lloyd de Mause, *The History of Childhood,* (New York: Harper Torchbooks, 1975).

88. Krafft-Ebing, *Psychopathia Sexualis* (1886), (New York: Putnam, 1965, reprint).

89. Karl Menninger, *The Crime of Punishment* (New York: Viking, 1969).

90. Alexis de Tocqueville, *Democracy in America,* Third Book, Chap. 1.

XVIII / *The Death Penalty: Arguments For*

91. *The American Scholar,* Spring 1962.

92. *American Economic Review,* June 1975.

XIX / *The Death Penalty: Arguments Against*

93. *New York Times,* March 23, 1975.

94. Cesare di Beccaria, *Dei delitti e delle pene* [Of crimes and punishments]

95. Ibid.

XX / *Fines*

XXI / *Who Should Be Imprisoned?*

96. Henry J. Steadman and Gary Keveles, *Am. J. of Psychiatry,* 129, 1972, pp. 364–70.

97. Kozol et al., "The Diagnosis and Treatment of Dangerousness," in *Crime and Delinquency,* 18, 1972, pp. 371–92.

98. "Psychology and the Criminal Law," 5 *Univ. of Richmond Law Review* 21, 1970.

99. "Crime in a Birth Cohort," *Proceedings of the American Philosophical Society,* Vol. 117, no. 5, Dec. 1973, pp. 404–411.

100. Ibid.

101. Ibid.

Index